THE FAMILY HERDS

THE
FAMILY HERDS

A STUDY
OF TWO PASTORAL TRIBES
IN EAST AFRICA
THE JIE AND TURKANA

by

P. H. GULLIVER, Ph.D.
Government Sociologist, Tanganyika

NEGRO UNIVERSITIES PRESS
WESTPORT, CONNECTICUT

Originally published in 1955
by Routledge & Kegan Paul Ltd., London

Reprinted in 1970 by
Negro Universities Press
A Divison of Greenwood Press, Inc.
Westport, Connecticut

Library of Congress Catalogue Card Number 79-129943

SBN 8371-5032-9

Printed in the United States of America

TO MY WIFE AND FELLOW-WORKER

PREFACE

THE research embodied in this work was made possible by a grant from Colonial Development and Welfare funds recommended by the Colonial Social Science Research Council. I was attached as a temporary Sociological Research Officer to the Governments of Kenya and Uganda whilst I was in the field, and this book is published with their permission. They are not, of course, responsible for the views expressed in it, which are my own. In its original form the work was accepted by the University of London as a thesis for the Degree of Doctor of Philosophy, and this book is a modified version of that thesis.

Field research covered two tours amongst the Turkana in Kenya of eleven months (1948-49) and seven months (1950) respectively, and amongst the Jie of Uganda one tour of seven months (1950-51) with one or two additional brief visits. In 1951 I published *A Preliminary Survey of the Turkana: a report compiled for the Government of Kenya* (henceforward to be referred to as *Survey of the Turkana*), the title of which is self-explanatory. A detailed bibliography was given there up to 1951; since then I have published a number of papers which contain data supplementary to the theme of this book and which may be of interest to the specialist.[1]

I wish to make two introductory points concerning the scope of this book which may prevent misunderstanding. To some readers it may perhaps seem that I have dealt at undue length with the physical environment and social ecology of these people. Like some readers of my earlier book, they may tend to neglect this part of my

[1] *A Preliminary Survey of the Turkana*, Cape Town University: School of African Studies, n.s. No. 26, 1951; 'The Karamajong Cluster', *Africa*, xxii, 1952; 'Bell-oxen and Ox-names among the Jie', *Uganda Journal*, xvi, 1952; 'Nomad Anthropologist', *Corona*, 1952; 'Jie Marriage', *African Affairs*, lii, 1953; 'The Population of Karamoja', *Uganda Journal*, xvii, 1953; 'Jie Agriculture', *Uganda Journal*, xviii, 1954; 'The Age Organisation of the Jie Tribe', *The Journal of the Royal Anthropological Society*, lxxxiii, Part 2. Also with Pamela Gulliver: *The Central Nilo-Hamites*. International African Institute, London, 1953 (Ethnographic survey of Africa: East-central Africa, Part vii).

vii

account in their search for more truly anthropological description. I would ask these readers to look again at Chapter 2, for I believe strongly that it is impossible to understand the social behaviour and institutions described in this book without due appreciation of ecological conditions. Amongst the Turkana most especially, environment is a conspicuous limiting factor in every aspect of social life, though not of course necessarily a determinant of social forms. It may be worthwhile to add that the environment and ecology of the Turkana are unlike those of the Nilotic pastoralists of the southern Anglo-Egyptian Sudan, which latter are so well known to all anthropologists due to the excellence of the work of Professor Evans-Pritchard.

My second point is that amongst both the Jie and Turkana ritual and religious phenomena associated with domestic animals (especially cattle) are of comparatively less importance than amongst most African pastoralists of whom we have reasonable record. In my concentration in this book on livestock as property and as an integral factor in kinship relations, it may be felt that there has been a neglect of this other, usually important feature of primitive pastoral life. Briefly, it may be said that both the Jie and Turkana have an essentially mundane and profane attitude towards their flocks and herds. As I have written elsewhere, 'the Turkana are typically prosaic, matter-of-fact and non-speculative and do not dwell on the mystical, the magico-religious aspect of life very much',[1] and much the same may be said of the Jie. It is of course true, for example, that for both people a meat feast is an essential part of any important ritual or religious event; and again, men have their individual and special beasts from which they take honorific names; but in these and many other cases these phenomena do not show the vital psychological and social significance so evident, for instance, amongst the Nilotic Nuer.[2] The Jie and Turkana have not developed strongly that certain 'cattle mentality' so commonly mentioned in accounts of the Masai or the Nilotes.

No attempt has been made to write Jie and Turkana words in a scientific orthography, and to facilitate the work of publication no special letters or signs are used. Since this is an anthropological account of these peoples, I have given only those native terms which

[1] *Survey of the Turkana*, p. 251.
[2] Cf. Evans-Pritchard's account of 'ox-names' among the Nuer (*Africa*, xxiii, 1953, pp. 182 *et seq.*) with my own account of Jie 'ox-names' (*Uganda Journal*, xvi, 1952, pp. 72-5) for an example of the difference in attitudes.

seem essential to that account. There appears to be little value in frequent or lengthy vernacular interpolations in a work of this kind.

I wish to thank members of The Bible Churchman's Mission Society in Uganda, and especially Canon and Mrs. R. Clark, who gave my wife and I much help and warm hospitality on many occasions; it is hoped that this book may be of assistance to them in their understanding of the people to whom they devote their lives. Many officers of the Governments of Kenya and Uganda gave us much appreciated assistance, especially towards the practical side of living in the field, and to them we are indebted. Mr. H. E. Lambert, O.B.E., formerly Senior District Officer, Kenya, who first introduced us to East Africa, and Dr. Audrey Richards, Director of the East African Institute of Social Research, have both in their different ways given prodigally of their advice and encouragement which were invaluable to me. Thanks are also due to Mrs. E. M. Chilver, Secretary of the Colonial Social Science Research Council (Colonial Office), for her work on the administrative side of this research scheme. I owe an especial debt to Professor I. Schapera, who has been my academic mentor during most of the period occupied by this work. Had it not been for him my first book on the Turkana would never have been published, and he has read the present work in draft at least twice, making many useful comments and criticisms. Professor W. J. H. Sprott, the editor of the International Library of Sociology and Social Reconstruction, has been my teacher and friend since the end of the war, which alone calls for an expression of my sincere gratitude here; but he has also given me considerable assistance in his editorial capacity, including reading and criticizing the final draft of the MS. Finally, I wish to thank my wife, to whom this book is dedicated, for her unfailing support, help and encouragement. She lived and travelled with me in this difficult region of East Africa, particularly in Turkana, where it was not thought that a European woman could easily withstand the necessarily rigorous life. She was especially important in obtaining information from the womenfolk, with whom I, as a man, found serious difficulties. She herself, in addition, wrote almost the whole of *The Central Nilo-Hamites* which was wrongly attributed to us jointly by the editor of the series in which it appeared.[1]

SONGEA, TANGANYIKA   P.H.G.
December 1953.

[1] See bibliography. I wrote only the essay on the Teso.

CONTENTS

xi

CONTENTS

ILLUSTRATIONS

LIST OF FIGURES

LIST OF FIGURES

CHAPTER ONE

INTRODUCTION

I

PRIMITIVE pastoralism has perhaps attracted the attention of European observers more than any other type of native economy and culture pattern. There is something about the pastoral way of life and those who follow it which appeals to the romantic in the Englishman. The Bedouin Arabs, the Masai, the Fulani and others are possibly the most widely known African peoples. However little an Englishman knows of East Africa, he is almost certain to have heard of the Masai, photographs of whom seem inevitably to form frontispieces to books on the region. The independent character of the warrior-herdsman raises greater admiration than the less exotic agriculturalist. In East Africa, too, it so happens that many of the pastoral peoples are of the Nilo-Hamitic strain, which tends to give them a more striking physique than their Bantu neighbours. In addition, these pastoralists have tended to be the slowest to adopt the white man's ideas and techniques. They have come to represent very often the romance of an Africa now fast disappearing.

In eastern Africa pastoralism is a recurrent cultural feature, especially in the drier parts. From these regions this great interest in pastoral peoples has produced a wealth of information ranging from the anecdotal to records of careful and lengthy observation. A great deal has been written on the ecological, economic, military, ritual and emotional concomitants of pastoralism. Surprisingly enough, however, relatively little information is available concerning the sociological factors connected with herds of domestic animals as forms of property—that is, as foci of social rights and obligations, and as indices of social relationships. Although most writers have commented upon the obvious importance of the herds in the social

A   I

activities of such peoples, yet they have usually passed over what is one of the most significant aspects of a pastoral society. In those tribes who are wealthy in stock, from which a large proportion of subsistence is obtained (but also even in many tribes whose economy is predominantly agricultural), the mode and standard of living, material culture, kinship and community affairs, religion, ritual, law and war are not only set against a background of pastoral activities and necessities, but they are directly and continuously affected in a most intimate fashion. Therefore the regulation of the ownership and use of the herds is critical in the working of the society, and we as observers cannot properly understand that society without an appreciation of the sociology of animal property. Isolated examples of the analysis of pastoral property relations are provided, for instance, by the Nandi and Kipsigis herding-exchange institution[1] and the Balovedu reciprocal bridewealth-exchange marriage system,[2] but some of the best works on pastoral peoples are curiously lacking in adequate treatment of these kinds of relations.[3]

This book aims at an analysis, in two pastoral societies, of the regulations governing herds and flocks of animals as property, and the interrelation of these regulations with the kinship system. The two tribes under discussion are, from the economic point of view, representative of two types of pastoralism common in eastern Africa. The Jie of Uganda have a mixed economy of millet farming and animal husbandry, the latter operated under a system of transhumance; the Turkana of Kenya are nomadic herdspeople with practically no agriculture who depend almost entirely on their animals for subsistence. By African native standards both peoples are wealthy stock-owners, and even the Jie depend heavily on their herds for the maintenance of traditional living-standards. Culturally and historically the two tribes are closely related.

In either tribe, any man is the centre of a field of direct, inter-personal, enduring relations based on agnatic, maternal and affinal kinship, with a residual category of quasi-kinship, viz. bond-friendship. This field comprises the network of social relations specific to

[1] Cf. Huntingford, G. W. B., *Nandi Work and Culture*, London 1950, pp. 52-5; also Peristiany, J. G., *The Social Institutions of the Kipsigis*, London 1939, pp. 150-2.
[2] Cf. Krige, E. J. and J. D., *The Realm of a Rain Queen*, London 1943, pp. 141-51.
[3] E.g. Evans-Pritchard, E. E., *The Nuer*, Oxford 1940, and *Kinship and Marriage among the Nuer*, Oxford 1951. These are undoubtedly the finest description and analysis of a primitive pastoral tribe, yet they do not contain an integrated account of the Nuer property system.

that man, and it is not entirely coincident with that of any other individual. These relations exhibit a variety of practical, moral and emotional contents, but they contain also a basic common principle by which they are brought together into a significant social system. Their chief mode of expression and a main thread of continuity lie in reciprocal rights over domestic animals. They are, from a vital point of view, property relationships. With each of these people a man maintains well-recognized reciprocal rights to claim gifts of animals for certain socially defined requirements. Thus a particular kind of inter-personal relationship is consciously translated into the right to seek stock in times of need, and the corresponding obligation to give stock in times of others' needs. For the Jie and Turkana this is a critical index of social relations, for in his stock a man not only finds the material content of life but also the supreme means whereby to express and maintain his social interests and development. Through the use and disposal of his animals he is able, in the most practical way, to express his relations towards others. In native conceptions, a man who is closely related is *ipso facto* one who gives and is given animals; and this shows not only mutual affection and confidence but also it makes for genuine co-operation in each other's life. In marriage, the birth and development of children, at times of death and disaster and in all the other essential ritual in which a man becomes involved, in the physical maintenance and improvement of his herds, in politico-legal affairs and sometimes even for food, a man seeks the assistance of his close kin and bond-friends, who themselves in turn expect his support.

In each tribe the heart of this social system lies in what is to be called the 'extended family', which group, based on agnatic kinship, contains the prime principles of ownership, inheritance and the control and use of the herds. After an ecological survey, analysis begins therefore with a study of this group. In dealing with the extended family we are concerned with kinship on a relatively small scale, and the only kin group which is larger, the clan, is but putatively agnatic and chiefly important as a unit of ritual prescription. The widest group within which agnatic kinship can actually be traced is normally based on the grandfather of the current adult males, who together with their wives and unmarried daughters, sons, sons' wives and children make up the extended family. This is, of course, not an uncommon group in primitive societies, but it is one which has received relatively little attention other than the purely

3

descriptive, and in recent years appears to have been overlooked by anthropologists in their concentration upon the analysis of larger scale kinship structures.

The Jie and Turkana extended family, being so small scale a group is particularly sensitive to the internal development due to the ageing of its members and the succession of one generation by another. Therefore an attempt is made to analyse the processes within the group which result from this natural development. Where kinship relations are also, and importantly, property relations, a change in the former necessarily causes a redistribution and redefinition of the latter. This is a constant process in both societies. In addition to a static, structural account of kinship and property, especial emphasis is therefore laid upon the diachronic analysis of these social relations and their interaction.

In so far as is possible, description and analysis of the two societies proceeds on parallel lines in order to facilitate comparison. These two social systems have a common origin and in many fundamental parts exhibit common features, structurally and dynamically. However, it will be seen that in other no less significant features they differ considerably. In so far as is possible these divergencies are traced to ecological, demographic and sociological factors which correlatively diverge. By this means it is hoped that a step forward is made in the understanding of kinship and property relations and of primitive pastoralism. This book, however, remains a particular study of only two societies and leaves the analysis of the wider theoretical problems until sufficient data are available for comparable peoples and cultures.

II

The Jie tribal area (*Ajie*, hereafter to be called Jieland) forms the larger part of the modern 'county' of Jie in Karamoja District, north-eastern Uganda.[1] The territory stretches from Koten Hill in the east (at latitude 3° 6′ N., just above the western escarpment of the eastern branch of the African Rift valley) to the Labwor Hills and Acoliland in the west, and between Karamajongland in the south to Dodothland and the Kapeta river in the north—about sixty-five miles from east to west, and twenty-five miles from north to south. Most of

---

[1] Also included in the Jie country are the Labwor (5200 people) living in the hills of that name to the immediate south-west of Jieland. The county chief, a Jie, lives at Kotido in the centre of Jieland proper.

the territory is common pastureland, settlement being effectively restricted to an area of some six miles radius around Kotido in the centre of the country.

The Turkana tribal area (*Aturkwen*, to be referred to as 'Turkana-land') forms the modern Turkana District in the Northern Province of Kenya, though some Turkana live elsewhere.[1] The territory lies wholly within the Rift Valley to the west and south-west of Lake Rudolf, south of Ethiopia and the Anglo-Egyptian Sudan.[2] It extends some two hundred and seventy miles from north to south and about one hundred miles from east to west, though narrowing sharply to the south.

After a hostile separation from the primordial Karamajong, the Jie lived near Koten Hill. Some time later the tribe split in two, but on a purely friendly basis; one part remained near Koten Hill and continued to carry the old name, the other part descended the Rift Valley escarpment into the western area of modern Turkanaland (Tarac valley). There is an explicit story of this event, known to both peoples, which describes it as a secession by some of the younger people of the old tribe, who went into unoccupied territory below the escarpment.[3] At a later date the Jie proper moved some thirty miles westwards to their present settled area around Kotido. No date can be suggested for either of these events beyond the general statement that it must have been at least two hundred years ago. The secessionists and their descendants—the Turkana—moved gradually eastwards, where they came into contact with the Samburu and Marile, who then lived west of Lake Rudolf, the Samburu to the south and the Marile to the north. There was probably a good deal of intermarriage with and absorption of these peoples as well as warfare[4]

---

[1] In the report of the East African Native Census, 1948, are quoted the following population estimates from the Provincial Commissioner, Northern Province: In Turkana District 69,400, in Isiolo District 1500, and in Samburu District 4000. Yet for the Turkana District alone, registered tax-payers (adult males) numbered 21,041 in 1948, which would suggest a population of at least 80,000. This latter figure will be used here.

[2] The north-eastern Turkana live in country gazetted as part of the Sudan, but by agreement administration there is maintained by the Kenya Government.

[3] This story is given in my paper, 'The Karamajong Cluster', *Africa*, xxii, Jan. 1952, pp. 5-6.

[4] Such intermarriage is not only described by Turkana, but would appear to explain the physical differences between themselves and the Jie. Turkana show a range of skin colours, for instance, varying from black to olive, in which a reddish hue is most predominant. Both Samburu and Marile also have reddish skins, though it is not likely that they are of the same physical stock.

during which time the Turkana became firmly established in what is now central Turkanaland. It is unlikely that strong contact was maintained with the Jie proper, for there was no common boundary. The intervening territory was more of a no-man's land disputed and spasmodically occupied by Turkana, Karamajong and Dodoth, but it was not too difficult for both Jie and Turkana to

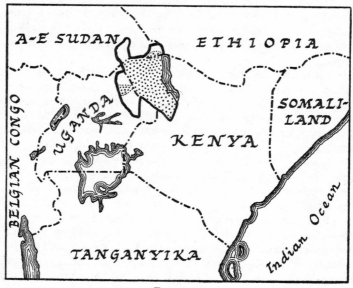

FIGURE I

THE LOCATION OF THE KARAMAJONG CLUSTER
IN EAST AFRICA

The thick line shows the limits of the territory occupied by the tribes
of the Karamajong cluster. Jieland and Turkanaland are stippled.

travel across it and maintain intermittent contact. Certainly it seems quite clear that the two peoples never made war on each other, and sometimes they allied against their common enemies, the Karamajong and Dodoth. Relations were also continued because of trading facilities. The Turkana were able to obtain iron-ware, grain, tobacco, gourds and pots, mainly from the Labwor (who were the outstanding blacksmiths and traders of this region), either direct or through Jie intermediaries. Probably some grain was also obtained from the Jie themselves. Each tribe refers to the other as 'paternal cousins', and they both claim to be 'one people'. It is significant that each tribe made continual warfare against almost all the rest of their neighbours, regarding them as inveterate enemies.[1] In the latter half of the nineteenth century the Turkana began a phase of expansion, pressing back their neighbours on all sides. Briefly, the reasons for this were, first, that they were isolated from the main brunt of the rinderpest epidemics of the end of the nineteenth century and were thus comparatively stronger; second, they were most probably forced to expand by the pressure of an increasing population (human and stock) on an increasingly arid country; and third, they obtained guns and ammunition from Abyssinia, whence they also received encouragement and help in initiating raids.

Meanwhile it appears that the Jie proper remained more or less static, a small tribe surrounded by stronger neighbours to the south (Karamajong), the north (Dodoth) and the west (Acoli). Indeed, when the British first arrived the Jie were hard pressed by the Karamajong in particular and were having to give ground slightly. Whereas the Turkana were expanding both population and territory, and also their stock wealth, the Jie were scarcely more than holding their own.

Early European explorers first entered Turkanaland at the end of the nineteenth century[2] and contacts were made with British administration in 1903. The first post was established on the southern edge of the country in 1909. Although political officers were stationed in Turkanaland, the area was gradually occupied and chiefly controlled by military forces, which, by constant patrols and several major expeditions, waged a lengthy campaign against the Turkana. The area was one of the last to come under British control in East Africa, and in the meantime became a refuge for ivory poachers and outlaws of all kinds, some of whom had bases in or assistance from Abyssinia.

---

[1] After their migration to Kotido the Jie proper split up again when a section moved north-eastwards and became the Toposa and Donyiro tribes. Jie profess a similar friendship with these two tribes to that with the Turkana, but they live so far away that contact lapsed and there was really no question of warfare, alliance or trading facilities. Turkana regard them both as enemies to this day. The Jie-Turkana pattern has parallels within the Karamajong Cluster in relations between the Karamajong and Dodoth, and between the Toposa and Donyiro.

[2] A chronological list of early explorers is given in Appendix No. 1 of my *A Preliminary Survey of the Turkana*, Communications from the School of African Studies No. 26, University of Cape Town, 1951. For brevity this work will be referred to throughout this book as *Survey of the Turkana*.

INTRODUCTION

Doubtless, Turkana resistance, made possible by the wildness of their country, was stimulated by these people and by Ethiopian efforts to gain control of territory claimed by the British. Not until 1926 was civil administration established, and even then military forces were retained in the north to protect the marches with Ethiopia. Even today, semi-military forces maintain a line of armed forts and constant patrols against external raiders from the east and north. Much of the time of the Administration is taken up in dealing with border affairs, and on the whole the Turkana, prevented from continued warfare only, have been left to themselves. The country is extensive, arid and wild, not easily to be developed along modern lines; administration is made difficult by lack of communications and meagre contact with the natives, who remain a backward people. Warfare apart, the indigenous economic and social life persists, little affected by modern ideas and techniques. Many Turkana see a white officer no more than once a year, sometimes less frequently[1]; some areas are seldom visited by officers. There is a rudimentary system of appointed headmen, but there are no native courts or local councils of any kind.

Early explorers, mainly elephant hunters, reached Karamoja in the last years of the nineteenth century. Some passed through Jieland but were either chiefly intent on travelling north, or they were based amongst the Karamajong and regarded the Jie as hostile. Similarly, the early civil administrators a decade later were chiefly concerned with the Karamajong, the government centre being at Moroto, in their country. A military station was established in northern Karamoja, in Dodothland, the function of which was to establish the *pax Britannica*, but it was mainly concerned with the belligerent Turkana and the outlaws. The Karamoja tribes submitted to British occupation with little opposition, possibly because their countries had for several years been overrun and despoiled by ivory hunters and traders[2] who had with some success established themselves in control there, and as elephants and ivory became scarcer coercion of the natives became more necessary for their purposes. One of the difficulties in bringing the *pax Britannica* to Turkanaland was the nomadic habits of the Turkana. Officers were neither certain at any

[1] Despite the fact that only administrative officers are empowered to collect poll tax.
[2] These were mainly Arabs, Swahili and Indians, who had large bases on the Manimani river in Karamajongland.

8

time where the people lived nor could they prevent the natives moving away into open country. In Karamoja this problem was overcome by stabilizing the bulk of the population in their settled areas and strictly demarcating tribal pasture areas. This policy was carried out in about 1914 by military forces.

Between the wars Karamoja was largely left to its own devices—a backward area, dangerous on account of its increasing aridity, but thought capable of little modern development. Administration remained centred at Moroto and little affected the northern areas, including Jieland. Since the end of the Second World War a programme has been begun which aims at the development of the pastoral resources of the District. Artificial water supplies (boreholes and dams), stock sales and inoculations against rinderpest are now all being pressed forward. At the same time beginnings have been made in local government. There is a system of appointed chiefs with administrative units at 'county', 'sub-county' and 'parish' level on the hierarchical Uganda pattern. Formal common assemblies are regularly held at these levels under the relevant chiefs, who are also heads of the local courts which deal at least initially with all judicial cases, subject to the superior authority of European officers. Jieland, therefore, in common with the whole of Karamoja, is rather more 'developed' than Turkanaland, but modern innovations are still in their infancy, and still very considerably behind the rest of Uganda. The indigenous economic and social life persists strongly, although modified in certain important ways—mainly in its submission to the authority of chiefs and courts which express the greater authority of the external government.

At this place it may be pointed out that in this book I am dealing principally with the two societies as I observed them in action. It is necessary, of course, to make use of individual histories and experiences by way of illustration, but the kinship and other relations here described are contemporary relations. This is not a circumstantial, reconstructed account of a former state of Jie and Turkana societies, but as near as possible an account of the period 1948-51.

Ecological and economic conditions are dealt with in Chapter Two and need not be repeated here.

The bulk of Jieland is common pasturage, occupied under a system of transhumance only by stock and herdsmen who live in mobile camps. Most of the population are to be found living permanently in the small settled area roughly in the centre of the country (see map, Figure 2). Homesteads are arranged into settlements consisting of from one to eight clan-hamlets. Each settlement occupies a specific area but does not own it as a group. Externally it is often difficult to distinguish settlement boundaries, as homesteads form continuous belts. Separation is social rather than geographical. Nearly all settlements are named groups; primarily they are distinguished by the possession of a ritual grove (*akiriket*) at which the ritual of the constituent clans takes place, but with the support and co-operation of all the members of the total group (or usually, all initiated male members). There is also common ritual for rain-making, warding off disease and disaster, and so on. There is a great deal of everyday economic and social co-operation. Each settlement has at least one excavated pond to provide catchment water in the wet season. Garden land normally lies in and around the settlement and plots are individually owned by the womenfolk. Unused land is free for anyone to take up, but usually a woman prefers to make a new garden near to her own homestead or near to the plots of her co-wives, and therefore the plots of adjacent settlements are not generally intermingled. Settlements are also the primary units for initiation and the arrangement of the men into age-sets.

Settlements amalgamate into seven named districts[1] which are geographically coherent though not necessarily spatially distinct from each other. The members of a district periodically combine for rain-making and other ceremonial functions, in particular the magical treatment of both males and cattle, symbolically marking the turn of the year when, in the wet season, all or most of the cattle herds have returned to eastern pastures. There are one or more ritual groves for each district which are distinct from the settlements' groves. Formerly the district provided military contingents in times of warfare.

Finally, there are two tribal ritual groves near the centre of the settled area. At least twice a year the whole tribe assembles at one of these for rain-making ceremonies and general supplication to the High God. One tribal grove is used just before the first rains break (March), and the other in the lull in rainfall between the two annual peaks (June).

---

[1] These districts and their populations are as follows: Panyangara 4862 (this contains also the area of Kadokin, whose people owe ritual allegiance to Rengen; but separate figures are not available), Rengen 3772, Kapelimuru 3684, Lothilang 1739, Kotido 1580, Kotiang 1304 and Kanawert 1270.

INTRODUCTION

All ritual activities are organized and led by the senior elders at the relevant level—settlement, district or tribe. This seniority is determined by the age-set system, which exists almost entirely to subserve the ritual life of the Jie. Only initiated men may take part in most ceremonies, and the fact that they are initiated is believed to make their participation in the ritual especially efficacious. Initiation and membership of age-sets has extremely little significance outside ritual affairs, for the age-sets are not connected with military or political organization. In everyday life the formal relations of age-mates, seniors and juniors, are of minor importance.[1]

In Turkanaland the mode of residence and the nature of all social activities are strongly affected by nomadism. Nowhere is any homestead permanent, nor under this particular nomadic system do groups of families necessarily move in concert. In any populated area at a given time there can be perceived three types of neighbourhood groups. Firstly, the primary neighbourhood is a small cluster of homesteads, geographically disparate from like clusters, and its inhabitants maintain for the time being daily face-to-face relations. The secondary neighbourhood is a collection of two or three such groups of homesteads, often based on a common water-point, often using common pastures to the temporary, *de facto* exclusion of other people, and geographically near to one another and distant from others. The tertiary neighbourhood is a wider, more vague socio-geographical region, within which from time to time social intercourse is maintained, its frequency depending on personal inclinations and requirements and the attractiveness of the activities (e.g. feasts and ceremonies, dances and general visiting) available. The primary neighbourhood seldom consists of more than five homesteads, often two or three, and they are not necessarily very close together. The secondary neighbourhood comprises two to four such clusters spread over an area of several square miles—i.e. between five and twenty homesteads altogether. The tertiary neighbourhood is too vague to allow of numerical description, but in general it covers an area of some twenty miles around any given secondary neighbourhood which belongs to it. Such neighbourhoods are sometimes coterminous with natural regions, such as a river valley, a

[1] The Jie age-set organization is described in a paper in *The Journal of the Royal Anthropological Society*, lxxxiii, Part 2. I do not give an outline of its rather complex operation here since it is irrelevant to present purposes, having little direct connection with either kinship or property rights.

mountainside, etc. The point of chief significance is that social relations in a neighbourhood are principally based on mere temporary contiguity which allows a degree of economic and social co-operation. At any time they may break up as constituent homesteads move away, or be added to as new families arrive. If a general move occurs, not all neighbours move together nor to the same destination, but they severally come to form parts of other neighbourhood groups in their new areas of residence. Neither do such groups re-form again at a later date—say, the equivalent time in the next year. A group of two or three families may sometimes move and keep together for a time, but such associations are always transitory, for the essence of Turkana nomadism lies in the individual freedom of each family under its own head. This will be described later.

The Turkana are loosely grouped into nineteen 'territorial sections' (*ekitela*, pl. *ngitela*) which are merely geographical groups to which a few minor social distinctions attach—e.g. details of female clothing, dialect and types of ornamentation. A man and his family belong to that section in which they normally spend the wet seasons. Sections have no political, economic or ritual significance.[1] There is an age-set system which is not particularly strong, endemically because of its subservience to the needs of nomadic pastoralism, and more recently because of the end of raiding. Unlike the Jie system, it provided the core of the primitive military organization. Today it exists mainly as a conservative continuation of the relations established by initiation, and by a certain fraternity amongst contiguous age-mates exhibited in feasts, dancing and some ritual activities.

III

In conclusion of this introduction some mention of the conditions of field-work is required. Amongst the Jie my work was straightforward, since I came from Turkanaland knowing the language and cultural background. No less important, however, was the fact that the people were friendly and generally helpful in my enquiries. When one was living in so constricted a settled area it was not difficult to make many contacts and some considerable friendships. People of both sexes and all ages became valued informants and my work was

---

[1] Leaving aside historical considerations, a similar quality attaches to these sections as in England is given to such regions as East Anglia or Wessex.

seldom impeded by opposition. In short, the Jie provided for me almost ideal subjects for anthropological research, and little more needs to be said here. In Turkanaland, however, conditions were vastly different. There the natives were often hostile to our presence, or at least apathetic to my enquiries. Many of the older men were still smarting under the necessity of submission to the *pax Britannica* and the losses of people and stock during the period of conquest. They frankly resented the cessation of warfare and the loss of independence which had provided much of life's value and significance. They have suffered the disadvantages of European conquest, but, in being left alone thereafter, have received little or none of the advantages. They still live for their past, unlike the Jie, who are genuinely glad of the end of the old days of warfare and who recognize their greater stock wealth, more reliable food supply and so on.[1]

Frankly, I never felt, with the exception of one or two cases, that I was ever entirely trusted by the Turkana amongst whom I lived. Men and women amongst whom my wife and I worked for many weeks during our eighteen months' stay there remained, under the surface, suspicious of our presence and never really understood our intentions. At no point, except that of warfare, was I able to stir their interest. Evasions and downright lies were the common practice to the last. I never had an old man as a regular informant during the whole time. Women who became friendly with my wife were more than once warned off by their menfolk. Men would come to beg from us, but refused to stay and talk; indeed, they sometimes merely tapped their mouths to indicate their desire for tobacco. To carry out a survey of a secondary neighbourhood took many days of tiring walking and gradual enquiries as to the whereabouts of homesteads and the number of inhabitants. My two best informants were both tribal policemen kindly loaned to me by the District Commissioner as guides and assistants—fortunately both were still unsophisticated. One of these men was a veritable mine of information and so far as I could discover never told me a conscious untruth. However, I have never relied wholly on the evidence of either and have neglected that which I cannot fully substantiate from elsewhere. Other noteworthy informants numbered no more than half a dozen, none of whom could I trust in the last resort.

A particular factor affecting field-work was the wildness and extent

---

[1] This does not mean that the Jie welcome all modern developments now beginning. They certainly do not, but at least they do not live regretting the past.

of this semi-desert land. We travelled by lorry and on foot with camels and donkeys, spending many days merely reaching a general destination and gaining little information *en route*. Unfortunately, the only possible centre was the administrative station at Lodwar, which lies in the central desert area with few Turkana near by. The eighteen months in Turkanaland could not be a period of intensive field-work, but was necessarily split up into spells of several weeks by lengthy, exhausting travel. It was invariably difficult to locate homesteads, even in regions whose geography we came to know. Water-points, tracks and passes were sometimes kept from our knowledge; they lied about the disposition of homesteads; at other times natives refused to have much to do with us, even moving away secretly at night to avoid us. It was therefore never possible to live with a group of people for periods of several months. Not only did groups of small size limit the possibilities of enquiry, but they were impermanent; and it was unusual to be able to stay in one place for very long because of the difficulty of obtaining supplies. We could not live off the land—even meat was difficult, sometimes impossible to obtain in the middle of herds of animals. The number of my immediate neighbours was seldom more than about one hundred people, and the total number of people within reach of my camp not usually more than two hundred to two hundred and fifty men, women and children. It was seldom that we had the opportunity by persistent effort and friendliness to break down the automatic suspicion and opposition.

Now these field-work difficulties as such are not important in this book and belong more properly to a discursive account of life in Turkanaland.[1] They must, however, be mentioned in order to explain if not to amend some of the deficiencies of my data. To take a few random examples: I witnessed only one complete wedding, but even then not the preceding bridewealth discussions; and at the only other one I was able to attend I was not able to watch events nor talk to the participants since I met only complete hostility, although we had been living in the area for about three weeks at the time. I never saw initiations, nor did I properly witness funeral and mortuary ceremonies. Usually it was not possible for me to meet all the members of an extended family. In addition, both of the wet seasons were poor whilst I was in Turkanaland, and therefore there

[1] See *Survey of the Turkana*, pp. 10-12, and also my, 'Nomad Anthropologist', *Corona*, April 1952.

was not the conventional intensity of social activities at either time. Consequently it was not possible to collect the wealth of evidence that could be desired. I am aware of my inability to give sufficient documentation and of the inadequacy of some that is given. Although I genuinely found a surprisingly high degree of cultural homogeneity for so dispersed a population, my specific data has perforce to be drawn from a relatively small number of particular areas.[1] I feel certain that my main analysis is substantially correct and can give a degree of documentation; on the other hand it is recognized, and the reader should be aware also, that more detailed data would perhaps have permitted further refinement.

[1] During my second tour of field-work in 1950 I made several extended trips by lorry and on foot to regions where intensive field-work had not been carried out. In extremely few cases did I discover anything but homogeneity in all important sociocultural features. Minor differences of dress, dialect, ornamentation and the lay-out of homesteads appeared to be the only common variations. Such homogeneity is probably maintained through the continual intermingling of people from many areas in the course of nomadic movements.

CHAPTER TWO

ECOLOGY AND PASTORALISM

ALTHOUGH this account of Jie and Turkana social life is to deal mainly with the complex of social rights over domestic animals, we must begin with at least a brief survey of the nature and influence of the indigenous environment. This will not only provide the background against which to set the sociological study but will immediately display fundamental differences between life in the two countries. Further, whilst it might be possible, though not necessarily desirable, to embark on a discussion of social relations in Jieland with but a brief mention of ecology and economics, this would be out of the question for Turkanaland. In this latter country there is such a notably harsh and difficult environment that its effect on social life is all-pervasive, inescapable both for the people themselves and for the observer of their lives and activities. For a proper understanding of any facet of Turkana social organization it is necessary to begin with an appreciation of the environmental limitations rigorously imposed on all social activities. To a certain extent any study of the Turkana is also an ecological study.

I wish, also, to provide some data on the place and importance of domestic stock in the daily lives of these two peoples which may throw light on their conceptions of property rights in these animals. For, after all, cattle, camels, goats and sheep are not mere symbols in which rights are vested. They are, especially for the Turkana, but only to a lesser degree for the Jie, the principal means of life and livelihood.

Ecological Survey of Jieland

Jieland is part of the undulating plains of north-eastern Uganda. These have an average altitude of some 4000 feet and dip gently to the west and south-west towards the Kioga-Nile basin. Except on parts of the perimeter, Jieland itself has no outstanding high land.

16

ECOLOGY AND PASTORALISM

The year is fairly clearly divided into two seasons—wet and dry. The rains usually break about the end of March, rise to a peak volume in May and there is a second and lower peak in July-August. The dry season continues from September till March. The average rainfall for central Jieland is about twenty-five inches, but is characterized over the years by a wide range of variation. At Lotome[1] since 1939 annual falls have varied between 19·3 and 37·4 inches—that is, a total range of about 66 per cent of the average fall.

Outside the wet season, rain does not usually fall in any quantity; December and January appear to be completely rainless and other months are dry in effect. Even during the wet season there are often dry spells of two to eight weeks without effective rainfall.[2]

The long, dry season causes the ground and vegetation everywhere to be dried and burnt up so that for at least five or six months there is no vegetal growth. Open water disappears; soils crack and crumble. Since most of the effective rain comes in fairly heavy, if prolonged storms, there tend to be floods of water followed by drought. Much of the country is 'black-cotton' soil, which is highly resistant to the absorption of water; and even elsewhere the hard, sun-baked earth cannot readily absorb large quantities of water. The run-off during and after a heavy fall is therefore great, with corresponding loss of water and depreciation in the effectiveness of the rainfall. At the same time the crumbled top-soil tends to be washed away as the whole countryside is aflow with water.[3] The

[1] Reliable statistics are not available for any place in Jieland. Figures have been recorded at Lotome in Karamajongland since 1939, and these are used here since the position of Lotome is in most respects similar to that of central Jieland. I have to thank Canon R. Clark, who has kindly allowed me to use his records.

[2] In 1950 and 1951, both only fair years, there were effective dry spells of some seven to eight weeks between May and July.

[3] Compare the following description: 'The track northwards from Karamoja was exhaustingly dry and hot; while returning to Moroto, however, I was caught in a rainstorm which lasted for about two hours. Within ten minutes of the initial downpour the whole surface of the plain for miles around was covered with a sheet of water moving westwards. Nowhere except on the rises did I find it less than ankle-deep, and small gulleys which, when they were dry, I had passed two days before almost unnoticed, were now roaring torrents against which it was impossible to stand. When the storm had passed I dug into the ground in many places to see how far the rain had penetrated; and nowhere could I find moist soil at a greater depth than 6 inches, and as a rule the earth was bone-dry and powdery at a depth of $1\frac{1}{2}$ to 2 inches from the surface. The sun-cracks, of course, retained water, but most of that was evaporated during the next day or two.' This extract was taken from a field geologist's report in 1928 and is quoted in *Soil Erosion and Water Supplies in Uganda*, by Wayland, Brasnett, *et al.*, Entebbe, 1938, pp. 37-8.

long, hot dry season and the relative ineffectiveness of low rainfall produce an arid grass and bush land and cumulative soil erosion. Erosion is accelerated in the settled areas by overcultivation and by the overgrazing by congested dairy-herds. The general aridity is aggravated by the proximity of the Turkana semi-desert to the east, whence comes a hot, dry wind during the dry season, causing heavy dust-storms in January and February.

Average rainfall in the east of Jieland must be about the same as in the centre, but to the west, however, it increases to between thirty and thirty-five inches a year on the Acoli border. The nature of the grasslands follows this rainfall pattern. In the east and centre grass is short and thin and tends easily to become overgrazed, with much soil erosion; in the west grass grows thickly and to a height of six or seven feet. Unfortunately its value is much depreciated by the long dry season when this tall grass is dried out and becomes useless for pasturage. Also, after about October, large areas in the west are completely waterless. Water cannot be obtained by digging anywhere there to a depth of some thirty feet. Such areas are necessarily closed to stock. At the same time the whole country east of Kotido is waterless in the dry season, and even in the centre water is very scarce. Therefore, in that season stock must be based on one of about eight water-points in the west. These are shown in Figure 2.

The pastoral pattern, then, follows a system of transhumance. In the dry season stock are concentrated mainly in the west and west-centre. As the rains come and new succulent grass appears there is a dispersal of herds far and wide over the whole of the western area now that surface water becomes available. By mid-June this grass is beginning to get thick and tall, while to the east, where also there is now surface water, new short grass is growing up. A movement is made to the east and east-centre at about this time, leaving the western pastures uninhabited. When the rains cease (September) the surface water in the east fairly quickly dries up and of necessity herds must begin to move westwards again. Here surface water lasts rather longer so that at first herds can remain fairly spread out; but by December the concentration on the permanent water-points again becomes necessary.

In pre-British days the system of transhumance involved the whole of the population, for as the dry season progressed the permanent homesteads became deserted, as almost all the people congregated in the stock camps. By at least February each year the Jie were concentrated within about seven or eight miles of each of the few permanent water-points. The reason for this lay primarily in the acute

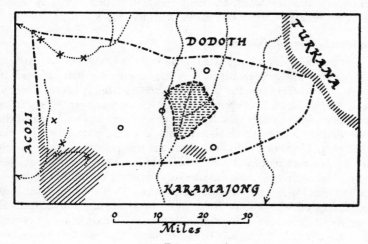

FIGURE 2

(*a*) SKETCH MAP OF JIELAND

—·—·—·—	Approximate boundary of modern Jieland. N.B. The boundary in the south-west (Labwor) is indefinite.
············	Water-course (usually dry).
×	Permanent water-point, indigenous.
o	Permanent water-point, bore-hole or dam.
/////	High land.
:::::::	Settled area.

(*b*) DIAGRAM OF COMPARATIVE AREAS

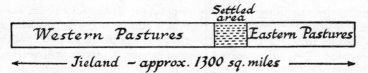

shortage of water in the settled areas. When the country was being pacified and conquered by the British this large-scale movement of population was prohibited by the military authorities in order to stabilize and thus more easily to control the tribes of this region. Thereafter the older men, women and children have lived permanently at the homesteads, and only the young men and boys with a very few women live in and move with the stock camps.

Ecological Survey of Turkanaland

Turkanaland lies wholly within the eastern branch of the African Rift Valley. The general altitude at the base of the Rift escarpment is about 3000 feet, and the land falls away gradually to 1230 feet at Lake Rudolf. As a first approximation the country can be regarded as a great plain, geographically an extension of the low lands of the Anglo-Egyptian Sudan, isolated from British East Africa for the most part. Scattered over this plain are ranges of hills and a few larger mountain blocks. These latter vary in height from about 4500 to 7000 feet. Dwarfing all the rest in size (and also in importance to the Turkana) is Muruapolon in west-central Turkanaland. This is an undulating tableland some forty miles by thirty miles in extent, all over about 4000 feet. Lorienetom in the north-east is about twenty miles by ten miles in area. The other mountains are largely solitary peaks with broad slopes and shoulders.

Almost everywhere, from whatever vantage point, the observer is confronted with a continuous stretch of plains in which the mountains are but partial breaks. There are, indeed, large areas of plains altogether free of high land. The 'black-cotton' plains in north-western Turkanaland are quite unbroken for a distance of some eighty miles; central Turkanaland, as it slopes gently towards Lake Rudolf, contains only a few isolated hills. Elsewhere the vast plains make sharp contrast with the relatively small area of high land. This contrast is reflected in the ecology of the inhabitants. There is always the dichotomy—the plains and the mountains. The Turkana themselves are people of the plains who make use of the mountains unwillingly and only by necessity. If one asks a man where he lives, he usually gives the name of the region of the plains in which he attempts to live in the wet season, though for much of the year, for all of some years perhaps, he may in fact not live thereabouts. This is his 'homeland', *akwap*. The mountains are not regarded as anybody's homelands. Men and women have told me repeatedly that they do not like to live in the mountains, and the beginnings of each new wet season, the beginnings of new pastures in the plains, are sufficient to draw them away from the mountains, although pastures there may be much better. This attitude is rationalized by the people, though not without some truth also. It is cold in the mountains, they say; the stock are more likely to contract disease, and predatory animals abound in the thick bush and forest; they assert that they know the plains better and that the mountains are full of capricious spirits, and so on. The mountains are indispensable to the Turkana way of life and the people recognize that much of their stock could not exist but for mountain pastures; but everyone agrees that the mountains are not pleasant areas to live in, compared with the plains. It may be noted here that even when stock and people are concentrated on the mountains they must usually look to the plains, or at least the foot-hills, for their water supplies, since natural supplies in the mountains are generally poor and temporary. The steep passes and paths to be climbed down and up at least every other day are another disadvantage of mountain life. In all this it is significant that it is the homestead which normally remains in the plains for most or all of the year, which is called the 'chief-homestead' and which is the home of the head of the family, together with his chief wife. They only live with their valued cattle when the latter descend to the plains in the wet seasons.

Temperatures are uniformly high throughout the year, between 100° F. and 70° F., seldom lower, even at night. Whilst Turkanaland has not the excessive torridity of some more northerly desert lands, it has nevertheless a steady heat which is little relieved at any time.

The Turkana divide the year into two seasons—the dry season, *akumu*, and the wet season, *agiporo*. These two terms, in keeping with realities, are used in an extremely elastic manner, meaning only in a general way the division of the year into rainy and non-rainy periods. More precisely they refer to the times when the rains have been sufficient to produce new and fairly well-established vegetation —the wet season; or the times when rain is absent or quite insufficient to produce or maintain the vegetational cover of the land —the dry season. In the general way the wet season extends from about April to August and the dry season from about September to March; but the rains in any year may break any time between March and June, and may fall off between June and September—there is little correlation between Turkana's rainfall and that of the higher regions of British East Africa. Not infrequently the rains more or less fail altogether—even by Turkana standards—and the growth of vegetation is so poor that the people say that no wet season occurs in such years.[1]

As a general statement, it may be said that the average annual rainfall in the plains is twelve to sixteen inches, falling to less than six inches in the central desert regions. The significant features of the rainfall are the wide range of variation over the years and the considerable degree of variation between successive years.[2] Figures are misleading as they stand since they afford no indication of the nature and effectiveness of the rainfall. Where rainfall is so small, the way in which actual precipitation is received is of high significance. Rain usually comes in sharp storms which occur in the latter part of the day or persist intermittently for a day or two. There is a high degree of evaporation due to the constant heat; and owing to thin and sandy soil covers and poor vegetation there is a rapid run-off. Consequently water retention is low. A day or two of rainy weather in the wet season may well be followed by a fortnight or more of cloudless drought, when the earth becomes dried up, cracked and reduced to an infertile, dry, crumbled mass. Since the growth of vegetation depends almost entirely on rainfall, it is clear that an average fall, broken up into short periods of heavy precipitation separated by long periods of drought, is inimical to permanent and strong growth and seeding. An average fall may produce a poor withered crop. The point of significance here is that in this arid country the quantity and nature of the rainfall is quite critical. Variations of a few inches can have a considerable effect not known in more fortunate lands; similarly, a fairly concentrated rainy period during the year can have much more effect than an equal fall spread out over several months. Rainfall is not only small, it is irregular both in quantity and effectiveness. These considerable variations in

[1] One of my Turkana staff, who knew the Kitale area of the Kenya Highlands, told me that it was the wet season up there all the year round. I explained that there was a dry season of at least about three months. He replied, 'It is not a matter of rain; it is the grass. Plenty of grass makes a wet season. There is no dry season at Kitale.'

[2] Since 1922 the average rainfall at Lodwar (central region) has been 5·75 inches; since 1933 the average at Lokitaung (north) has been 16·1 inches; over a shorter period the average at Kaputir (south-central) was about 12 inches. Rainfall at Lodwar has varied between 2 and 10 inches in general; but 1933 had only 0·73 inches, and this was the worst famine year in memory; 1936 had 14·5 inches, and this was about the best year in modern times. Lokitaung figures range between about 5 inches and 22 inches, with one phenomenal year (1947) of 40 inches. Figures have been obtained through the courtesy of the East African Meteorological Department, Nairobi.

rainfall—and thus in the supply of vegetation—are important in causing corresponding variations in the movements and dispositions of the nomadic Turkana over the years. Turkana say, with truth, that only about one year in four or five has a 'good wet season', i.e. with rainfall well above the average paucity.

Attention has already been drawn to the physical dichotomy in the country, and from the point of view of rainfall there are significant differences between plains and mountains. No rainfall data are available for any mountain area but about twenty-five inches appears to be an average fall over about 4000 feet.[1] There is the same division of the year into two seasons and to a lesser extent there is irregular distribution during the wet season, and variations from year to year. However, variations and irregularities are rather smaller in the mountains than in the plains. Rainy spells last longer, intervening dry spells are shorter, and precipitation at any one time is usually heavier. Probably these higher masses tend to foment their own storms, and since—except for Pelekec—they are situated towards the periphery of the country, relatively nearer to higher external lands, they tend to share to some extent the better rainfall of the Kenya Highlands, Uganda and Abyssinia. Whereas the lower plains and barren hills tend to be foci of hot air, inimical to rainy conditions in contrast the mountains tend to be foci of cooler, damp air, both because of the change in altitude above the floor of the plains and also because of the thicker cover of vegetation. Evaporation is lower than in the plains, and owing to a better soil cover and thicker vegetation the run-off is less. The November short rains are invariably unreliable in the plains, but frequently provide a most valuable stimulus to vegetation on the mountains at a time when the effects of the previous wet season are slackening.

The vegetation of Turkanaland, which is mainly a product of this distribution of rainfall, follows the same natural dichotomy. In the plains there is semi-desert bush which in the east-central regions deteriorates into almost sheer sandy or rock desert, and in the better regions in the north-west and north-east develops into semi-desert grasslands with relatively less bush. The typical state is one of bare sandy or rocky soil with a sparse, intermittent cover of low bushes, shrubs and scattered small trees in which acacias

---

[1] This estimate is based on comparison with other arid areas in East Africa, the evidence of natives and Europeans, and my own observations regarding the relative frequency and intensity of rainfall in the mountains compared with the plains.

predominate.[1] Most water-courses support some larger trees (mainly thorn), and over 3000 feet there is much sanseviera and cactus. There is a virtual abscence of permanent grass except in some better parts in the north, where nevertheless there is much bare ground. Much of this vegetation is dormant in drought, but with the wet season temporary grass and herbage appear for longer or shorter periods according to the effectiveness of the rainfall. At this time useful grazing is provided along the banks of the larger water-courses.

In the mountains over about 4000 feet (sometimes lower) there is permanent grass which grows several feet high in the wet season. Bush is often thick and trees plentiful, and in many places they appear to be increasing at the expense of grass cover. In the better areas a thick grass cover grows, of the type usually associated with dry savannah lands. As the dry season progresses these mountain grasslands become increasingly arid and burnt up by sun and hot winds; nevertheless, grass of a kind does persist the whole year except in certain infertile parts and in the worst years. The bulk of the grasslands are between 4000 and 5500 feet. See Figure 3.

Running across the plains, each water-course forms an outstanding belt of thicker vegetation in contrast with the surrounding plains. There are no permanently flowing rivers and the two major water-courses (Turkwel and Kerio), which flow more or less continuously from April to September, receive the bulk of their water from the Kenya Highlands to the south. Because of this they have especially thick belts of vegetation on either bank. Those on the upper Turkwel (and its main tributary the Malmalti) are composed of gigantic thorn trees, dense forest and bush with grass, up to nearly three miles wide in places. They provide dry-season pasturelands comparable to those of the mountains.[2] Other water-courses, the largest of which all depend on sources outside Turkanaland, seldom flow for more than a day or so at a time, often a few hours only. Immediately after a storm they rage in flood, flow for a brief period, and then cease, leaving pools of water and deposits of silt and debris.

Water supplies are taken mainly from the water-courses. After the rains, ponds are formed, rock-pools are filled and local springs gush,

[1] For a detailed, though incomplete account of the vegetation of Turkanaland see Edwards, D. C., *Report on the Grazing Areas of Turkana*, Government of Kenya, 1945. Also see sketch-map No. 1 in my *Survey of the Turkana*, p. 40.

[2] The upper Turkwel riverain belt and a few other favoured plains areas will be included as 'mountain grasslands' for simplicity of exposition.

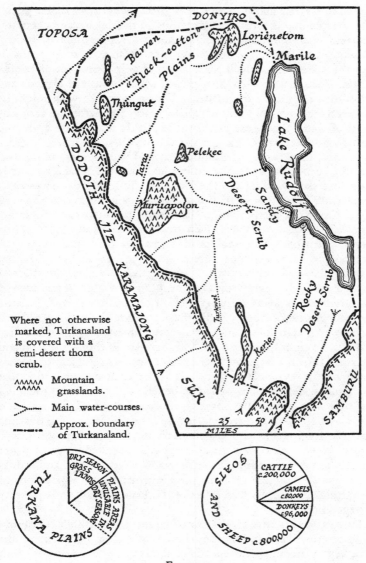

FIGURE 3

SKETCH MAP OF TURKANALAND

but no more than about three weeks' drought exhausts them. Thereafter people find their water by digging in the dry beds of the water courses; and the number of points where digging is fruitful diminishes as the dry season progresses. It appears most probable that the water-table which these tap is largely a product of rainfall outside Turkanaland—to the west and south in eastern Uganda and the Kenya Highlands respectively. Thus contrary to what might be expected there are few areas which, by native standards, are seriously short of water. There are cases, but relatively few, where graze and browse outlast water. Except for the north-west, where sudanic savannah plains begin, it is unusual to find water-points more than ten to fifteen miles apart, i.e. rather less than a Turkana can easily walk in a day. Neither are there commonly found the excessively deep water-holes typical of Boran and Somali country to the east, or of Karamoja to the west, where from three to ten people are required to form a human chain to draw up water. Most of the larger, permanent water-points in Turkanaland are not more than two people deep, and not infrequently one person can carry out watering of stock on his own. In saying that few areas are short of water I am deliberately avoiding European standards. It amounts to the fact that few areas are ungrazed, or only partly grazed, because the people cannot obtain sufficient water for their animals. Each permanent water-point can provide for homesteads up to a radius of seven or eight miles around, and there are in the wet season and early dry season a large number of minor points sufficient to outlast much of the available pastures. It is, of course, quite true that additional water supplies would be beneficial, especially in reducing the time and strenuous physical effort required of humans and animals in going to and from water, and thereby increasing the time available for grazing and also conserving the stamina of all concerned. Nevertheless, it must be emphasized that shortage of water scarcely reduces the effective use of available vegetation, and it does not primarily regulate or limit the movements and dispositions of these nomadic people. The cause of Turkana nomadism is poverty of vegetation.

Turkanaland is an arid, desiccated country, probably undergoing some progressive deterioration, though at a slow rate which must have begun before the present inhabitants came to occupy it. Both human and stock populations have probably increased during the period of British occupation, although there is an annual crop of deaths of stock due to underfeeding and overexhaustion. On the other hand, Turkana cattle appear to have been isolated from the main ravages of East African epidemics. In addition, due to the territorial expansions over the last seventy-five years or less, the Turkana occupy and use a far larger area today than was available to their grandparents. This has involved not merely a general increase of territory, for some of the best grasslands are included in the new regions.[1] Effective dry-season grasslands have been increased by as much as 100 per cent. However, it is obvious that there is considerable pressure on the country's resources in the second half of the dry season at least; vegetation is poor even by Turkana standards, and probably deteriorating.

Stock must be herded in areas where there are both pasturage and water. Nomadic movements are largely the result of conventionalized attempts to maximize the supply of these necessities. From the foregoing description of the country it is obvious that at certain times of the year some areas are quite unable to contain herds, whilst the vegetation of other areas is such that only scattered, thinly distributed herds can live there. As vegetational resources become exhausted, movement must be made to areas where better conditions exist; conversely, as new resources become available following the rains, herds can be moved to hitherto barren areas. But this is by no means the whole case, for all types of animals have not the same dietary needs. At one extreme are cattle which must have grass (or certain types of herbage usually associated with grass); at the other extreme there are camels, which need browse (i.e. the leafage of bushes and trees) and which seldom graze if only because they are anatomically unfitted for it. Both sheep and goats are capable of both grazing and browsing, though sheep fare better on grass.

To some extent these dietary requirements determine the areas in which the kinds of stock can be kept. Cattle are strictly confined to grasslands, which means the mountain areas all the year round and the banks of water-courses and the lower hills in fair wet seasons. In accordance with the Turkana traditions of living in the plains whenever possible, the cattle are driven down from the mountains as soon as the new rains have produced sufficient graze in the plains, and are

[1] For example, there are included western Muruapolon, the bulk of Lorienetom, Thungut and Mogila mountains, and also the forward plains grasslands of the northwest and north-east. On the expansion of Turkanaland see *Survey of the Turkana*, pp. 150-5, and sketch-map No. 6.

moved back only when compelled by exhaustion of graze there at the beginning of the dry season. There tends, therefore, to be a distinct difference between the localities of cattle herding in the two seasons—a decisive movement from the mountains to the plains and back again. In the poorer wet seasons some of the cattle herds may not be able to move down to the plains at all since little or no grass grows there. At such times movement is restricted to leaving the better—usually the higher—parts of the mountains for those parts which had been grazed out earlier. Thus, whether the rains are good or poor, there is some movement in response to the appearance of new vegetational resources; and in any case, whether in the mountains or the plains, there are likely to be minor movements in adjustment to changing resources and changing demands upon them at any one time.

Browse, however, is ubiquitous, or almost so, in Turkanaland, varying only in quantity and quality. Even the worst of the central shrub desert region affords some browse in the wet season, whilst extensive areas of the plains provide some kind of supply right through the dry season. Thus the Turkanan are usually able to keep their camels and goats in the plains, although some areas cannot maintain herds throughout the year. Camel and goat herds tend to make gradual movements, going from part of an area and then moving on elsewhere. The worst parts of the plains gradually empty as the dry season progresses, or perhaps a few widely scattered homesteads only may remain. There is a gradual concentration in the better parts of the plains and in the mountains. Probably less than half of the browsing herds reach the mountains, outside of the worst years. When the new rains break, bush leafage quickly returns and browsing stock are able to disperse again fairly soon.

These conditions mean that a family's herds must be split up—for all (or very nearly all) families own all types of stock. The typical arrangement is that the cattle are kept in one homestead and the goats and camels in another. If there are sufficient, the camels may occupy a separate homestead, or milch cattle may be separated from oxen and immature cattle. It is a matter of the convenience of herding, watering and general organization. In addition, an over-large herd may necessitate too frequent movements, as it more quickly exhausts local vegetation. The division of the family's herds is purely a practical measure and not socially conditioned, though it has of course important social consequences. For any single family this is not an absolute necessity, since the browsing herds could be kept along with the cattle in the mountains in the dry season; but it would not be possible for all families, since the mountain areas are restricted and could not maintain all of the Turkana stock throughout the dry season. The tradition of attachment to the plains serves to support and rationalize the system. Quite apart from this, however, the Turkana, realizing the general poverty of their natural resources, do not wish to leave any browse unused, and it is a firm principle that less persistent pastures should be utilized first and that more persistent pastures should be reserved until worse times of the year when the rest are more or less exhausted. Thus the goat and camel herds remain in the plains, apart from the cattle, whilst browse persists, moving to the mountains only when pastures in the plains can no longer contain all the herds. Similarly, the cattle can take advantage of new but purely temporary grasslands off the mountains in the wet seasons, thus leaving the latter pastures for intensive use in the dry season—and also, of course, allowing an interval in which the mountain areas may recuperate, free of stock, during the period of new growth.

Thus the natural dichotomy of plains and mountains is broadly followed in the pastoral organization. Cattle spend eight or nine months in the mountains each year (and not infrequently the whole of the year), whilst the camels and goats remain in the plains, although tending to shift towards the mountains by the end of the dry season. It may be convenient to speak of the cattle following a system of transhumance between mountains and plains, so long as that term does not obscure the movements within each region. This may be contrasted with the more truly nomadic movements of the browse homesteads, which tend to move about all the year in response to gradually changing conditions of vegetation.

Figure 4 illustrates diagrammatically the disposition of the three main types of stock over the year. This must be taken as a rather abstract, ideal scheme with which no particular one of the thousands of patterns of individual movements may agree. It gives only the major dispositions of stock, for camels and goats are to be found in scattered herds almost everywhere at all times.[1] If it be objected that the diagram is somewhat complicated, the reader may be assured that the actual position in Turkanaland is a good deal more complex

[1] The genuinely empty areas of Turkanaland are the mountains in a fairly good wet season, and the central desert and 'black-cotton' plains in the dry season.

as it appears to the observer who attempts to detect some system in the intricate web of movements in so large a country. Indeed, this diagram presents an oversimplification in the attempt to summarize,

FIGURE 4

CYCLICAL SCHEMA OF THE DISPOSITIONS OF TURKANA STOCK

	Early wet season	Climax of wet season	Early dry season	Development of dry season	Consolidation of dry season	Climax of dry season
MOUNTAIN BLOCKS FORWARD PLAINS	Cattle	—	—	Cattle	Cattle	Cattle Goats Camels
LOWER HILLS FOOTHILLS	Cattle	Cattle	Cattle	—	Goats Camels	—
TURKANA PLAINS	Goats Camels	Goats Camels	Goats Camels	Goats Camels	Goats Camels	Goats Camels
BANKS OF WATER-COURSES	—	Cattle	Goats Camels	Goats Camels	—	—

This shows an ideal cycle of stock dispositions. All herds do not pass through every stage in every year because rainfall, and therefore vegetation, varies so widely. The duration of the wet season is approximately from April to August, but the rains may break any time between March and July, and may fall off between June and September. The rest of the year is the dry season. A 'good wet season' occurs only about once in four to five years. In some or all of the other years cattle may not be able to leave parts of the mountain blocks at all.

Only the major disposition of each type of stock are noted here. Camels and goats (including sheep) are to be found everywhere with cattle, but in relatively minor concentrations. Movements are not restricted to those between the four geographical-vegetational regions as shown in the table. There are more or less frequent movements within each region according to local conditions there at the time.

Cf. map showing principal cattle movements; End-paper, *Survey of the Turkana*.

for the purposes of this present account, the complicated situation with its multitude of variables. It must be emphasized that we are not dealing with a fairly straightforward system of transhumance such as that practised by the Jie and companion tribes in eastern

Uganda, or by the pastoralists of the Nile basin in the southern Sudan; nor is it a migrational system controlled by strong, corporate territorial or kin groups as in the case of some of the North African camel-herders. The irregular distribution and effectiveness of rainfall, the complex distribution of plains and mountains and the dietary needs of the different types of stock cannot be reduced to a simple formula, nor is there any indigenous authority to enforce such a thing in practice.

Each year conditions are different enough to alter the details of individual patterns of nomadic movements and the timing of successive 'stages' of the annual cycle. In Figure 4 I have not attempted to assign specific months to each 'stage'. A few examples may illustrate how variability of rainfall affects basic movements. In 1949 the rains were so delayed that cattle could only descend to the plains in late July, and many herds did not descend at all. Goat and camel herds remained relatively concentrated in the better parts of the plains until about June, and were able to disperse throughout the plains for only about three months. In 1950 the rains were earlier and the ideal wet-season pattern was established by early May; but the rains fell off again so seriously and plains grasslands became so poor that many cattle herds returned to the mountains again in June and redescended in July and early August. In 1951 the rains were earlier still and wet-season dispositions were taken up by mid-April, and were somewhat precariously maintained during the rest of the season. There are also often distinct regional variations. A fixed time-table cannot therefore be established for either cattle or browsing stock.[1]

The Use of Pasturelands

In both tribal areas there are the same indigenous conceptions regarding the use of pasturelands. The first principle is that there are no specific pasture rights attached to any individuals or groups of any sort. All pasturage is common to all members of a tribe.[2] A herd of stock can be moved anywhere at any time. The second principle is that movements are made primarily at the discretion of the 'owner'[3] of a herd, or of his agent in charge. Furthermore, a herd is not

[1] For a more detailed account of the physical environment and the patterns of nomadic movement see *Survey of the Turkana*, pp. 37-52.

[2] This principle of general commonage operates also amongst the Karamajong, Dodoth and Donyiro.

[3] In Turkanaland an 'owner' is the head of a nuclear family—see Chapter 5. In Jieland a herd is owned by a group of full-brothers, but at the moment for the sake of simplicity, I speak of 'an owner'—see Chapter 3.

necessarily to be found in the same place at the same time of successive years; most importantly, particularly in Turkanaland, conditions of rainfall and therefore of grass and water are seldom the same two years together, and in any event there is no especial reason why an owner should establish his herd in any one spot.

The principal reasons for the movements of herds are lack of grass or browse, lack of water, or both. Since, especially in the dry season, the relative adequacy of these at various places is a matter of opinion, there may well be a variety of opinion amongst owners. One man, for instance, may consider that his present area can no longer adequately support his animals and he moves to another area believed to be more satisfactory; another man, although he realizes the poverty of the area's resources, does not consider that sufficient advantage is to be gained by moving. Each man attempts to provide for his herds as best he can in the light of his experience and the needs of his animals. He must take into account the quantity and quality of vegetation, facilities for watering, distance between pastures and water, and future prospects of both. There are certain times when movement is essential, e.g. in the early dry season—in Jieland, herds must move westwards as water supplies cease in the east; in Turkanaland, cattle must move to the mountains as the plains grasslands are exhausted. At other times movements are conventionally prescribed though not physically essential, e.g. when new pastures and water are available with a new wet season—in Jieland, herds scatter over the west and later move eastwards; in Turkanaland, flocks of goats and sheep scatter over the inferior plains areas, and cattle descend from the mountains. The timing of both essential and conventional movements is, however, entirely the concern of each owner, and so is the new location to which he moves. In addition to opinion on purely pastoral grounds, there may also be personal considerations. The availability of labour to an owner may limit movements. A man may prefer to go near to a kinsman or bond-friend when the decision to move has been made—though this must not be overemphasized. Some men appear to prefer to move as little as possible; others seem to like to shift at every opportunity. In all this there is no controlling authority to override personal choice and inclination.[1] An owner

[1] In recent years in both countries some slight restrictions have been imposed by the Administrations through the appointed chiefs. These only prohibit the use of certain areas at a certain time, and so far no new element has been introduced into the indigenous individualistic system except in the marches between Kenya and Ethiopia, where very strict frontier control exists in respect of the local Turkana.

may be influenced by the decisions of his kinsmen or even of casual neighbours; he may accede to the opinions of other owners with whom temporarily he shares a common camp (Jie) or homestead (Turkana), but such pastoral alliances are always a matter of mutual convenience, and strong disagreement causes their dissolution. There is no particular reason compelling kinsmen to co-operate, and very often in both tribes an owner asserts his independence of his near kin by deliberately following an independent course in pastoral affairs.

In Jieland I have recorded the locations of all cattle and goat homesteads during the dry and wet seasons for inhabitants of the Kotido district June 1950 to August 1951, and for many of those of Kapelimuru, Panyangara and elsewhere over the same period. It was not difficult to obtain such information or to check its accuracy. No pattern of pastoral organization appeared other than that already described, and the Jie themselves invariably insist that it is purely a matter of the decisions of individuals. No basis of control of general organization in pastoral affairs is provided by membership of extended family or clan, settlement or district. In the concentrations in the dry season and in the scatter at other times I have always found a tribe-wide intermingling of herds in any area. Neither does a herd, or camp, move in a fixed orbit each year, for the semi-nomadic movements vary from year to year according to the conditions of rainfall and vegetation and according to personal choices. In the early days of my field-work I asked men where they had their cattle camps in, say, the wet season. They invariably found difficulty in telling me more than, 'in the east', and some informants would name several places where their camps had been in different wet seasons. Indeed, such questions led to informants explaining to me the nature of their pastoral system. Over a period of years a man may establish a convention of tending to put his camp in a certain area (based on a certain permanent water-point) in the dry season, but this location can always be changed and is in no way binding.[1]

In Turkanaland the situation is more complex on account both of the much greater extent of territory and of the more variable patterns of rainfall and vegetation, of plains and mountains, and of the requirements and capabilities of the various kinds of stock. The basic principles have been sketched in the previous section of this chapter, but as far as the stock-owner is concerned it is a matter of

[1] See the Appendix, Part 1, to this chapter.

individual, or at the most small group, movements depending on personal opinion. Essentially the Turkana nomadic pattern stems from the reaction of the head of each nuclear family to his immediate environment, in the light of his accumulated pastoral experience. Detailed evidence cannot be given here, but it will, I trust, become clearer later when the organization of the nuclear family is described.[1] A few examples only will be given here by way of illustration.[2]

People who occupy the same wet-season area, roughly speaking, do not necessarily send their cattle to the same mountain area in the dry season. For example, men living in the comparatively well-populated, wet-season plains region of the Koteruk river (central Turkanaland) send their cattle north-west to various parts of Murua-polon, south to the Malmalti basin, west to the foot-hills of the Suk Mountains, and a few go east to the banks of the Turkwel river. Thus cattle herds which tend to be near together in the wet season may be up to one hundred and fifty miles apart by the end of the dry season. These men's browsing stock spread in all directions as the dry season develops and a few families remain more or less permanently in the vicinity because local vegetation is sufficient to support a few herds all the year round. In each dry season, Koteruk area stock mingle with herds from other plains areas. For instance, in the Malmalti basin will be stock (not only cattle) from much of central Turkanaland and from the lower Kerio valley; so that herds which are near together in the dry season may be a hundred miles apart in the wet season. This sort of thing occurs almost everywhere. I carried out systematic observations in various areas and at various times over two years (in so far as the natural difficulties of field-work in Turkanaland allowed) and invariably found a complete inter-mingling and remingling of herds of many areas. This means, of course, a similar intermingling of the people also. These facts are borne out by what the Turkana themselves say. 'We can move any-where, everywhere. Are we not all Turkana? You own stock and things; you do not own the country.' Further, a man is not prevented from changing his areas of pastoral operations, nor need his brothers or sons follow his geographical cycle. The only time of the year when movement is at all restricted is towards the end of the dry

---

[1] See Chapter 5. A discussion of some of the available data will be found in chapters 6, 7 and 11 of *Survey of the Turkana*.

[2] A discussion of the nature and frequency of movement, with examples, is given in the Appendix, Part 2, to this chapter.

season, when pastures are becoming critically impoverished. A new-comer, especially a group of newcomers, may arouse inchoate public opinion to common opposition on the grounds that a further strain on available vegetational resources would exhaust them before the next wet season. Even this action is condemned in theory, and Turkana say that no man should be denied pasturage (and water) for his animals.[1] Nevertheless, at these drastic times men are driven into temporary alliance to protect their own welfare; and fights do some-times occur, especially when a dry season is unusually severe and protracted.[2]

It is to be expected, however, that men do not wander relatively aimlessly about the countryside as these genuinely tribal ethics would allow. On the whole, each man settles in an approximate, annual nomadic cycle. His detailed knowledge and experience of terrain, vegetation, water supplies, paths and passes, and so on, will apply only to a restricted territory, and the risks of moving elsewhere are increased by relative ignorance. The inertia of convention (though purely individual convention) is considerable, and if a certain territory is satisfactory there is little reason to change it. A man obviously does not wish to send his cattle to a mountain fifty miles away when there is an equally suitable area only thirty miles away. Though there may be a practical choice of areas (as e.g. at Koteruk), once the choice is made, it is unlikely to be changed frequently. A man may be well aware (or at least he may fully believe) that in a particular year another mountain has better vegeta-tion than his normal territory, but he weighs up the relative advan-

---

[1] So strong is the expression of this moral principle that in my first tour I was temporarily convinced that there was seldom, if ever, any restriction whatever on movements. Men and women everywhere had stressed this so forcibly. Cf. *Survey of the Turkana*, pp. 64-6, for a case in point. This is the only major factual error in that introductory account of Turkana social life.

[2] Some years ago when rainfall had been unusually poor for two years consecutively, dry-season grasslands on Pelekec mountain failed before the dry season ended, and most cattle had to be moved. Some went west to parts of Muruapolon, some north-west to Thungut, Mogila and the Dodoth Escarpment, and some north, to Lokwanamur. In most cases men were able to go to areas where they had bond-friends or kinsmen. One group, however, attempted to move *en bloc* to Naitamajong. Following early brawling, a serious fight occurred, and some serious injuries were incurred on both sides. The 'invaders' retired, split up and separately found entrance elsewhere. Naitamajong, the nearest mountain to stricken Pelekec, had suffered almost equally badly, and the men there were genuinely afraid of the grave consequences if more stock came to graze there. It is important to note, however, that here, and at other times, spears were not used in the fighting—it was not war as Turkana understand that word; or, as we might say, it was not really civil war.

tages and disadvantages. Is it practicable to move cattle on a three-
or four-day trek where grass may not be available *en route*, and water
uncertain? Is it worth the effort and the reduced stamina of the
cattle? Perhaps other men move there, making the danger of overcrowding; or perhaps sufficient herds will leave the current area and
so reduce the pressure on existing resources. A man may be
influenced by his neighbours' opinions and actions. Often, although
the alternative area is believed to be better, a move is not made since
the relative advantages are not considered to be worth the effort and
risk.

When a man becomes independent he tends to maintain an established routine which varies only in details—e.g. the time when the
various moves are made each year, and the precise location of homesteads in an area. He may always move his cattle to a certain mountain area, but his homestead may in any one year be ten or fifteen
miles away from its location the previous year. Again, a man may
say that in the wet season he lives in a certain area, but his actual
location in any year can vary considerably. This means that his homestead is likely to be found within a fairly wide field, and his stock
watered at one of two or three water-points. One cannot locate a
Turkana more specifically. These decisions of detail and the less
frequent major changes in the cycle are fundamentally individual
ones. Opinion can vary a good deal; needs vary also. A small flock
of one hundred goats can manage in a rather poorer area than a large
one of three hundred animals. When a move seems to be necessary
there is often lengthy discussion amongst the neighbours, and there
is, as I have frequently seen, a good deal of disagreement. For
instance, amongst one group in the early dry season near Karibur,
north-east Turkanaland, it was generally agreed that local browse
was exhausted. One man moved off a fortnight before the others, and
joined his half-brother elsewhere. Of the remaining six family heads,
two moved about forty miles due west to where some late rains had
recently fallen and where therefore they thought some fresh browse
would appear, one moved east to the shores of Lake Rudolf, one
(the poorest) moved a short distance westward and stopped there,
one decided on gradual movements westwards, and one began
gradual movements due north. The following wet season all the men
were back in roughly the same region, but they were not all together,
for their homesteads formed parts of three separate neighbourhoods.

It will be clear from the foregoing account that neighbourhood (i.e. residential) groups are only temporary associations, continually forming and breaking up. Two or three men and their families may keep together for a time because of ties of kinship or friendship and co-operation, but such collaboration is always liable to be broken off and there is no reason to believe that any Turkana goes through life bound to others in pastoral and nomadic activity. One informant put the situation thus: 'A man lives next to his brother-in-law. They live together, perhaps they herd together; they move to one [part of the] country. Later the man wants to go this way—his affine wants to go elsewhere. They part and each moves to his [chosen] area. There are no [hard] words; it is finished.'

In Jieland possession is not even 'nine points of the law', and that principle holds in Turkanaland only during the worst time of the dry season and may in any case be set aside if a newcomer has the support of men already in the area (i.e. a kinsman or bond-friend). In the same way water is considered a free good, a resource common to all tribesmen. Specific rights do, however, lie where water resources have been artificially developed. If there is a running spring, or an open, natural pool, anyone can water his stock there on the principle, 'first come, first served'. But such water is always scarce even in the wet season; soon after the last rains holes must be dug in the beds of water-courses. This involves considerable initial labour, especially in view of the absence of proper digging tools, and a certain amount of upkeep is required. In Jieland, where water is more of a problem generally than in Turkanaland, holes go down as much as twenty-five to thirty feet, and both digging and upkeep is correspondingly greater. The people who dig such a water-hole are taken to be the owners, with prime rights to the water. Sometimes the herdsmen of a single camp or homestead do all this work, but often two or three groups combine. Other people may use the water-hole only at the permission and convenience of these owners. In congested areas several herds may water at a single hole one day, and several others on alternate days.

The usual system is that a new arrival attempts to gain permission to use an existing hole. In extremity he may beg permission from any owner, for it is considered wrong to refuse unreasonably. Usually a newcomer approaches a friend or kinsman, and the presence of such a person may be a good reason for a man moving near to that water-point, since he thus feels assured of gaining watering facilities. Rather than become beholden to a stranger the newcomer will, if possible, make a new hole for his own use. If a man attempts to use a hole without prior permission (unless it is abandoned) it is likely to lead to a fight. It is a grave breach of manners, an unwarranted assumption, and, in the dry season, a threat to the welfare of the herds already dependent on that water-hole. Minor brawls do sometimes occur on this score.

I do not want to overemphasize these water-rights. They do exist, and men will explain them clearly; but it is seldom that a person finds great difficulty in obtaining water at a permanent point of any size. So long as people are willing to be considerate and to help in the upkeep, there is little difficulty. At bottom, both Jie and Turkana feel that, like pasturage, water is free to all. Every man has the right to water his animals and no one should deny him that right.

Animal Husbandry

Here is not the place to give a detailed description of the pastoral life of these two peoples, and I shall confine myself to as brief an account as seems consistent with the need for background material.[1]

For neither tribal area are there any reliable statistics of domestic animals; the following are my own rough estimates, which claim no high accuracy:

Turkana

200,000 cattle, 80,000 camels, 800,000 small stock, 96,000 donkeys. In terms of numbers of animals per head of population, we get the following:

3-4 head of large stock (cattle and camels)
10 head of small stock

Jieland

60-65,000 cattle, 70,000 small stock. In terms of numbers of animals per head of population, we get the following:

3-4 head of large stock
4 head of small stock

These figures are rather lower than those for the Masai,[2] who are, like Turkana, purely pastoralists, or for the Ngwato,[3] who have, like

---

[1] Some information is given for the Turkana in *Survey of the Turkana*, chapter 3.

[2] Human population 50,000, cattle 700,000; i.e. about fourteen cattle per head of population. Cf. Kenya Native Affairs Report, 1946-47, p. 39.

[3] Human population 40,000, cattle 351,000; i.e. about nine cattle per head of population. Cf. Schapera, I: *Native Land Tenure in the Bechuanaland Protectorate*, Lovedale, 1943, Table XIX.

the Jie, a mixed economy; but they are considerably higher than for many African pastoralists. In very general terms both the Turkana and Jie may be said to be wealthy stock-owners. The Turkana are particularly wealthy in small stock, which are usually in good condition. Their cattle, however, suffer badly in each dry season, despite their good recuperative powers during reasonable wet seasons. Their camels, which are treated precisely the same as cattle but which can live in non-grassy areas,[1] are perhaps best suited to the environment. They are relatively few in numbers and many families have only about half a dozen. Jie cattle fare better than those in Turkanaland because of better pasturage.

In Turkanaland, though there are wealthy men with up to one hundred cattle and over three hundred small stock, there is on the whole no great variation in wealth. An 'average' family owns about twenty-five to thirty cattle and perhaps about one hundred to one hundred and fifty small stock. Very few men indeed have no stock or only a mere handful, for life is impossible, or almost so, without stock in that semi-desert land.[2] Certain regions are probably more wealthy than others, but not to any great extent. In Jieland wealth is rather less evenly distributed. The wealthiest families live at Wertakow settlement, Kapelimuru, where the most prosperous houses have one hundred to one hundred and fifty cattle. Throughout the country similarly wealthy men are sprinkled. On the other hand, everywhere there are houses which have but a handful of cattle. Small stock are particularly unevenly distributed, and many houses of average cattle wealth, possess none at all. Poorer people can to a considerable extent fall back on agriculture and trade. However, it would be incorrect to lay too great a contrast between the two tribes. It is obvious that with a social system wherein cattle serve a multitude of non-economic ends and are thereby frequently passed from owner to owner (chiefly through the mechanism of bridewealth), any owner's wealth is liable to considerable fluctuations. A poor owner with unmarried sisters and daughters will in due course receive stock at their weddings; a wealthy man expends stock upon his own and his sons' marriages. In both tribes many wives or many animals are in practice synonymous with wealth; and

[1] Camels are not used for riding or pack purposes.
[2] A very few paupers eke out existence on wild fruits and occasional labour for more wealthy people. The small Ngebotok section, next to the Hill Suk, on the upper Turkwel, do practise a good deal of agriculture, but they are quite atypical.

it is a general principle that bridewealth is given according to the wealth of the bridegroom and his kin, so that a wealthy owner must surrender more stock at marriage, and, if his sons-in-law are relatively poorer, he will receive less at his daughter's marriages. We cannot therefore speak as if wealth in stock was an entirely fixed matter or only slowly changing. This is one of the most important respects in which property in animals differs from property in land.

The Turkana have been fortunate in their relative isolation from bovine epidemics. The Jie have shared the common fate of most pastoralists of eastern Africa; rinderpest in particular, but other diseases, also, have taken heavy toll. To the present day most years witness at least local outbreaks, though compulsory inoculations against rinderpest seem (1951) likely to become accepted now. Such fortuitous factors, quite beyond Jie control or remedy, do affect holdings of stock and so cause varying fortunes amongst men, which amongst near kinsmen are often a source of jealousy and trouble.

Under the Jie transhumantic system there is a contrast between the fixed homesteads, *ere*, pl. *ngireria*, and the peregrinating stock camps, *awi*, pl. *ngawie*. At the former live the older men, women and children, with a dairy herd for some ten months of the year; and there is the centre of agriculture and of social activities in general. At the camps live the young men and youths in charge of the stock. It is seldom nowadays that a wife or girl lives in a camp. A homestead is a permanent, firmly built structure, still bearing the stamp of the necessity for defence against raiders in its stout pallisades. Internally in its division into enclosed yards and kraals it is a material embodiment of the social structure of the family group which inhabits it. A camp is a transient affair, a mere ring fence of low bushwood. There is only a hut or shelter in the wet season, and no possessions that men cannot carry in their hands or on their shoulders. It is purely a subsidiary of the settled homestead.

Under the Turkana nomadic system the contrast is less obvious. No habitation is anywhere permanent. A family is typically divided, as we have seen, into at least two parts—one with the cattle, one with the browsing stock (camels and small stock). Owing to the nature of the distribution of vegetation and the different requirements of these two types of stock, the division is more fundamental. Each type of herd is kept at a homestead such that physically there is little or no difference between the two habitations. At least one wife (of the family head, a son or a dependent) should live at each homestead, and at least one adult male; these two supervise the domestic and watering, and the pastoral and herding sides of life respectively. Fences, huts, kraals, etc., are essentially similar at each homestead and there is but one word for both, *awi*. Each is the home of people of each sex and all ages. A wife keeps her utensils and property with her wherever she lives. Neither is like the 'camp' of the Jie.[1] On the other hand there is always a 'chief-homestead'—that at which the family head and his chief wife live. I have already mentioned that the family head, so long as it is possible, lives in the plains; that is, he lives with the browsing stock throughout the dry season and transfers his residence to the cattle homestead if and when the cattle descend from the mountains in the wet season. The homestead at which he does not live at any time, the 'secondary-homestead', is regarded as subordinate and is not the centre of family life and social activities as the chief homestead always is.

For present purposes the distinction to be drawn is between the Turkana situation, where the nuclear family is permanently (or nearly permanently) divided amongst at least two residential units, which may be many miles apart and subject to quite different conditions, but each is the home of its members; and the Jie situation, where home is quite specifically at the fixed homestead, with the stock camp a mere ancillary unit containing only the young men and boys, and in which the pattern of life is of a purely transitory nature. There is, of course, the similarity that both Jie homestead and Turkana chief-homestead are the natural centres of family activity by reason of the presence there of the men who are heads of family groups and who are the owners of stock.

In conclusion of this brief survey of animal husbandry, the chief values of stock may be mentioned. They are basically the same in each tribe. Firstly, stock are of economic importance in providing both food and material for clothing, utensils and decorations. In Turkanaland almost the sole means of livelihood lies in the herds of animals. The Jie, however, have a mixed economy in which cereal (sorghum) agriculture plays an equally important part with pastoralism. Secondly, animals are essential for ritual purposes. Scarcely any ceremony, and no important one, can occur without the slaughter of a beast—e.g. rain-making, marriage, initiation, the prevention or

[1] The word for the Jie 'camp' and the Turkana 'homestead' is the same, *awi*. Actual similarity refers only to the quality of mobility, not to real physical or social resemblance.

alleviation of disease and disaster. Only through such slaughter can the High God be properly entreated or appeased. There is also the social importance of the meat feast at a ceremony. Thirdly, stock, and cattle in particular, provide in native conceptions the principal expression of all social relations of real and lasting importance. A relationship, whether established by birth (kinship) or by conscious effort (affinal kinship and bond-friendship), is given meaning and significance in so far as it rests upon mutual rights and obligations concerning stock. This social value of domestic animals will be a main theme of the present account of the Jie and Turkana.

Some Demographic Considerations

Jieland has an area of roughly 1300 square miles, and a total population of 18,200; therefore there is an overall density of human population of about 14·0 persons per square mile. Owing to the nature of settlement and transhumance this figure is only useful in general comparison with the equivalent figure for Turkanaland (see below), for it is, significantly, over four times larger. The size of the small settled area has already been noted,[1] and within it, apart from minor breaks here and there, is a more or less continuous stretch of permanent homesteads. Assuming that about four-fifths of the population are resident there, the density of population would be about 129 persons per square mile. The remainder of the population —mainly young men and boys at the stock camps—live in either the eastern or western half of the country, broadly speaking, according to the time of year; and density of population is between six and ten persons per square mile. In the latter half of the dry season there is, of course, relatively high concentration of stock camps around the permanent water-points.

Turkanaland has an area of some 24,000 square miles and a population of about 80,000[2]; therefore there is an overall density of population of about 3·3 persons per square mile. Such a figure has little internal significance, however, because the pattern of population distribution varies widely according not only to the seasons but also to the nature of rainfall and vegetation in any year. In an average or good wet season all the mountain areas are quite deserted and both human and stock population are spread over almost the whole of the plains. Conversely, in the late dry season many parts of the plains are

---

[1] See map and diagram in Figure 2.
[2] Cf. p. 5, footnote 1.

uninhabited, but there is a relatively high density of population in the mountains and in the better parts of the plains.

In the wet season (unless as so often happens it is poor, even by Turkana standards) there is an overall density of three to four persons per square mile (area IV, Figure 5), with some higher

FIGURE 5

POPULATION DENSITIES IN TURKANALAND

	I	II	III	IV
	Nangoleki	*Oropoi*	*Kanamut*	*Logiriama north*
Region . . .	Mountain	Plains	Plains	Plains
Season . . .	Late dry	Mid wet	Mid dry	Early wet
Area: sq. m. . .	20	18	60	40
People . . .	400	280	180	150
Persons per square mile	20	15·5	3·0	3·8
Cattle. . . .	2000	1300	480	None
Camels . . .	1200	300	160	125
Goats, sheep . .	4000	None	1700	1100

Neighbourhood I is one of the best mountain grasslands in Turkanaland. Neighbourhood II is an exceptionally well-favoured plains area in the north-west. Neighbourhoods III and IV are typical of the normal Turkana plains, although the former contained in part some mountain grassland.

Each of these neighbourhoods was fairly clearly demarcated by geographical features and by spatial separation from others. Some details of neighbourhoods II, III and IV are given in Figure 12.

densities locally in favoured areas (area II). In the dry season, population density in the mountains may be as much as fifteen to twenty people per square mile (area I) and up to four or five persons per square mile in the better areas of the plains.

In so far as population density is an indication of the relative intensity of inter-personal contacts and relations, these approximate figures must be read against the background of the continuous movements of the people and the essential individualistic nature of Turkana nomadism. Seldom, if ever, does a Turkana spend the whole year in daily and constant contact with the same group of people (beyond the members of his homestead, and even they may vary), for residential ties are invariably temporary and indeterminate.

As Figure 5 shows, the range of contacts at any one time is limited. The effective community is seldom more than two hundred people and in the plains in the dry season is usually about one hundred. A man may therefore have day-to-day relations with only a dozen other men, none of whom may be more than casual and temporary neighbours.

From this brief analysis the following factors are to be emphasized. In Jieland there is a high concentration of homesteads and settled population in the centre of the tribal area. Here live the bulk of the people, and all the older people; and inter-personal contacts tend to spread over the whole tribal society and to persist (with the important assistance of strong ritual inter-dependence and co-operation). In Turkanaland the poverty of pastoral resources compels fairly frequent movements, which are not organized systematically on any kind of group basis. At any one time inter-personal contacts are limited, and those contacts are not normally persistent over a period. Finally, the nature of Turkana nomadism demands that a family's herd, and in consequence the family itself, be divided amongst at least two separate homesteads. Even the basic social unit has no residential integrity.

APPENDIX

THE NATURE AND FREQUENCY OF PASTORAL MOVEMENTS

1. *Jieland*

Taking the year as a whole, there are certain times when movement is usually necessary. The Jie see their year begin in the latter part of the wet season (July-September). Starting from that period, the movements are: (1) from the eastern pastures as the rains cease and surface water disappears (c. October); (2) to one of the permanent water-points in the west as temporary water supplies fail (c. late November)—these two moves may be telescoped into one; (3) adjustments following local deficiencies of grass, maldistribution of herds at permanent water-points, etc.—these continue through the rest of the dry season; (4) dispersal of herds over western pastures following new rains, surface water and new grass (c. late March); (5) return to the east as grass and water become available again there (c. late June).

Most camps make about five moves during each year of two seasons; not a few move seven or eight times covering up to one hundred and fifty miles. A few men short-circuit these ecological constraints by settling their camps near to a permanent water-point and remaining there for at least the whole dry season and early wet season. Such immobility, though not rare, is not common. Only in the second part of the wet season (eastern pastures) are the great majority of camps fixed for as long as three months.

2. *Turkanaland*

Each independent man has, very roughly, an established cyclical routine which in basic outline is not often varied, but in which details vary considerably from year to year in response to variations in natural conditions and the man's personal opinions about them. Of the multitude of individual routines two broad types are to be distinguished.

The first type of nomadic routine occurs where wet- and dry-season areas are roughly contiguous and where the browsing stock tend to follow over the same country as the cattle. Migration is in the form of general progressive and regressive movements, with the cattle always tending to be more forward (i.e. nearer the better parts). In these cases the two homesteads belonging to the nuclear family tend to move in the same direction in the same region, and often contact and co-operation between the two is more or less constant.

In the second type of nomadic routine the wet season area is geographically separate from the cattle pastures of the dry season. Cattle homesteads must make a decisive move away from the plains to the mountains at the beginning of the dry season, leaving the goat and camel homesteads which therefore move in a different nomadic course and are subject to quite different conditions. In this case the two homesteads of a single family are kept apart for much of the year, and co-operation is slight and intermittent.

Speaking generally, in the first type of routine two to four moves by each homestead (not necessarily in concert) will usually take the herd from peak wet-season to peak dry-season pastures, and a similar number takes them back again; and there may be minor movements of adjustment in each area. This gives between five and ten moves each year. Equally generally, in the second type of migration the cattle make bi-annual movements between plains and mountains, and there may be minor movements of adjustment in each area. In some years cattle may not be able to descend to the plains at all, and then they must make minor moves in the mountain area. Browse homesteads in the plains may move more frequently in attempts to ensure adequate feed for the stock, although some may become established fairly early in the dry season and remain for as long as six months. In the worst regions moves may be made every month or so, and sometimes after only a few weeks.

No Turkana homestead, for whatever kind of stock, is anywhere permanent. The longest period in which a homestead did not move, of which I have record, was eight months. As an approximation for the whole country, most homesteads move five or six times a year of two seasons, at least two or three of which will be major movements.

As concrete examples of the kind of movements to be found, schedules are given here of the locations of the homesteads of two men whose routines are typical of the two kinds mentioned above. (Numbers give the distance moved in each case in miles.)

(*a*) The homesteads of Lokorke, north-west Turkanaland:

Browse homestead—about 150 goats and sheep, 8 camels.

1. March 1949	.	Middle Oropoi	Late dry season location.
2. Late April	.	Muruita Hills 20	Early rains: new browse.
3. July	.	Kalobeyei 8	Wet season had set in tardily.
4. Late Sept.	.	Lokicel Hill 15	Early dry season.
5. December	.	Upper Naitera 10	Dry season well established.
6. Feb. 1950	.	Kabalabalai 3	Advanced dry-season conditions: minor move to allow stock more easily to reach pastures.
7. April	.	Lowatum 8	Early rains: new browse.
8. May	.	Kalobeyei 20	Improved conditions. (Homestead about two miles from site in 1949.)

From the end of the dry season 1949 to the end of the following dry season this herd moved approximately fifty-six miles.

Cattle homestead—about 25 cattle.

1. March 1949	.	Ngiputiro	Late dry-season location in foothills.
2. Late April	.	Middle Oropoi 5	Early rains: new grass at foot of mountains, more water. The eight camels join the cattle from the browse homestead.
3. July	.	Lowatum 8	Wet season established.
4. September	.	Kalaperto 6	Early dry season: grasslands deteriorating rapidly.
5. November	.	Upper Oropoi 6	Dry season established. Camels rejoin browse homestead.
6. April 1950	.	Lokolopus Hills 5	Minor move to allow cattle to graze new mountain area. Sheep joined cattle.
7. Late May	.	Middle Oropoi 4	Wet-season pastures: poor rains. Sheep rejoin goats: camels rejoin cattle.
8. July	.	Kalaperto 3	Move made out of Oropoi valley at orders of local headman, under grazing control scheme.

From the end of the dry season 1949 to the end of the following dry season this herd moved approximately thirty miles, but it remained in a restricted area during the whole period. The wet season 1949, and also that of 1950, was only fair. Lokorke said that had the rains been reasonably good he would have shifted his cattle almost as far eastwards as his goats and sheep. This statement was borne out by information from a large number of other men whose pastoral routines were roughly similar to that of Lokorke.

This is an example of the first type of migration. In this particular region, grasslands are above average for Turkanaland. The dry-season cattle pastures are on the slopes and ridges of the Dodoth (Rift) Escarpment (2000 ft.) at an altitude of 3500 to 5500 feet.

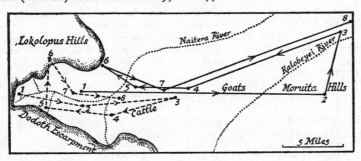

(*b*) The homesteads of Coloma, north-east Turkanaland:
Browse homestead—c. 500 goats and sheep, 20 camels.

1. Aug. 1948	.	Karibur	End of wet season and into dry season.
2. Mid-Nov.	.	Kakalai	15 Dry season well established.
3. December	.	Middle Katome	20 Continuing move westwards to where 'short rains' fell in November.
4. Late Dec.	.	Upper Katome	8 Minor move as conditions worsen.
5. Feb. 1949	.	Upper Lomogol	35 Advanced dry season conditions. Return eastwards. Pastures so bad that Coloma lost many goats.
6. April	.	Kalin	15 Early wet season location. Remained here until at least August.

From the end of the wet season 1948 to the end of the following wet season this herd moved approximately ninety-three miles.

Cattle homestead—c. 35 cattle.

1. Aug. 1948	.	Western Labur	End of wet season.
2. September	.	East Lorienetom	30 Early dry season—move to mountains.

47

3. December . Maiyen river 10 Forward plains area (near international boundary) opened by D.C.: gave access to hitherto untouched pastures.

4. Feb. 1949 . East Lorienetom 10 Maiyen pastures exhausted—return to mountain area.

5. c. July . . Lower slopes of Lorienetom 3 Wet season too poor for cattle to leave mountains entirely.

From the end of the wet season 1948 to the end of the following wet season this herd moved approximately fifty-three miles.

This is an example of the second type of migration. This plains area is about average for Turkana; the wet season 1949 was well below average. Movement to the north-east was restricted by Administrative frontier control.

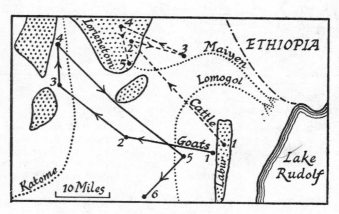

CHAPTER THREE

FAMILY AND PROPERTY IN JIELAND

(a) THE HOUSE

The Structure of the House

The Jie word *ekal* primarily means the fenced, enclosed 'yard' belonging to each wife inside a homestead. This yard is provided for her when she comes to live at her husband's homestead. She is thereafter responsible for its upkeep. It contains her huts, her granary-baskets and all her other possessions and stores. There she lives, cooks, eats, sleeps and carries on much of her normal work; there she looks after and brings up her young children and caters for her husband. It is essentially her private domain. As a full-wife she has the right to her own yard. *Ekal*, by extension, means also the group of people who live in the yard—the wife herself, and her children. If the husband has no other wife he also normally belongs there; if he has several wives his allegiance is divided, giving him a kind of *ex officio* membership of each *ekal*. These two uses of the word are very similar, being the physical and social aspects of the same thing. From the first, it may be noted, a child lives in and belongs to a different yard from that of its half-sibling, though both have the same father.

There is a further extension of the same word, *ekal*, sociologically, which has no physical counterpart. This usage will be translated here as 'house'. A house is founded by a set of full-brothers, all the sons of one woman, who, at the death of their father and his full-brothers, have become independent of parallel sets of men who stand in the relations of half-brothers or paternal cousins. A mature house contains several yards, i.e. several sets of a wife and her children. A yard itself becomes a house when the greater unit that contains it dies out; a house dies out when the original full-brothers are all dead. Their sons then divide up on the basis of maternal affiliation, so that

D   49

the former house now becomes a group of new houses. Basically, then, a house is grouped round a set of full-brothers. A man therefore belongs first to the house of his father and his father's brothers, and afterwards to the house of his own full-brothers. The two houses are not contemporary but strictly consecutive.[1] Whilst the father's house is still intact the whole range of sons are subject to the authority of its head, who is its most senior man. When each set of sons (full-brothers) form their own house, they become independent of other sets each under the authority of their own most senior man. Parallel to this authoritarian structure goes the ownership of domestic stock. A house owns its own stock, over which it exercises sole rights of use and disposal, through the authority of the eldest brother.

Occasionally the word *ekal* is used to refer to the group of men who, though divided into several houses, were originally united within the house of their immediate fathers. This usage here will be referred to as the 'house-line'.

A daughter who has married and become a full-wife leaves her father's homestead and lives thereafter with her husband, being ritually incorporated into his clan and thus into his family and house. She is no longer a member of her mother's yard. Until such time a girl belongs with her mother and brothers. In what follows, however, we shall often ignore the sisters and daughters of the men, since they all eventually marry and leave and then have no longer a significant status in the Family structure. On the other hand these various groups, at their different levels, are not wholly agnatic since they include the mothers and wives of the men. Indeed, women are the foci of differentiation within the house and have structural and ritual status in it. There is the not uncommon paradox that in a strongly agnatic society, descent is organized through a woman who strictly genealogically belongs to a different agnatic descent line. By ritual performance and the facts of residence her allegiance is transferred, and by the process of living together her interests as well as her status become increasingly and irretrievably bound up in the agnatic structure of her husband's Family. Nevertheless, sociologically the patrilineal principle predominates and men are the important social units, so that quite logical continuity is maintained

---

[1] Sometimes, of course, a boy belongs to the house of his grandfather when that man or one of his full-brothers are still alive. For the moment we may neglect this possibility.

in the total Family structure. Whereas a woman is lost to her natal Family, a man automatically remains in the Family of his fathers. Further, although the differentiation and distinctiveness of a house is determined by descent through a woman, yet the Jie do not primarily think of a house as a woman and her sons, but as a set of full-brothers and their wives and children. Any wife who is barren, has only daughters or whose sons die in childhood, does not found a new house. The essence of Jie Family structure is the line of continuity and the parallel relations amongst generations of males. Although abstractly the grandmother may be said to found a house-line, in fact no middle-aged or old man that I met could remember his grandmother's name. That woman is merely an anonymous turning-point.

Only in the household do the females have a role equal to that of the men. This is the sphere of domestic activity where females play an important part, whether as mother, wife or daughter. The herd of stock are almost as much their concern as the men's. Women in the homestead, though not in the camps, are the principal dairy-maids and are chiefly responsible for the care of the calves. Women are, of course, the chief domestic workers and they own and cultivate at least nine-tenths of the garden lands. The household or yard has a common food supply which is only partially shared with the husband-father, unless he has no other wife or mistress. There is sociable and conventional sharing both of food and work with other yards, but this is a result of good relations rather than of compulsion. Although she cannot own animals, a woman has specific rights in the herd. Prominent is the right to food from them, especially milk, but also blood and meat. Hides and skins are also used principally by the women. Just as a man in fear of witchcraft, supernatural danger or chronic illness may take an animal from the herd for ritual slaughter, so may a woman—or rather a man will do it for her; but she has the undeniable right to this ritual privilege.

The yard and the house (which is only a yard become independent) are groups of people amongst whom there is considerable affection, esteem and mutual consideration. Since this present account of the Jie is to be chiefly concerned with some of the structural aspects of their society, derived from analytical study, it may be useful at this early stage to lay some emphasis on the very real importance of these emotional feelings and attitudes which are the fertile soil in which grows the immense solidarity of the house. We shall later examine the yard and the house as units in the process of the development of the Family and in the strictly parallel development of the complex of rights concerning domestic stock. Here it must be recorded that the house has roots other than can be gained from its purely structural position and from its possession and use of stock. Fundamentally it grows out of the uterine ties between a mother and her children. The nucleus of the herd of the house-to-be comes, as we shall see, from the milking stock allocated by the father to his wife for the provision of milk for herself and her children. The children grow up under the care of their mother, who, in Jieland as elsewhere, has a deep, natural affection for them and a great concern for their wellbeing. The pattern of affectionate ties established in childhood continues into the adult life of the sons. Gradually all the daughters leave the group, though established feelings persist even so; but *vis-à-vis* her sons a mother remains in close and constant contact with usually very real affection on both sides. Until a son marries, indeed until his wife finally comes to live with him, his mother is mainly responsible for cooking for and feeding him, storing his possessions and, in general, providing a home for him. Even when his wife is living with him at his homestead, a man often returns to his mother for food, assistance and sympathy, and continues to regard her yard as his home. Jie are not notable for their external show of affections towards one another, but the genuine attachment between a woman and her adult sons is obvious to an outside visitor in the general atmosphere of the yard—the friendliness of members, the sharing of work and the performance of odd jobs for each other, combined with intimate and easy conversation. At times of sickness men express deep concern for an ailing mother, and on such occasions the real feelings break through to the surface. Men and women do not normally mix together much in normal daily life, but a man always feels (as we should say) 'at home' in his mother's yard. Men have often gone out of their way to introduce me to their mothers when I have been visiting. It obviously seemed to them important that, if I knew them well, I should also know their mothers. There are no reservations in this attitude, no latent hostility or rivalry; and that is more than can be said of other kinds of relationships in the Family. Even between father and son, where the two men are typically closely attached, there is a certain underlying tension born of the resentment of an adult son towards the continued authority of his father and the latter's strict control over the domestic stock. The aims and ambitions of father and son are in some ways quite contrary. As between half-brothers and cousins, only too often the hostility motif is the stronger part of the relationship.

Between full-brothers there is similarly unreserved affection which may go to the extent of self-denial of rights in the other's interests. This is tempered by the strict, autocratic authority of the eldest brother—an authority which reaches a peak when the set of brothers establish an independent house. Younger brothers allow the eldest very considerable freedom of action without criticism, though it may perhaps be against their own personal interests. It is the supreme moral law of the Jie that full-brothers live and work together and present a solid front to all other people. This is enhanced by their joint ownership and absolute rights in a herd of stock. Ideally, and very frequently in practice, this herd is used in the best interests of them all. In addition to this most important common property there is what amounts almost to common ownership and use of other property, clothing, ornaments, weapons, cash, etc. It would be unthinkable to refuse to share freely with a brother, and it is taken for granted on both sides that a man will share any good fortune with his brothers. Half-brothers and cousins also come and request shares in these things, but they must make a strong and specific demand, and deception is often used to evade it, or even a blank refusal. Between brothers demands scarcely need to be made. It is a question of giving, not demanding.

Jie say that brothers always live together, and in fact they almost always do. In modern times members of a Family sometimes do not live in one homestead, but even where a Family has become most divided spatially, full-brothers continue to live together. This, of course, has its roots partly in the basic economy of the house which is dependent on a common herd; but also exists in deep fraternal affections and the belief in the real need to keep together. I discovered only three cases where full-brothers had come to live apart, and in two of these cases the quarrel was not between the men themselves but between their wives.

The sole case of drastic disruption of fraternal relations occurred in Lukori settlement where, as the result of a tremendous disaster, a group of three brothers split up. As the result of severe rinderpest, the Family herds were almost wiped out. This was followed by the deaths in rapid succession of the father, a brother, the chief wife of the eldest brother and two children. Happening so closely together, and so disastrously, the deaths of both humans and cattle were put down to witchcraft, and the survivors, brothers and half-brothers, began to suspect and finally to accuse one another. The half-brothers went off to live elsewhere, and eventually, in an intolerable atmosphere of fear, suspicion and economic difficulty, the eldest brother, Loputukwa, moved away with his remaining wife, all his children and two or three cattle. The other two brothers, Lokwalo and Anoka, shifted the old homestead a short distance, but because of continued fears of witchcraft they eventually decided to move to Lothorgut settlement, each with his wife and about five cattle in all. I am not clear how these few remaining cattle had been divided up, but most likely it was on a basis of the stock allocated to each yard.[1] This was a disaster on the grand scale in Jieland, for before it occurred that Family had been at least of average wealth; and it has been the subject of much comment ever since. It is interesting that in 1951, several years after the original cleavage, Loputukwa, the eldest brother, moved with his wife, children and cattle to live with Lokwalo at Lothorgut. He had been advised by a diviner that the witchcraft was finished and that he ought to live with his brother again. Further, although he was the eldest brother he had been the one to break away, and therefore he must make the move which was to restore unity. Apparently Loputukwa, even before the diviner's advice, had felt rather uncomfortable in living apart from his brothers. There are, as far as could be ascertained, no more cattle today than there were at the time of the trouble, and economically the house remains in considerable hardship. It was a clear illustration of the feeling that brothers should keep together. Lokwalo was quite prepared to accept his brother, and a good deal of physical labour was involved in the reconstruction of the homestead at Lothorgut. On the other hand there appeared to be no inclination on the part of the other members of the Family to re-unite, and they remain with their respective maternal kin.

A full-brother is referred to and addressed as *lokato*, which means literally, 'he of the place of the mother' (*lo*—'he', *ka*—locative affix, *itoto*—'mother'). This term may be compared with that for a half-

---

[1] Such division of the herds of a house whilst the full-brothers are yet alive is not only exceptionally rare but is strongly condemned by the Jie on moral grounds. This is the only case of its occurrence that I ever heard of, and is of course a direct consequence of this singular case of disaster and acute fraternal dissension.

brother or paternal cousin, *lokapa*, literally 'he of the place of the father' (*papa*—'father'). Linguistic recognition is thus given to the special status of full-brothers whose close relationships are through the mother, as compared with a close agnate with whom the relationship is through one or more men. It is of interest that half-brothers and paternal cousins are referred to by a single term irrespective of precise paternal connections. Structurally speaking, a man is rather the son of a house than the son of a particular father.[1] Whilst relations between a man and his son are usually close and friendly, they stand outside the structure of the house, in that the father's death does not affect the son's status and social role so long as a father's full-brother is still alive. Sociologically there is a group of 'fathers' for a man. All of them must be dead before he and his own brothers can achieve their inheritance and independence. A man does, of course, prefer his real father to his other fathers, and commonly a man takes greater interest in the welfare of his sons than in the welfare of his brothers' sons. Inter-personal relations follow physiological connections and the facts of upbringing in the yard. A father may support his son against his nephews, though he is severely restricted in such partiality by his relations with and obligations to his brothers. Nevertheless, a classificatory 'father', the brother of the deceased father, holds a precisely similar status and authority towards his brother's sons as the dead man did himself formerly. Indeed, the authority of father over son is in some ways subject to the overriding authority of the head of the house, the father's eldest brother.

The ultimate authority of the head of a house is absolute, both over his younger brothers and all their children. He has certain ritual

[1] We need not lay too much significance on kinship terminology in this matter. Another tribe of the northern Nilo-Hamites, the Lotuko, makes the same distinction, although the Bari do not, nor do the southern Nilo-Hamites, e.g. Masai. Terminological differentiation between full-brothers and other agnates of the same generation is also found amongst the Acoli and Shilluk. Whilst separate terms exist for half-brother and paternal cousin among the Dinka, yet in practice they appear to be called all by the term for half-brother. Cf. Seligman, C. G. and B. Z., *Pagan Tribes of the Nilotic Sudan*, London, 1932, *passim*. See also Evans-Pritchard's comments on Nuer terminology in this matter in *Kinship and Marriage among the Nuer*, Oxford, 1951, pp 171-2. Too little is known about the kinship structure of, say, the Lotuko or Acoli to discover whether the terminological grouping of half-brothers and paternal cousins may be related to a house system as amongst the Jie, or to some other structural or historical features. Amongst the Jie it is to be noted that no difference is made between father and father's full-brother on the one hand (i.e. senior members of one's own house) and father's half-brother and paternal cousin on the other. All are termed *papa*.

powers, and flagrant flouting of his decisions is believed to put a man in danger of automatic, supernatural punishment. Where the all-important stock are concerned, the word of the head cannot be gain-said. His approval of all transactions involving stock must be obtained, if only in tacit agreement. Thus, for instance, any man of the house cannot hope to marry against the wishes of the head, nor may a girl be promised in marriage.

The head of a house is the eldest living brother. He is succeeded at his death by the next oldest, and so on down to the last survivor. This man is the representative of the house in all its dealings as a group with other groups, whether inside the Family or not. For instance, if someone begs a contribution to his bridewealth from the house, the gift is always described as having been made by the head. Similarly, the head always accepts for the house any shares of in-coming stock payments. When a case arises that the house should exercise a rightful claim to a share of, say, an incoming bridewealth of some other house, the head of the house is expected to take the initiative in the matter. The younger brothers excuse themselves on the grounds that they are relatively junior in status, though in fact they may be fairly old men with their own wives and children.

The age of the head of a house varies a good deal according to accidents of survival and death. Quite often the eldest son of the eldest brother is not so very much younger than his father's youngest brother, but that does not affect the latter's legal position when he becomes head of the house. Thus the eldest of a set of brothers may have to wait until middle-age or beyond before his yard becomes a house and he becomes its independent head. On the other hand his paternal cousin may be a young man when his yard simultaneously becomes a house. For both men the position is the same irrespective of age. They are both subject to the unitary authority of the oldest surviving 'father' and each becomes independent of the other when the last 'father' dies. The older man may have a wife and children, the younger may not; it is irrelevant structurally. In practice the older one, who is perhaps near the age of the head of the old house, may be able to exercise some influence with that head which the younger man would not presume to attempt. An old man who is head of the house may be willing to allow the oldest of his 'sons' to exert a good deal of authority, especially in day-to-day and economic affairs. Nevertheless, at bottom the power of the head of the house remains inviolate. I have seen middle-aged men whose 'father's' word is implicitly followed, even when they disagree or feel disgruntled, and when in other ways they are allowed a free hand. It would be dangerously subversive of the fundamental moral premise of Jie society actively and openly to flout the authority of the head of the house, since it would involve a negation of the principles of the house and the ownership and control of the herds.

The Allocation of Stock amongst Wives

To the outside world the independent group of brothers possesses its own herd of cattle and flock of sheep and goats; and it has been seen how the head of the house titularly and authoritatively represents the group as a whole. On the other hand, the herd of animals belonging to a house is not, internally, an undifferentiated one, for whilst general and ultimate rights are retained by the head for the total group, specific rights attach to the constituent yards. For purely domestic purposes a large proportion of the herd is allocated amongst the wives of the house—the wives of both the founding brothers and of their sons. When a wife comes permanently to live at her husband's homestead she is allocated a number of cows from which to obtain milk to feed herself, her children, and, in part, her husband. Such an allocation is arranged by her husband, whose prime responsibility it is to provide for his wife, at the agreement of the head of the house. The main allocation is of cows, but with them usually go an ox or two and some sheep and goats,[1] and possibly a donkey. The number of stock that can be allocated to a new wife depends directly on the size of the house's herd and the number of other wives to be accommodated. Unless the founding-brothers are old men they usually retain unallocated the bulk of the male stock—bulls, oxen, rams, buck-goats and castrated sheep and goats—and some of the female stock. As far as possible a new wife is allocated animals out of this 'residual herd'. If, however, it is small or deficient in female stock, the new wife must be provided for by a redistribution of all stock amongst the wives. A wife must be allocated a fair share of milking-animals, and no other wife (or man for that matter) can deny her that right. There is no distinction made in respect of the relative seniority of the wives or of their husbands.

---

[1] At the homesteads, Jie do not milk ewes and goats, but children are expected to take off some of their milk either by milking into the palms of their hands or by sucking directly at the animal's teats. This is conventional procedure by which children obtain extra food. Adults disdain to do this as being fit only for children.

FAMILY AND PROPERTY IN JIELAND

The new wife of the son of a younger brother has equal rights with her co-wife who has long been married to her husband's father's eldest brother. Indeed she may well have a greater moral claim, since she will probably have babies or young children to feed, which her older co-wife no longer has. Allocation is not once-and-for-all, and can always be modified in the light of new circumstances, for behind the allocations lies the principle that the herd belongs to all for the benefit of all.

Such allocation is a social and not a physical act, for it does not affect the pastoral organization of the house. All the animals are kept in one kraal, which may or may not be used in common with other houses. All the animals are herded and watered together in so far as they are kept at the homestead or at the camp. Except for the division between the dairy herd and the camp herd a house's animals remain one physical unit. Only calves are temporarily withdrawn, for they are kept at night in the respective calves' huts of the various wives. Until the cow runs dry a calf is always kept in that hut whilst its dam is around the homestead. The wife responsible must see that the calf has neither unrestricted suck at its dam nor insufficient opportunity.

All offspring, male and female, of a wife's animals are considered to remain a part of her allocation unless there is redistribution at a later date when a new wife has to be accommodated. Even those finest of male young which are not castrated but are retained as serving-males (bulls, rams and buck-goats) remain part of the wife's herd, though in maturity they will serve the females of the whole herd. Thus the bull of the dairy herd, an animal selected with all the care that Jie animal husbandry can afford, may 'belong' to a wife, or it may be part of the 'residual herd'.

There are other additions to a wife's herd. In so far as it is possible she gets an extra cow or two when she bears more children. The conscious ideal is that a house's animals should be so distributed that everyone, especially children, shall have fair shares in the milk supply. The wife with the most young children ought to have the most milch cows.[1] Whenever animals are received into the house wives usually receive shares. For instance, when a girl marries, her

---

[1] Should a wife be unfortunate enough to have no cow in milk, or to be obtaining only a small quantity of milk, her co-wives are expected to help her in so far as their means and needs allow. To the Jie it would be criminal if a wife were not able to give her young children milk whilst a co-wife was feeding older children or even adults. As the milk supply falls off in the dry season only young children receive a regular supply.

mother will usually receive about five of the bridewealth cattle, and as many as fifteen or twenty goats. The mother's co-wives receive one or two head of cattle each and a few goats. A wife sometimes receives gifts from her father or her brother, from her sister's husband, or from her daughter's husband. Her sons will receive gifts from time to time and may also receive individual shares of in-payments of stock. Her sons, from the age of about four years, each begin to have their own special bell-oxen. The first of these are usually given to a boy by his father or uncles, but as he grows up he often prefers to beg them from elsewhere as his fancy lights on a suitable, half-grown animal and as he exercises the claims of friendship and kinship outside the house. An adult man will have at least four or five of these special oxen to which he is individually and emotionally attached.[1] These animals are all considered as part of the herd of the men's mother, although like all her animals they may be taken at any time for the use of other members of the house, at the authority of the head.

There are also adult sisters and daughters of the house living in the homestead. These are either young wives ('bride-wives') who have not yet gone to live with their husbands, or girls who have borne children to their lovers. They usually continue to use their mothers' herds, but sometimes an unmarried mother may have a sub-allocation from her mother from which to feed her children—particularly if it is thought likely that she may remain unmarried for a long time. She becomes, as it were, another wife of the house. When a mother dies her herd is kept on by the eldest daughter still living in the homestead, who acts as foster-mother to her brothers and sisters. The mother's herd gradually fades out as daughters go away to live and as her sons are all married. If the deceased woman leaves only sons, what remains of her herd will be re-allocated among her son's wives, subject to no other overriding requirements within the house.

A son's wife is allocated stock from the herd of the house and not only from her mother-in-law's part of it, for she is a wife of the house and was married from the whole herd of the house. Her mother-in-law will in fact usually give up one or two animals, since she no longer need provide for her son. When a mother is dead and all the sisters have gone, bachelors cluster round the wives of their

[1] See my article, 'Bell-oxen and ox-names among the Jie', *Uganda Journal*, xvi, March 1952.

married brothers. Such a wife is then expected to cook for and feed them and provide them with a home in her own yard.

Although the primary motive in this allocation of stock is the organization of the milk supply for each yard, there are certain other rights attaching to each wife in respect of the animals. When an animal dies the wife to whom it had been allocated (if any) has the sole right to its skin. This she needs to make clothing for herself and her daughters, for mats, covers and bags, and for sundry requirements such as thonging, thread and sandals. She supervises the cutting up of the meat and its distribution amongst the yards in the homestead. She also makes gifts to neighbouring wives. A large part is retained for her own use in her yard. If an animal is required for ritual purposes both its meat and skin are lost to the wife, for a ritually slaughtered beast may not be skinned and the meat is largely consumed at a purely male feast. Very occasionally an ox is killed for eating purposes. This is not frequent, as it is regarded as bad economy. It can only occur at the permission of the husband, and if the house is only average or poor in wealth the head would also have to give prior agreement. In the last few years there has begun a tendency to kill oxen for meat, since there is now a fair cash market for it. The wife then retains the cash (or other goods) obtained, though at the discretion of her husband. Whether an animal is killed for home consumption or for sale, a wife is morally bound to share some of the meat with her co-wives of the house, and also of the wider Family. At times a wife may wish to barter (or nowadays perhaps to sell) a goat or two in order to obtain grain, seed, iron, foodstuffs, etc. This is a legitimate desire and, with caution, a proper use of her animals. She can thereby improve the economy of her household.

We may contrast the rights of a wife in respect of her stock with her rights over agricultural land and its produce. A wife owns her garden land absolutely and in no way at the discretion of her husband. How much land she is to cultivate in any year, and where and what she grows, is entirely her own decision. The produce of the gardens is her own to use or dispose of as she wishes. Basically even her husband has no prime rights here, although where normal marital relations exist no woman would think of excluding her husband from the consumption of her garden produce. If a woman barters or sells some of her grain she retains all the goods or cash obtained. The returns on the sale of beer made from her grain is at her own sole use. Her husband may ask but he cannot demand the use of her profits. She may insist on buying beads and decorations or a new pot, rather than giving the cash to him for other purposes. In practice the whole thing works out in the normal give and take of marital relations; but whereas the husband's word is law in regard to stock, a wife has the last word concerning gardening and garden produce. As regards her co-wives, a woman is not bound to share her store of grain or to give up garden land. Because of cordial relations she may in fact do so, for the co-operative, communal spirit is strong in Jieland. Nevertheless, the produce of the gardens is most clearly regarded as belonging to the wife and her yard. It may be added that success in gardening is often the results of hard work and wisdom on the part of the woman and her daughters, and they are the principal beneficiaries of this. Purely at her own discretion a woman may give or lend both land and produce to other women, even outside the house and Family—e.g. her married daughters, her sisters, her mother's brother's womenfolk, etc. It is recognized that she should be able to continue practical relations with these kinswomen.

Where the domestic stock are concerned, a wife has none of these powers as of right and even her *de facto* control is strictly limited however well established a wife and mother she may be. Jie often say, 'Women do not own cattle. They own gardens,' or, 'Grain is the stock of women.' Men do not attempt to deny that women have certain well-defined rights in the animals of their house and yard, but they always affirm that such rights are at the supervision of themselves and that control of the major uses of stock is unreservedly held by men. At no time in her life does a woman have prime control over animals. She may be given a special cow or ox by her father (which is characterized as being her grandfather's) when she leaves his homestead for good. But her husband can take it and dispose of it should the need arise, e.g. for ritual slaughter. She may protest but she cannot prevent it. 'Her husband would beat her,' is the typical Jie formula. Whereas a husband may take an ox from his wife's herd to make a gift, to sell or barter, etc., without her consent, she has no chance of acting similarly. In fact, if an animal is taken from the cattle camp the wife may scarcely know what is happening, since it is the result of purely masculine dealings outside her sphere. When I or my wife have asked women about future marriages, or often indeed about past ones, we have generally been referred to the men

61

of the house. 'It is words about the stock. Ask the men,' they say. A woman's claim to a share in an in-coming bridewealth is put up by her menfolk and received by them, and ultimately controlled by them.

In all this we should clearly distinguish between formal, legal principles and the actual state of affairs. The account given above, and such native statements as ,'He can take her cow (given by her father). Has he not given stock (bridewealth) for her?' may seem to give a picture of overweening tyranny of husbands upon their wives, and to a lesser extent of sons over their mothers. This must be set against the men's ready recognition of the interests and rights of the women and of their value and status in the house, the men's dependence on their wives and mothers, and the general cordiality of marital relations. All this modifies the purely legal pattern as, indeed, it does in many societies where the dominance of men is often so stressed. The Jie woman is always ready to air her opinion and to stand up for what she considers her rights, and few men can afford to turn a deaf ear. In any case, it is my strong impression that genuine respect for and acknowledgment of the value of women would prevent most men acting in any high-handed fashion. Equally, a woman expects her menfolk to take charge of major matters concerning the stock and to carry out the pastoral duties connected with the herd, and she is prepared readily to accept their decisions. It is an aspect of the social division of labour within the house.[1]

This inferior legal position of a woman continues throughout her life. Whilst the house of her husband persists, she is subject to his authority and that of his brothers. When her sons become independent she comes under their authority. Her former allocated herd and its accretions are by now split up amongst her sons' wives' yards and even perhaps a wife or two of her grandsons. She herself is left with what is still an allocation from the herd of the house—just enough to provide her with milk and occasional meat. From a structural

---

[1] As an example of how a wife may interfere in stock matters which are, strictly, outside her concern, the following account is illustrative. A wedding was being held up because a kinsman of the bride was demanding another head of cattle in addition to the cow he had already received. As a mother's half-brother he had received his due, but since the bridewealth was a large one he obviously felt he could stick out for more. In the middle of the argument, at the time when the groom's people began to grow restive, the man's wife got up and told the groom in a loud voice, 'It is good that you have given us a cow. We are glad; we are very glad. It is the cow of the marriage. We want no other animal.' The crowd applauded and the discomfited husband retired amid some laughter. His greedy obstructionism had been defeated by his wife's more acute perception of the circumstances.

point of view she is still only a wife of the house, although her own sons founded it. In fact, as an old woman, whose children are all grown up and married, she will have her allocation drastically reduced in order to help her daughters-in-law who have young children, and to make up her sons' and grandsons' bridewealths. On the other hand her agricultural rights continue untouched except in so far as old age and infirmity compel a reduction of activity. Her connections with stock gradually decrease; her function in the house structure is completed. It must be recorded also that ties of affection between middle-aged sons and their aged mothers begin to slacken and she is no longer identified with the development of their house. In most things they depend on their wives and sons and daughters. Once her sons gain independence, the mother, if she is still alive, goes into a kind of retirement, for the sociological development of her life is mainly completed. Her sons may accord her prestige and affection still, but it is tempered by the process of events in which they are still active but in which she herself has played her part out. She has little if any authority over her daughters-in-law, whose yards and households are, for the most part, quite separate.

Seniority in the House, and the Order of Marriage

One of the more important, if not the most important, factors in the identity, unity and independence of a house is that it possesses its own herd of cattle, sheep and goats. Such ownership is primarily exercised by the set of full-brothers under the leadership of the eldest, but it can be said in truth that the stock belong to the whole house since it is a vital principle that they are used in the interests of all members. We have seen how this is translated in the domestic, economic sphere by the allocation of animals to each wife, from which she can feed herself and her children; and the sizes of allocations are as far as possible in keeping with the mouths to be fed. At first oxen and other male animals are mostly retained unallocated since their values and uses are relatively unconnected with feminine, domestic activities. These values and uses are chiefly in connection with the ritual, legal and other social spheres pertaining to external relations beyond the house.

It follows that, from this principle of the joint use of the herd, there must be some regulation of the claims and demands of the various members. This comes out most clearly in the rule that men may only marry in strict order of seniority. This for the founding-brothers is simply a matter of age. For their sons, however, there is a range of brothers, half-brothers and paternal cousins amongst whom rights must be regularized. To this end they marry in turn in order of seniority, and no one ought to take a second wife before they all have a first wife. Only occasionally is this modified in practice when at any particular time there is no unmarried son of an age to marry; then an older brother or cousin may be allowed to marry a second time. This is rare, however. All this is controlled by the fathers of the men under the headship of the eldest survivor. Morally and in practice there is no possibility of this rule being broken. It would be a complete negation of the spirit of unity in the house if it were. There is no distinction made according to immediate paternal affiliation. The son of the eldest brother cannot claim extra privilege against his younger cousin, the son of the youngest brother, except that he has superior seniority and therefore an earlier claim. It is believed that every man has the undisputed right to marry at least once and to propagate children of his own.

Seniority is reckoned according to the order of birth of the men, but modified sometimes according to considerations of the relative seniority of the yards. The principles of ranking are as follows:

1. Yards are ranked in the chronological order of the marriages of the mothers to the founding-brothers of the house.
2. Sons are ranked in a single yard according to their order of birth— the births of sisters are ignored for this purpose.
3. Where the age-difference between agnates is large—over about five years—seniority ranking follows age (order of birth) irrespective of the relative positions of their yards, or of the men's positions inside those yards.
4. Where the age-difference between agnates is small—less than about five years—age (order of birth) is modified in the seniority ranking as follows:

   (a) A man is ranked senior to *older* agnates in junior yards who occupy positions in those yards equivalent to his own position in his own yard; e.g.

   the first son of a yard is ranked above the first son of a junior yard; the second son of a yard is ranked above the second son of a junior yard.

   (b) A man is ranked senior to *older* agnates in senior yards who occupy relatively lower positions in their yards than he does in his yard; e.g.

   the first son of a yard is ranked above the second and third sons of senior yards; the second son of a yard is ranked above the third and fourth sons of senior yards.

Examples of seniority ranking are given in Figure 6. It will be seen that large age-gaps do occur owing to the intervening births of girls and also (not shown in Figure 6) to the deaths of sons in infancy. Age-gaps between sons in equivalent positions in their own yards

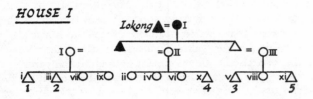

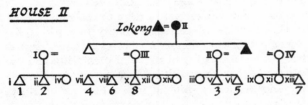

FIGURE 6

SENIORITY RANKING IN A HOUSE

The two houses in the extended family of Lokong: Lokaicil, Kotido.

Large roman numerals—order of yards (i.e. order of marriages of wives).
Small roman numerals—order of birth of children.
Arabic numerals—order of seniority of sons.

In House I—seniority follows the order of birth. On the other hand, the eldest 'son' was about 10 years older than the eldest son of another yard. After the marriage of his own full-brother he was allowed to marry a second time before 'son' 3 married.

In House II—the order of birth is modified at the following points:—

son vii takes precedence over son vi.
son xiii takes precedence over son x.

are frequently a result of long intervals between successive marriages by the founding-brothers. In such a small, compact group as the house, not only is the order of birth of all the sons easily remembered but also the extent of gaps between births, to a fair degree of accuracy.[1]

This somewhat complicated method of assessing seniority in the house is controlled by the 'fathers'. It is an attempt not only to regularize the claims of sons but also to equalize the opportunities and development of each of the yards. The eldest son of a yard, in being made senior to the second son of a senior yard, is thereby allowed to marry first—i.e. to have the use of the house's herd in order to make up a bridewealth. To a certain extent, therefore, there is something of a parallel development among all the yards. Just as a senior man ought not to take a second wife before all his juniors have taken a first, so a senior yard ought not to take another wife before more junior yards also have wives. This latter principle is, however, much subject to considerations of individuals' ages, so that a man of marriageable age does not have to wait whilst a much younger agnate of a wifeless yard grows to the right age first. The principle is a mixture of the ideal theory of equal and parallel development and the common sense of practical issues. It does, however, illustrate the real belief of the joint ownership and use of the herd of the house, together with the recognition that the group will eventually and inevitably split up into a number of independent, descendent houses based on the present yards. It illustrates also what membership of a yard means in terms of the solidarity of the full-brothers. If the eldest brother marries, that is, in some ways, thought of as a marriage into the yard, the house of the future.

It must be interpolated here that the Jie as well as the external observer may only speak figuratively in saying that a yard takes a wife, for there is no notion of polyandry involved. Quite definitely one brother marries the wife and the other brothers have no sexual claim upon her, though she may be expected to cook and provide for them. Adultery is a very grave crime in Jieland, and none the less so between a man and his brother's wife. Nevertheless, with due regard to this, we are justified in speaking of a yard taking a wife, so strong is the solidarity of brothers and so vivid their structural antithesis to parallel groups.

[1] The Jie year is divided into the major seasons, which can further be subdivided according to the timing of certain activities, e.g. the digging-up of garden land, the return of the home dairy herd, the various annual ceremonies, etc. In fact, due probably to the continual and close intercourse of a small, dense population, relative orders of birth are commonly known even beyond the confines of a settlement; and to some extent they are embodied in the age-set structure.

Amongst the set of full-brothers who found the independent house there is, in theory at any rate, the same respect for equality tempered by seniority. Here the matter is simple in principle, as it is purely a matter of the order of birth of the men to their mother. Thus the Jie say that full-brothers ought to marry in that order, and the eldest should not marry twice before all his younger brothers have married for a first time. There is, however, frequently a serious inconsistency in fraternal solidarity at this point. It has already been noted that the eldest living brother has ultimate authority in the house, and although he should and usually does exercise that power in close consultation with his brothers, he can also abuse his position by taking advantage of it. His status is in some ways thought of as a temporal extension of the authority of the 'father' before him and before the house became independent. Just as the 'father' had absolute control over the herds, so now the eldest son has inherited that authority in respect of the members of the house. He can therefore marry twice or even three times before his next brother marries once. This is not regarded by the Jie as a laudable action, but they admit that it sometimes happens, for the senior brother is 'like a father'. Of course, the senior brother cannot do this if he is still subject to the authority of a living 'father', for then he and his brothers form only a yard and must accede to the principles of seniority already discussed.

When it does occur that an eldest brother takes such an advantage over his younger brothers, it is accepted philosophically by the latter. Longoli had four wives though his next brother, Loycing, aged about thirty, had no wife at all. When I first learnt of this (for it was the first case of its kind that I came across) it appeared to contravene all that I had been told of the ideal theory of equality, and I queried the circumstances in detail. No one seemed to think that it was particularly odd; Loycing himself said, 'He is the head [of the house]. They are his stock. I am small [junior, young]. It is [a matter of] his words.' Outsiders commented that Longoli was within his legal rights as the eldest brother—younger brothers could only accept his decisions. Yet Loycing had a mistress with living children, and this woman was waiting until such time as her lover could get stock to pay bridewealth. Sometimes the younger brother's rights are recognized to the extent that a few cattle may be made available for betrothal (one to ten cattle) to the woman, a pledge of ultimate marriage by both parties.

FAMILY AND PROPERTY IN JIELAND

In the majority of cases the moral principles are observed in practice and elder brothers give due recognition to the aspirations of their juniors. The irregular case here quoted, and many others recorded in my notebooks, seem to be results of greed and selfishness on the part of the eldest brothers concerned. Longoli was doubtless affected by such motives, for he was avaricious and grasping in many of his dealings outside the house. He had fairly recently been, and still was, involved in bitter relations with other senior members of his Family, based partly on his uncompromising attitude towards his close agnates' demands. More typical fraternal relations display a good deal less self-regard and more observance of moral standards. Such a position may be illustrated by the remarks of one of my best informants, Logwela, the elder of two brothers. I once asked him why he had only one wife, though he was about fifty years old and head of his house. He replied, 'Our cattle died from rinderpest. Logono [the younger brother] had no wife. There were few cattle. You know the disease has been very bad in the country. Logono took the cattle for his wife; she ate many stock and there are not enough for me to marry. I could not take the stock for another wife —he remained [without a wife]. So I must wait for another wife. Who knows, the cattle may never be enough for that. Now there is one wife each. That is good, for are we not full-brothers? Is it not right that we are the same? I married first, then he married. Those are the words [i.e. that is how it happened].' Logwela was an upright man who took a pride in following the moral strictures of his tribe. His house had suffered badly from the rinderpest epidemics, but he did not allow resentment against his half-brothers and cousins, who had been more fortunate, to embitter Family relations, much less to affect relations with his younger brother.

Although the selfish brother is not typical nor even very common, it is worth emphasizing these irregular cases, since they show the real strength of the authority of an eldest brother in the house organization. On the other hand I discovered no instances of the seniority regulations amongst the sons of the house being contravened. It might well be suspected that the head would attempt to favour his own sons against the sons of his brothers in the same way as he had taken advantages for himself. That the strong moral unity of a house is not threatened in this way is, I think, the result of the nature of the growth of the group. When a man takes advantage of his status to deny, at least temporarily, his younger brothers their rights, there are few practical sanctions to prevent him. He is independent of the rest of the Family, who in any case do not care to intervene in the affairs of another house. The younger brothers are in a weak position to oppose him. When, however, the house has developed in its later years, the younger brothers are supported by their wives and by adult sons, and it seems that even a selfish head cannot go against their combined opposition and flout the moral standards of house unity. His autocratic authority is reduced more nearly to leadership and his whole position impels him towards the maintenance of the solidarity of the group in the face of potential cleavages. His authority cannot well be challenged where it is exercised towards the end of ensuring the strict adherence to the proper rules of seniority. In that policy the conflicting aspirations of the various sub-groups are resolved in supporting him.

What is the significance of these principles of seniority in an account of the structure of a house?

The Jie themselves primarily regard the house as the stock-owning unit in their society. The herds and flocks of a house are separate from and independent of other herds and flocks in that they are used principally for the exclusive advantage of the members of that house. There are, as will be seen later, quite definite reciprocal rights and obligations recognized in relation to other houses, but these are always subject to varying conditions of cordiality, respect and mutual convenience. Structural relations between houses may be fairly fluid. Inside the house, inter-personal relations are relatively unimportant in the structure of relations, although it is not of course denied that houses do differ through time, or compared with one another, because of individual personalities and particular relationships between members. Quite obviously Jie are not all alike and the pattern of the house cannot suppress their various personalities, antipathies and affections. Nevertheless, to a great extent these are kept under control by the overriding necessities of the solidarity of the house, stemming as it does from the primary principle in Jie social life—the solidarity of full-brothers.

Now the principal use of stock, as any Jie loves to assert, outside basic economic needs, is for marriage. Even though the Jie are wealthy stock-owners,[1] the sizes of bridewealth payments are such that a marriage is usually a considerable strain on the resources of the house. The institution of bridewealth is described in Chapter 8,

[1] See p. 39 above.

and here it may be sufficient to state that at least one-half of the total bridewealth must be found by the house—an average bridewealth being about fifty cattle, plus many goats. It is most unusual that two members of a house can marry at the same time, let alone the four or five men who may all wish to marry in any particular season. It is necessary, as it were, to ration the resources of the house for these purposes, and there are also other demands occurring from time to time as well as the constant need for food.

When a man wishes to marry he must first gain approval of his intentions by the head of his house so that he may be allowed to have the use of stock for his bridewealth. This given, he has a claim on all the stock of the house wherever allocated or in the 'residual herd'. This right is exercised for him by the head of the house, who decides which cattle, goats and sheep are to be taken. The suitor's half-brothers and paternal cousins can in no way deny him this right nor prevent him from using stock allocated to their mothers and, therefore, ultimately to themselves. The herd is treated as a single unit for use in this way. The head of the house will, of course, see that no wife is left drastically short of milking-stock, whether she be the suitor's mother or some other woman. Nevertheless, where economies in domestic allocation are to be made, they should fall as equably as possible on all yards. Usually the 'residual herd' will be principally depleted, but that may be too small or it may contain too few female stock. An acceptable bridewealth should contain a good proportion of cows,[1] and each yard must surrender some. It will be noted that the share of each yard is not determined by considerations of friendliness or animosity, approval or disapproval, but by actual requirements as decided by the head. Special considerations of friendliness may be marked, over and above such requirement, by the gift of a bell-ox (not hitherto required) to the suitor by a half-brother or cousin. The unity of the house's herds and the authority of the head are re-emphasized at the time of the actual wedding, when he and his full-brothers ceremonially hand over the stock to the bride's people. A marriage payment would not be properly made if the head of the house did not perform this ceremonial act.

At this point some mention may be made of other uses of the

---

[1] There is no fixed proportion between cows and oxen, but it would be almost an insult to offer only a few cows, and doubtless the bride's father and her kinsfolk would strongly object. About half of the stock should be females.

house's herds by members. The house as a unit will from time to time be approached by other members of the Family with requests for contributions to their bridewealth. These requests are an important practical aspect of intra-Family relations. The house contributes as a group; the size and composition of the contribution is determined by the head. At other times various members of the house are approached to contribute towards other men's bridewealth—e.g. a close affine, a bond-friend, etc. These are well-recognized claims against a man and thus against his house. He has the right to take some of the animals from the herd, subject always to the ultimate approval of the head. It may only be a matter of a goat or two, or it may involve cattle. They are, if possible, taken from the allocation of the man's yard, but he may dip into the 'residual herd'. It is recognized by members of a house that one of their number has a right to use and dispose of stock in pursuance of normal social relations—relations, moreover, which do not affect all members of the house equally closely. Similarly, there are occasions when a man requires one or more animals for barter purposes or to obtain cash (to buy goods, to pay tax, etc.) or to provide a feast at some ceremony. Occasionally an animal is required for meat or for its skin. These kinds of requirements occur continuously in ordinary life, and each time the right is acceded to, the basic unity of herd is reaffirmed.

To sum up, I wish to emphasize that the Jie house has its birth in the birth of children, particularly sons, to a wife; it reaches its maturity and full independence when these sons together become independent of their half-brothers and cousins; and it dies with the death of the last survivor. In all this the solidarity of the full-brothers is paramount, and from that stems the egalitarian principle so much in evidence and which is expressed *inter alia* in the unity of the herd which those men jointly own and use. The death of one or more of the founding-brothers leaves the house intact, precisely as it was before as a corporate group, so long as one of their number survives. With the death of the last one, and only then, do the various sets of their sons (yards) become independent, and only then is the herd permanently divided up. There is a strict and well-recognized correspondence between the solidarity of the full-brothers and the unity of their herd.

APPENDIX

THE DISTRIBUTION OF HOUSES, THEIR MEMBERS AND STOCK IN THE HOMESTEAD 'LOREKALI', LOKATAP SETTLEMENT, KOTIDO DISTRICT

This is one of the old-type homesteads with a population of 96 people in April 1951. It contained the majority of the members of a large extended family. For the genealogy see Figure 9.

For each house the founding full-brothers are given first, as they do not belong to any yard. The figures in brackets give their approximate ages.

Numbers of cattle allocated to each yard are shown opposite the wife's name. In some cases a daughter (married, or an unmarried mother) occupies a separate courtyard, but she and her children remain a part of her mother's yard as far as stock are concerned. The yards are shown in the accompanying diagram of the homestead.

House A (21 people)

Theoretically this group forms a house-line of two houses, for the father, Ila, is dead and there was no brother. The junior house is represented by an unmarried mother and her younger sister, and it tends to be submerged by the senior house headed by a young married man.

Yard A1— 1. Athike, widow of Ila.   5 cattle
        2. two unmarried adult sons.
Yard A2— 3. Lopui, married daughter of 1.
Yard A3— 4. Murinyang, wife of 5.   6 cattle
        5. Nakong, eldest son of 1.
        6. three children.
Yard A4— 7. Moicam, unmarried mother, daughter of
           deceased wife III of Ila.   12 cattle
        8. five children.
        9. younger sister of 7.

                Unallocated stock *c.* 15 cattle
                      Total c. 38 cattle

Yard A5—10. Ethin, married daughter of deceased wife
           II of Ila.
        11. four children.

(This yard belongs to a house of another family and settlement. The wife returned to her paternal home because of fears of witchcraft. She continues to be supported by her husband, but her dairy herd is kept in the kraal of her half-brother.)

FAMILY AND PROPERTY IN JIELAND

House B (19 people)

	1. Nadenya (65): 2. Longerun (50).	
Yard B1—	3. Nakoro, wife I of 1.	8 cattle
	4. adult son.	
Yard B2—	5. Dukun, wife of 6.	5 cattle
	6. Dengil, eldest son of 3.	
	7. two children.	
Yard B3—	8. Lokwel, wife II of 1.	9 cattle
	9. adult son.	
	10. three younger sons.	
Yard B4—	11. Nakut, wife of 2.	8 cattle
	12. adult married son (wife not yet living with him).	
	13. adult son.	
Yard B5—	14. Aicing, daughter of 11, unmarried mother.	
	15. two children.	

Unallocated stock *c.* 30 cattle
Total c. 60 cattle

House C (4 people)

	1. Etau (25).	
Yard C1—	2. Mudung, wife of 1.	
	3. two children.	*Total c.* 20 cattle

House D (17 people)

	1. Kidemoi (55): 2. Lobalang (45).	
Yard D1—	3. Atokora, wife I of 1.	11 cattle
	4. married son (wife not yet living with him).	
	5. two children.	
Yard D2—	6. Loyo, married daughter of 3.	
	7. one child.	
Yard D3—	8. Ibura, wife II of 1.	9 cattle
	9. three children.	
Yard D4—	10. Nakot, married daughter of 8.	
	11. one child.	
Yard D5—	12. Nadure, wife of 2.	5 cattle
	13. two children.	

Unallocated stock *c.* 30 cattle
Total c. 55 cattle

House E (15 people)

	1. Logwela (50): 2. Logono (45).	
Yard E1—	3. Abanyo, wife of 1.	8 cattle
	4. six children.	
Yard E2—	5. Nakalio, wife of 2.	6 cattle
	6. four children.	
Yard E3—	7. Aicila, mother of 1 and 2.	2 cattle

Unallocated stock 14 cattle
Total 30 cattle

73

House F (Loyamoi and three of his wives lived in an adjacent homestead, where their stock are kraaled. The wife of yard F1 quarrelled with her co-wives and has refused to live with them.)

Yard F1—1. Kamera, wife III of Loyamoi.   5 cattle
        2. three children.

House G (9 people)

        1. Kire (55).
Yard G1—2. Erueta, wife of 1.
        3. adult son.
        4. six children.   *Total c.* 15 cattle

House H (5 people)

        1. Lodungo (35), brother of wife II of
            Nadenya (House B).
Yard H1—2. Nakwol, wife of 1.
        3. three children.   *Total c.* 15 cattle

Stock camps

At the time there were three cattle camps wherein houses co-operated as follows:

    1. Houses A, B, C and H.
    2. Houses D, E and G.
    3. House F.

There were also three goat camps arranged on the same basis. Each house had some of its stock in each of the other two camps. The arrangements of kraals in the homestead is shown in the accompanying diagram.

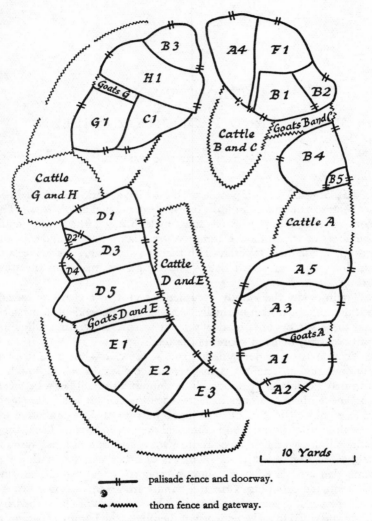

10 Yards

— palisade fence and doorway.

thorn fence and gateway.

The letters denote houses, and the numbers denote yards within a house: thus,
A1—house A, yard 1.

THE HOMESTEAD OF LOREKALI, LOKATAP SETTLEMENT, KOTIDO DISTRICT

CHAPTER FOUR

FAMILY AND PROPERTY IN JIELAND

(b) THE EXTENDED FAMILY

Introduction

The largest group of people within which agnatic ties are claimed to be traceable genealogically is the 'extended family', *eowe*.[1] The core of this group is a shallow, male lineage, the senior adult members of which have a common grandfather, the founder of the group. These men, together with their wives, sons, sons' wives and children, and unmarried sisters and daughters, make up the total group.

Traditionally the Family occupied a sector of a clan-homestead, but in modern times it normally occupies an independent homestead and there has begun a tendency for it to spread over the whole or parts of two, or even more, homesteads.

There exists a wider agnatic group—the clan—but here ties are putative and no attempt is made to trace them. Thus although a clan may be physically divided into a number of Families—between one and eight in number in fact—sociologically it has little significance. Since Jie cannot remember beyond their grandfather in genealogical reckoning, and commonly not even that far back, they cannot link together two or more Families in one rational system; neither do they attempt to. Members of other Families within the same clan are placed in a common category of 'clansmen', an undifferentiated grouping. Clan and Family are groups based on overlapping, but not coincident criteria. The real basis of clan solidarity lies in the ritual interdependence of members; the Family is based on

---

[1] Sometimes this group is simply designated *ngitungakothi*—'our people', although this term may equally well refer to the whole field of a man's kin and kith or only to the house. To avoid needless repetition I shall usually refer to the 'extended family' as 'the Family'. Normally in my account of the Jie I shall not use the term 'family'.

76

known agnatic links and interrelations are principally expressed in certain, fairly specific, reciprocal rights over domestic stock. Both are residential, face-to-face groups. In respect of the clan, members of a man's Family are fellow-clansmen. Clan membership has no special significance in respect of Family relations.

Although clustered round a crucial agnatic core, the Family is not wholly agnatic since quite specifically it includes the wives of the men, following their ritual incorporation into their husbands' clan at the culmination of the lengthy marriage process.[1] Wives play important parts in certain ritual connected with their adopted Families, but they have no role in the ritual activities of their father's Families. Women have an important structural position in a Family. To them, in the name of the sub-section which they found with their children—the 'yard'—are allocated portions of the Family herds. A wife become mother is a critical point of essential differentiation within the Family, and eventually her sons form a new and autonomous section of the group. For these reasons, stated here only briefly for the moment, I shall not refer to the Family as a lineage.[2] In any case such a term might be misleading, since the recent spate of discussion connected with lineages has dealt mainly with groups of greater spans, which are also significantly arranged in relation to one another in a segmentary structure. It has been mentioned that clans are neither part of a larger system nor apexes of smaller segments. Normally genealogical knowledge only goes back about two generations before the current senior adults—i.e. the limit of the Family. Almost always, if a man does remember the name of his great-grandfather, that knowledge adds nothing to the horizontal range over which the remembered genealogy stretches. Quite commonly a middle-aged or old man does not recollect the name of his father's father.

The use of the term 'extended family' (or 'Family') will therefore, by terminological difference, be a reminder that we are not dealing with a lineage system nor with any wholly agnatic descent group. No less important is the fact that Jie themselves conceive of their

---

[1] See pp. 227-8.

[2] In his study of the Tallensi of the Gold Coast, who have an especially far-reaching, segmentary lineage system, Fortes clearly distinguishes between small-scale lineages (agnatic descent groups) and 'families' which also contain women married to members of such lineages. A 'joint family' is generally clustered around an 'effective minimal lineage'; an 'expanded family' is generally based on a 'nuclear lineage'. See Fortes, M., *The Web of Kinship amongst the Tallensi*, London, 1949, p. 9 and p. 64 *et seq.*

Family as quite literally an expansion through time of the original polygynous family of their grandfather; and they have explained it to me as such many times. Exactly parallel with this development has gone that of the grandfather's herd of cattle, goats and sheep. He had a single herd of stock which his grandsons now own and use. Although physically and legally the herd (or rather its descendants plus accretions) is no longer a single unit, yet in some ways and at certain times it is still thought of as if it were. Thus men say, 'We are all grandsons,' or as an exact equivalent, 'Our stock are all one. There is only one herd. Other people's stock are different [separate].' Both are significant indices of the group.

Briefly, the ideal structure and development of a Family is described by the Jie as follows. Long ago the grandfather had his own wives and children and herd of stock. His sons were directly subject to his authority. There was a single group with him as its head. When he died the group broke up, and the sets of sons of his various wives became independent 'houses', and each house took its share of the father's herd. In their turn these men died and their houses broke up into a number of descendent houses each founded by the sons of a wife of the old house. In Jie theory the founders of these new houses, the grandsons of the first man, are the adult men of today. Their houses are loosely grouped together in 'house-lines', which are each composed of the descendants of a grandmother, a wife of the founder of the total Family group. The next phase of the process—for Jie see it as an on-going continuum—will be marked by differentiation based on the wives of the present adults. A house, at whatever stage, was or is an independent owner of a herd of stock, under the authority of the senior man—i.e. the eldest brother. The ideal structure of the Jie Family is illustrated diagrammatically in Figure 7.

The head of the Family is the most senior man alive. His position affords little or no authority. He is titular head, and in that capacity should both perform certain ritual and always be present to ratify any ritual performance or major social transaction by a member house. For instance, he should lead ritual performance at the incorporation of a wife or any member of the Family; he should ceremonially assist in the handing over of all bridewealth payments. There is further an idea that he acts for the Family as a whole, looking to its interests as a corporate group, attempting to maintain amicable relations amongst members. In theory, for instance, one of his agnates should not marry and alienate stock in bridewealth without the agreement of everyone else, including the Family head; and Jie say that the head could bring down supernatural punishment by an appeal to the High God. In fact, the authority of the head is usually far too slight and it might endanger Family relations further to appeal for supernatural punishment. In any case, if there is important disagreement in the Family, the head of the group is almost always deeply involved with one or the other of the disputant parties and cannot properly act as conciliator or counsel. However, just as

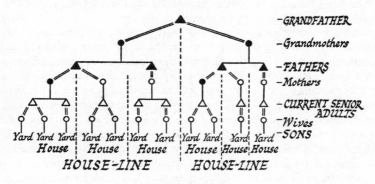

FIGURE 7

THE IDEAL PATTERN OF THE JIE EXTENDED FAMILY

the head of the Family represents the group in ritual performance, so he represents the ideal of Family unity and amity.

A Family is commonly known as 'the children of ——' (naming the grandfather), and the Family homestead is sometimes referred to by his name. Between the members of the group there is usually continual co-operation in pastoral affairs, residential and day-to-day intercourse and much assistance in all activities. Above all, there is recognition of reciprocal obligations to assist each other in transactions involving stock such as bridewealth, compensation, gifts and the like. Although this introductory account begins from the genealogical basis of the Family, from the facts of agnatic descent, yet structurally we might, as later we shall indeed, regard the Family as a complex of social relations between a body of men, and their wives and children, dependent on and primarily expressed in mutual rights and obligations in respect of a group of herds; both the ownership

79

of the herds and the relations being defined agnatically. Since the integrative principles operative in the Family are agnatic principles, and since men only can own stock and they are principally involved in the system of relations concerning rights and obligations over stock, we shall frequently have cause to speak as if the Family were purely an agnatic descent group. This will be done as a matter of convenience in exposition and does not in any way invalidate the fundamental Jie conception that wives are essentially full members of their husbands' Families, and not of those of their own fathers.

It may be pointed out here at once that in what follows we shall have occasion frequently to point out the continual and direct correlation between descent and stock-ownership, and between close agnatic relations and reciprocal rights over stock. This is not primarily an abstract rationalization as a result of objective observation and analysis. The Jie see it fairly clearly, and my better informants explained the elements of it to me at an early stage in my fieldwork. That is not to say, of course, that any native, however intelligent, could present a comprehensive account of Family relations and rights in regard to domestic stock. None can, any more than they can of other relatively complex aspects of social life; the natives are not accustomed to dealing in general and comprehensive terms, nor is there any need for them to do. Nevertheless, it is important to realize that as an ideal scheme the two systems are interwoven so that one could not well be understood apart from the other. The basic content of agnatic bonds, that which gives them value and significance for the people, and which provides the continuum in the Family through the generations, lies in reciprocal rights over herds of animals.

It may be convenient to add at this stage that this fundamental significance of property rights is largely unchallenged by other social institutions. There is no notion at all of an ancestor cult or of the supernatural influence of ancestors upon their living descendants. Although for some purposes close agnates combine in Family ritual, the basic ritual group is the clan and most ceremonies specifically connected with a Family are undertaken through the agency of the clan and the co-operation of clansmen and clan elders. Neither agricultural nor pastoral land tenure presents problems of ownership, inheritance or mutual adjustment of formal claims and obligations within, or without, the Family. The group receives no corporate exclusiveness in opposition to comparable units within an inclusive system. In so far as Families are founded on cores of agnatic descent and as such are owners and users of domestic stock, they stand alone and independent of one another except for the largely fortuitous links by marriage and bond-friendship. Families come together as parts of residential and ritual groups, but in these they are not identified as segmentary units. Political and judicial mechanisms operate in terms of the total kin group of any person involved in proceedings of that nature.[1] Close agnates are of course some of the most important members of a person's range of kin along with his close maternal kin and close affines. But the participation of such agnates in a judicial matter is only partly determined by group membership as such; for, as Jie see it, it is also a function of the reciprocal relations between each of the members and the person involved. Inter-personal relations are at least as important as intra-group bonds. From the economic aspect a Family gains little or no integration. The house is the real economic unit, being both a stock-owning and a garden-using group. Beyond the almost self-sufficient house, economic co-operation is not necessarily organized on Family lines. Close affines are almost as commonly found in pastoral co-operation as are close agnates; agricultural working-parties in the wet season are mainly composed of a house's affines, and seldom even include agnates. The Family, finally, is not even residentially isolated. Formerly a single homestead contained all the Families of a clan, together with their kraals. Today a Family's homestead is part of a clan-hamlet; and a homestead is not usually reserved to one Family alone.

To conclude this introduction to the Family, the group which is to be the subject of detailed analysis in this chapter, some account will be given of its internal and external recognition as a specific, corporate unit in certain circumstances, chiefly ritual.

Just before harvest-time, if the rains have continued to be poor and the outlook for crops is therefore bad, a last-minute attempt may be made in each settlement to temper the situation by invoking once again the intervention of the High God.[2] For this purpose all the adult men visit the homestead of each Family of that settlement in turn, and there blood, milk and porridge are provided by the women-folk of that Family. Communal supplications are made to the High God in the name of that Family for the welfare of its gardens and

---

[1] See Chapter 7.
[2] The normal and even the emergency tribal and district rain-making ritual will have been completed by this time.

crops, and also for its stock. On the other hand, and unfortunately less frequently, if there has been a good year thanksgiving is made to the High God for his blessings. Each Family in turn arranges a ceremonial feast in the central cattle kraal of its homestead, for which an ox is slaughtered. These feasts, held on different days, are attended by all adult males of the settlement, and public acknowledgment of good fortune is made, and opportunity taken to pray that next year's rains may come quickly and equally abundantly. The motif of each of these sets of ritual is the distinctiveness of the various Families in the name of each of which requests or thanks are made to the deity by all the men. 'There must,' said one informant, 'be words and ritual for each Family. Each one is different. We beg *Akuj* [the High God] for each one. There is our Family, the Family of Locoto, of Apalopua, of Komul and of Lotiowi' (naming the various groups of his own settlement).

During ceremonies within a settlement the names of the constituent Families are often mentioned in the detailed supplications of communal prayers. After asking for fertility, rain, good crops, fat animals, etc., in general terms, the list is repeated in the name of each Family. At any important ceremony the man who, in competition, spears the ritual ox earns for his Family the privilege of a special ceremony the following day when the district elders assemble at his homestead. On such an occasion any special difficulty or trouble which has affected that Family is taken up, and the High God's intervention sought in prayers. Certain stages of the long marriage ceremonial are confined to or especially associated with the Family of the bride or groom. At one particular ceremony, *lobwo*, every member (male and female) of the bride's Family must be ritually anointed by the head of the age-set of the bride's father. At this time the head of the Family dresses in a wife's clothing and decorations, to represent 'the mother of the Family', for, 'are we not all children of one woman—the mother of our grandfather?' On all occasions when a person is involved in particular ritual all members of his or her Family (or sometimes all the male adult members) are expected to give him (or her) full support, materially and morally, otherwise the ritual would not be efficacious. 'We do our ritual all together. It is good then.'

Although we shall not be much concerned with this aspect in what follows, the Family is so much regarded as a close, corporate unit by outsiders that in judicial proceedings an injured person (or his heir) is completely justified, in Jie law, in seizing compensatory stock not merely or only from the herd of the offender but also from the herds of any members of the offender's Family. The injured party is not, on the other hand, justified in seizing stock of any other person whatever his relation to the offender, e.g. clansman, maternal uncle, affine. The idea of the common herd of the unitary Family not only appears therefore in the system of internal rights and obligations but also in its recognition by outsiders.

These few examples demonstrate that the Family is thought of as a specific group of people who besides co-operating through reciprocal rights with each other, also have a unity beyond that which is regarded as essential to ritual efficiency. A man has reciprocal rights with a wide range of people outside his Family, some of whom are not even kin. Such relations are, however, relative only to the particular individual and may scarcely, if at all, involve the rest of his Family. Within the Family the system of rights and obligations is an interdependent network in which all are involved irrespective of external conditions.

The Metamorphosis of a House and the Formation of a House-line

It has been described how a house begins, develops and ends with the birth, development and death of its founding full-brothers. We have seen also that the life and unity of a house are inextricably bound up with the ownership of its domestic stock. Whilst at least one of the full-brothers is alive, the house, the wives and children of the brothers, is a unified corporate group under a single authority, and the stock form a unitary herd under a single control. When the last brother dies this corporate unity disappears, in respect of both humans and stock. In its place there are a number of separate groups and separate herds. What was a single entity becomes a kind of coalition of independent groups in the house-line.

This brief summary oversimplifies the process, for it is evident that, even before the old house dies out and is succeeded by the less explicit house-line, there is internal differentiation. There are the various yards which in due course will become the new independent houses. Everyone recognizes this inevitable process, not least the members of the yards themselves; and one of the significant functions of the seniority system is the regulation of this differentiation. At an early stage in the life of a house, most or all of the yards are composed of fairly young wives and children, who accept the authority of their husbands or fathers without question. As the sons of the wives, the men of the yards, grow to adulthood and to a recognition of their status and roles, they begin to think in terms of the development of their own sub-groups in which their future is bound up. A tradition grows up of the attachment to a yard of the cattle, goats and sheep allocated to it by the 'fathers'. There is the beginnings of the idea of 'our cattle' as against the cattle of other yards. They are the animals which have been directly attended to by the mother, and they have been augmented from time to time by rightful shares of in-payments and by gifts. They include special animals of particular value to the men, e.g. their bell-oxen, and gifts from maternal kin and from their own friends. This emergent feeling is of course restricted by the legal structure of the house and by the actual physical unity of the whole herd in the homestead, and at the bush camps in respect of kraaling, herding, watering and pastoral movements. Nevertheless, the seed is planted and continues to grow.

There is a wide range of important relationships outside the confines of the house, and for members of different yards these are not all the same. From the first the maternal kin of yards are different, and these include the important mother's brothers. The natal house of the mother is closely associated with her yard. The mother's brother's homestead is a second home where in childhood a person can find food, shelter, sympathy and encouragement. The first two children of a yard have been born and reared there before their mother moved to the paternal home. Enduring bonds have been set up which remain important through life. In adulthood men begin to marry and to establish vital affinal relations with the natal houses of their wives and to a lesser extent with their Families. Relations with a father-in-law and brother-in-law are particularly important. In a similar way there are affinal ties set up with the husbands of the sisters of the yards. In addition there are numerous ties of bond-friendship and it is common that if one is the bond-friend of a man, one is also linked with his full-brothers.

Only slightly is a man linked to the maternal kin of his half-brothers or paternal cousins, and similarly with their close affines. Friends and bond-friends of those agnates are more or less unconnected with the man. In short, the spheres of social relations of the various yards by no means coincide; indeed they tend progressively to diverge. There is less dependence on members of other yards and an increasing awareness of and dependence on relations which are focused on one's own yard. And in the background persists the notion that sooner or later the yards will become independent of one another.

It has been shown how the demands for stock for bridewealth are regulated according to a strict order of seniority, and how that cannot be evaded whilst the authority of the founding full-brothers (the 'fathers') persists. Nevertheless, as the men reach adulthood and begin to assume the responsibilities of marriage and children they become increasingly jealous of their own rights and suspicious of the claims of others. Whilst accepting, under compulsion, the claims of half-brothers and cousins, men are (to put it at its mildest) sorry to relinquish stock from the allocated herd of their own yard for the bridewealth of those agnates. The pride and care expended in one's own herd are frustrated by accedence to those claims, so that there is something of an idea of the development of other yards at the expense of one's own; it would be pleasant, furthermore, to take another wife into one's yard rather than see the animals go for the wife of a cousin; but for the moment there is little that can be done about it. Feelings and attitudes cannot be translated into actions. As the men of the various yards reach responsible ages (and in fact some of them may no longer be young men), they may begin openly to express these attitudes before their fathers at times when stock transactions are being discussed. An old man, head of the house, may listen to their opinions, and in many ways may give the men a free hand; but, apart from exceptional cases, he does not surrender his real authority, and the use of stock for bridewealth is still strictly governed by the moral principles of house structure. I have explained earlier that the death of one or more 'fathers' does not materially affect the situation whilst one survives.

Structurally it is inevitable that sets of full-brothers should diverge in ownership of stock, spheres of relations and general interests; and to a significant extent attitudes and feelings are canalized into that structural pattern. Structural opposition becomes expressed in a degree of rivalry between agnates which may develop into jealousy, hostility and obstructionism. The logical development of such attitudes will be discussed presently. First, however, it needs to be recorded that intra-house relations are not all or wholly tending to deteriorate, nor are they all or only composed of opposition rather than of co-operation. Were that so, the essential unity and solidarity of the house would be seriously threatened, and it is probable that there would be cases of houses breaking up prematurely. In fact, I have never heard of a house dividing up whilst one of its founding-brothers was still alive.[1] On the other hand I know many cases where an old man, the last of the founding-brothers, is the successful head of his house, many of whose sons and nephews are middle-aged with adolescent sons of their own, and even married daughters. Examples of such situations will appear later in this chapter during examination of genealogical evidence and elsewhere. These dependent adults do not contest the authority of their 'fathers' in their opposition to each other, and in any case they actively co-operate on many occasions. Half-brothers and cousins are often exceedingly friendly, and a man may find his firmest friendships with such agnates rather than with his younger full-brothers. Such friendships often grow out of joint experiences in the bush camps. As between such men, whose structural affiliations and developments diverge, there can still be fruitful relations which deny any possibility of inter-personal hostility, opposition or resentment.

When the last of the founding-brothers dies, the house dies. The former members automatically become divided into independent, corporate groups. Each such group, the former yard, is now a complete house under the headship of the eldest brother. This means that there is no longer a single herd, but an equal number of independent herds. Each new house takes the stock that had formerly been only allotted to the mother, plus all increments by births, shares of in-payments and gifts. There can be little scope for serious difficulties over this since the former allocations were quite precise even though physically kept together. Structural opposition is not aroused over matters of inheritance. There may, it is true, remain the problem of the 'residual herd' which at the moment of break-up of the old house belongs to no single yard. This problem is often short-circuited by the last head of the old house who allocates all the remaining stock before his death. Most old men, who are the last surviving founding-brother, take care to do this at a fairly early stage in order to preclude any possible trouble later on. If the house is rather below average in wealth there may already be no 'residual herd', though it will be renewed from time to time as fresh in-payments are received. Only

---

[1] See pp. 53-4 above for an example of hostility between full-brothers. Nevertheless, even there the moral unity of the house remained, and in the most serious case I quoted the brothers came together again after some years.

the wealthiest houses contain such a reserve for any length of time if the head is an old man with no fraternal successors. However, the sudden death of the head may discover a 'residual herd' which he had intended should be only temporary. If, for whatever reason, there is a reserve when the old house dies, it must be distributed amongst the new houses following joint discussion in which, perhaps, respected men of other related houses join. Whether the final allocation occurs before or after the death of the house, it follows the same principles. The rule is that the most junior yard (or house) should get the largest part, and other shares decrease according to increasing seniority of the yards (or houses). This, say the Jie, is because the most junior group has not only had the least time in which to accumulate stock, but also its needs are greatest. The men of the senior-most yard should have had opportunity for marriage and of using the stock of the whole house; some or all of the men of the most junior yard are likely to be still unmarried. If, however, all the sons are married at least once, and if the most junior yard has had reasonable opportunity to accumulate stock, then final distribution can be more nearly on a basis of equality. As an example, Uwongawo of Wertakow settlement had two surviving sons, one by each of his wives, and there was a single surviving son of his deceased full-brother. When he died all three sons were over thirty years old and had one wife each. This was a simple case, and the final distribution of the reserve stock, made after this death, was on the basis of exact equality. I was told that each son got fourteen cattle in addition to the animals already allocated to his mother. Uwongawo's half-brother, Owunyut, who is still alive, has no brothers who lived to marry. He himself has four wives, of whom one is barren. The sons of the first two wives are all married with one wife each. The two sons of the fourth wife are still youths. Owunyut is a very old man and married this last wife in his old age. He is not likely to live many years more. His eldest son, Ibokwel, was one of my best informants and friends. He told me that so far his father has not distributed all the stock of the house; and as far as I could discover some seventy cattle remain in the 'residual herd', for this is an exceedingly wealthy house. Ibokwel and his brothers feel that the time has come when their father ought to make the final allocations, and I was told how it should be done. Of these seventy cattle the junior yard ought to get about half, the remainder to be shared equally amongst the other two yards. If Owunyut does not make the allocations before his death, that is how it will be done afterwards, according to Ibokwel.[1]

If such a final distribution is made by the head of the house, there can be very little dispute over the matter as the old man's word is law. I have never heard of decisions of this sort being questioned openly by the sons of a house, although it is possible that there might be some private discussions at the time which could have some influence. If final distribution is made after the death of the old man there is more room for dispute, for each of the new houses may wish to exercise its independence, to improve its own position, and to increase its wealth as much as possible. Nevertheless, at this stage relations between the various groups of men are still largely determined by the mould of the old house.

This final distribution (if any) usually affects only a small part of the total herd, for the bulk of the stock have already been allocated. No one outside the house has a right to or claim on the herd at this juncture. Other members of the Family have no material interest in the result, but are concerned only that it should be such as to maintain maximum agreement. Senior members of the Family may therefore be acceptable mediators in the discussions.

Jie describe a yard as a wife (or mother) and her children and it is usually known by her name; but they describe a house as a group of full-brothers with their wives and children. Logically the house also includes the mother and her unmarried daughters, but at this stage these are usually of minor importance. Sisters eventually marry and leave the group, and thereafter are members of alien families and houses. The mother occupies a position of high prestige; she has some authority over her daughters-in-law and is accepted as an expert in family ritual and taboos. She cannot, however, own stock, for this power is reserved solely to men. In most of the important features of the organization of the house her sons take control, determining pastoral and economic arrangements and the use and disposal of animals. The future of the house is specifically bound up with the future of these brothers and not with their mother. Her structural role was chiefly concerned in the founding of the original yard, when her sons were subject to their fathers' overriding

---

[1] I may add, in view of what has been stated earlier, that Ibokwel is at least forty years old and his eldest half-brother is only a year or so younger. Neither felt able to bring pressure on their aged but highly respected father, whose word is their law. 'They are his stock,' said Ibokwel simply.

authority and ownership and control of the herds. Thus, although, at first at any rate, the actual membership of the new house is exactly the same as that of the old yard, yet the structural balance is shifted.

Whereas the focal position was the mother, now it has become her sons, the full-brothers; and, in parallel terms, whereas stock were attached to the mother, now they are owned by her sons. The link of maternal affiliation becomes implicit rather than explicit. It is to be noted also that although the subdivision of a house into yards and its subsequent cleavage into new houses is based directly and consciously on maternal affiliation, yet the patrilineal principle is not thereby submerged. This appears quite clearly where inheritance is concerned, and inheritance provides the seed from which flowers the property-owning distinctiveness of the house. Groups of full-brothers inherit directly from their fathers, not from their mothers, for women are allowed no more than a limited usufruct of stock, and always at the discretion of their menfolk. The focal status of brothers in a house, which largely excludes the mother structurally speaking, follows from the canon of patrilineal descent. The decisive line of continuity is ultimately between fathers and sets of their sons, in which their wives (or the mothers) are but differentiating links.

With this division of the herd into independent parts goes the cancellation of the former rights and obligations so rigidly maintained in the old house. That is to say, a man can no longer demand as of right, some of the stock of his half-brothers or full-cousins, nor is he himself compelled by any authority to surrender any of his own stock in their favour. Concomitant with this goes the abolition of the seniority ruling in regard to marriage. Now, as already explained, marriage is the chief occasion of the expenditure of stock. It is not the only occasion, but it is the most frequent and involves greater numbers than all other transactions. It also deeply involves the future development of the houses, since it concerns the natural increase brought by wives and children. To the goal of marriage, above all, men carefully tend and preserve their large herds, which exceed the mere economic demands put on them.

Jie say that a man can afford to marry if his own house has at least twenty cattle over and above minimum requirements for economic purposes. That means the agreement and assistance of his kinsmen and friends, and primarily of his near agnates, who together provide the remainder of a bridewealth. To a considerable extent, therefore, a man is dependent on his agnates and finds it difficult to go against their opposition. So, and especially at first, the men of the new houses—the house-line—are still bound together although their legal unity has disappeared. For instance, the old order of seniority in marriage tends to be followed still. A wifeless man is not likely to accede to or support the claims against his house's stock when a half-brother wishes to marry a second time. This practical, mutual interdependence is backed by the belief that every man ought to be able to marry at least once. It is significant that there is seldom much rivalry over the series of first marriages, but that the rivalry tends to break out over second and third marriages. A man may feel that he is no longer bound to follow the order of seniority since he is increasingly aware of the independence of his own house. He may therefore consider a refusal to assist the second marriage of a cousin, preferring to harbour stock for his own approaching second marriage. He is unlikely to refuse entirely, though it may be clear that he would like to; but rather he will be niggardly in the extent of his assistance. If it comes to a matter of third or even fourth wives the strain is even more apparent. The head of one house may be middle-aged and may be less considerate of the demands of youthful cousins.

These kinds of problems are regularly raised at the beginning of each wet season, when new marriages are discussed and arranged. Consequently each year the rivalry and degree of tension tends to increase. There is the fundamental notion, recognized by everyone, that a near agnate *ought* to assist, especially where the order of seniority is not violated. There is the strong desire to further the growth of one's own house. The development of a parallel house is conceived of almost as a threat to the development of one's own. There is conflict between the ideal and the practice. Each house, as the years go by, becomes increasingly more conservative in its expenditure of stock other than for its own advancement. Jie realize that concession to the demands of others reduces the animals available for their own purposes. A man feels that he would almost like to refuse the demands of others, yet he realizes that he cannot except by cutting himself off from the advantages of future help. Although the value and need of reciprocal assistance is recognized, there is the strain involved by temporarily or even permanently halting one's own plans in order to further the plans of others.

Similarly there are tensions concerning stock received in bride-wealth for a sister or daughter of the house, for close agnates are entitled to receive shares. Then a man wishes to conserve stock received, until he himself, or another man of his house, is ready to marry.

There is then a gradual development of house independence from the original, compulsory unity in the old house to the stage when the order of seniority is no longer recognized and reciprocal obligations are seriously threatened. This stage is reached as the men become middle-aged and when they begin to be concerned with the marriages of their sons rather than with those of the sons of parallel houses; and this is an important new element in the structure of a house-line. For the interests of the new generation in a house are relatively divorced from those of new generations in parallel houses. The house-line link becomes stretched and therefore less intense. To a certain extent the founding-brothers of a house are looking back-wards to the time when they formed a single house with their half-brothers and cousins; their sons are looking forward to the future development of their own particular house and yard.

The separation of houses is quite often emphasized by the physical separation of their herds. Though all the men and their wives live in the same homestead, there may be separate kraals there for each house. Usually the herds are herded and watered together in the day-time, but are separated at night. Unless the houses are exceptionally wealthy, they will probably share a common camp, but here again each house has its own kraal. Each is expected to provide what herdsmen it can. Sometimes there will be two or more joint camps in each of which are some of the stock of each member house; one or two houses will then be responsible for a camp and its herdsmen.[1] Any house is entirely free to make what other pastoral arrangements it desires—such as the spreading of its herd amongst camps owned by maternal or affinal kinsmen. Should a dispute arise over specific decisions regarding movements, etc., the members of a house are always able to break off and start a new camp following their own preferences. It is principally a matter of current and temporary convenience that houses co-operate in these things. There is also the important belief that on the whole close agnates are more to be trusted in charge of one's animals than are other people.

---

[1] Cf. the herding arrangements amongst the Family described in the Appendix to Chapter 3.

Inter-house Relations in the Extended Family

The structure and development of the Jie house has been traced to the point of its metamorphosis into a house-line—a group of increasingly independent, descendent houses. This life-history of a house and house-line is the paradigm of the life of the extended family, for that latter group is but a system containing one or more house-lines.

Between men and houses of different house-lines there exist the same sorts of relations which exist between men and houses of a single line.

Whether men of one house-line feel closer to one another than to other men of the Family depends on the stage of growth within the whole group. Sometimes there undoubtedly is a strong feeling that with a half-brother or first cousin one has shared a common herd of a single generation age—therefore mutual relations and rights are stronger. This is contrasted with the feeling that with the son of a father's half-brother one has shared a common herd which existed two generations' age—a stage further back, thus tending to make relations and rights more attenuated. This contrast is particularly strong at first when an old house has broken down into a house-line, but it tends to weaken as the men grow older and increasingly differentiated into independent groups with diverse life-histories, fortunes and extra-Familial bonds. The house of a half-brother becomes as distinct and as different as those of more distant paternal cousins.

There is a ranking of the men of one generation in a single range of seniority on precisely the same principles as have already been described for the individual house.[1] For the Family as a whole, houses are ranked by the order of marriage of their mothers to their 'fathers'. The order of birth of men is modified according to this.[2] This ranking is related to an ideal order of marriage, which in my experience never works in practice except in very small Families; indeed the Jie scarcely expect it to work, for they appreciate that the solidarity of a Family is far less than that of a house, and that there is no overriding authority to enforce compulsion. Members of

[1] See pp. 64-6.

[2] This same order of seniority within a genealogical generation of a Family is followed in the order of initiation of men and their placement in age-sets. Though a man be older, say three or four years older, than his cousin he may not be initiated first if he is ranked junior. The younger man may even be placed in an age-set senior to that of his elder. See my paper 'The Age-set Organisation of the Jie Tribe', *Journal of the Royal Anthropological Institute*, lxxxiii, Part 2, where actual examples are given.

different houses can afford to be independent of one another to a large extent. Nevertheless, this seniority pattern does set a moral standard on which to judge agnates' actions and the strength of feeling in their relations. When a man marries he expects to receive material assistance from all of his agnates. The readiness and generosity he meets with will, from one point of view, be based on this moral standard. His cousin may feel that his (the cousin's) house has only, say, one wife whilst the potential groom's house already has three, and therefore he cannot give support. In fact, some assistance will be given, but it will be reduced. More importantly, it will be given grudgingly and will not help to improve relations between the two houses. There is a notion of compulsion to assist an agnate even though he is not acting in an entirely approved fashion, and this necessity is resented. The resentful cousin is, of course, not an unprejudiced person, for he is thinking principally of his own house and its marriages, and he may be wishing to act equally irregularly when the time is opportune. Nevertheless, the resentment is no less important for all that. From the opposite point of view a potential groom resents the moral stricture to hold up his own plans until his agnates have all acquired equal status with himself.

Through time the material fortunes of the various related houses may vary. The herd of one house may prosper; its calves do well and disease is slight. Large bridewealths are received for sisters and daughters; friends and affines are generous. There may be many births and relatively few early deaths. Another house may have a run of bad luck. Disease takes a heavy toll; bridewealths are small. Perhaps one of the girls becomes an unmarried mother of long standing and thus, for a period, brings in no stock. These two instances are extremes, though not entirely suppositional; most houses have a history of more varied fortune. The point is that relative fortunes can and do change.

The Family process will be illustrated with detailed reference to the Family of Longoli, the genealogical skeleton of which is given in Figure 8. This group as it exists today is composed of the descendants of four men, the sons of one man, Longoli. Without giving a strict chronological account of the recent history of the group, I shall confine myself to a description of factors which have brought an advanced state of dissension, for the circumstances of this particular Family well exemplify the state of agnatic relations often to be found and the sorts of tensions which can arise.

One factor of great importance in the recent history of this Family was the varying fortunes of the different herds. House D had prospered whilst several other houses suffered severely from the

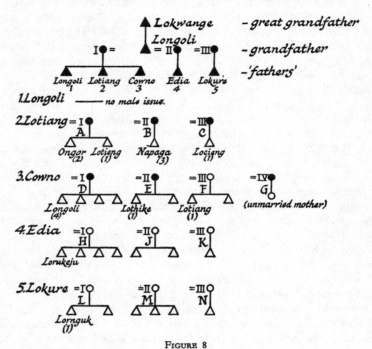

FIGURE 8

THE FAMILY OF LONGOLI

Contemporary houses are lettered for convenience of reference. Daughters are omitted from the genealogy.

Underneath the names of the current adult generation are the numbers of their wives, in brackets.

Ongor, the eldest 'son' and head of the Family, was a little over 45 years old: Longoli was nearly 45: Lorukeju and Lornguk were both about 30.

Total membership of Family—122 people.

effects of rinderpest and pleuro-pneumonia. House D, as far as I could discover, had missed the worst effects of these diseases during the last fifteen to twenty years. Its heaviest losses were in goats, which, although extremely unpleasant, were not so serious as heavy losses of cattle. Longoli, the head of the house, appears to have inherited much of the shrewdness and ability, which must have been the cause of his father's former successes, and he has supervised his estate more carefully and efficiently.[1] Associated with these differences of fortunes have been differences in marriages. Longoli had married four times, the last two bridewealths being made up in the teeth of considerable opposition in the Family. The head of the Family, Ongor, had only two wives and he resented his cousin's fortune and persistence. Neither was he at all pleased that his younger half-brother, Napaga, had two wives plus what amounted to a third in the former bride-wife of his deceased brother.[2] Another source of rivalry existed between Longoli and his half-brother, Lothike, who strongly resented Longoli's later marriages whilst he himself had but one wife. Lorukeju, the head of House H, feels a general resentment because he had so far been unable to marry owing to severe stock losses. His elder sister was an unmarried mother of some four years' standing and had not therefore brought in the bridewealth stock expected of her.

There have been what the people consider unusual unexplained deaths of people in the Family.[3] About the early 1930's Cowno died in suspicious circumstances and it was feared that the traditional homestead (of at least two generations' standing) contained some malignant influence. As yet there were no specific accusations of witchcraft against anyone, but it was thought best to shift to a new site and to build a fresh homestead. Just before this move of about half a mile, House B moved away independently to another site nearby. At this time Houses A to G were independent, but the 'fathers' Edia and Lokure were alive in the other half of the Family. After the move, cattle disease, which had been intermittently trouble-

[1] Longoli's father, Cowno, had been one of the foremost war-leaders of the immediately pre-British era. My estimate of Longoli is rather an impression than proved fact. My camp was next to his homestead for many months and I knew him well for over a year.

[2] This woman had only just been married when her husband died. Ever since, she had consorted with Napaga and had borne him several children, who are of course the legal off-spring of the house and of her dead husband and her pro-husband. For all practical purposes she was a wife of Napaga's.

[3] Jie recognize that death can be due to disease, old age or accident, and thus out of the control of mortals; but sudden death is always a matter of suspicion, and several such deaths in fairly rapid succession frequently lead to accusations of witchcraft or sorcery. Such feelings are inevitably heightened when the human deaths are contemporary with fatal stock disease.

some, became acute. About ten years after the move both Edia and Lokure died in quick succession, and another shift was made, back near to the old homestead. Houses C, E and L decided to join up with House B, thus leaving the main homestead. There existed a good deal of tension between the four seceding houses and House D (especially its head, Longoli), and also between House A and House D. The situation became acute when the head of House B and a younger brother (neither shown in Figure 8) died within a short time. The surviving brother, Napaga, was ready to make accusations of witchcraft, which, although not specifically directed, were believed by everyone to point to Longoli. Napaga decided to move again, and was supported by the other secessionists. He determined upon an unusually drastic move, to a newly opened garden area some two and a half miles away, where homesteads had not been built before. This brought underlying ill-feelings to the surface, and they were translated into action. Houses A, C, E, K, L and M all moved simultaneously with Napaga of House B. There was common hostility to, rivalry with and fear of Longoli and House D in particular and those others who supported him in general. But amongst these migrants there was not an overwhelming solidarity of feeling. Suspicions and jealousies could not be quitted even amongst themselves, and therefore they divided amongst three new homesteads— one for House A, one for House B and one for the remainder. Meanwhile in the old settlement the rest of the houses moved into a new homestead. These movements occurred in 1948.

The main rivalry emerged as that between Ongor and Longoli— the first was the formal head and senior man of the Family, the other the fortunate possessor of four wives and good herds. This particular rivalry had become crystallized as each man took the leadership of opposing factions of the Family, though such leadership had been only partly accepted by some of their respective adherents.

Against all these rivalries must be put one outstanding example of several cases of co-operative relations. The heads of Houses C, E and L were great friends who have for several years co-operated in many activities such as herding, movements of camps, occupation of a joint homestead, etc. Each had one wife, and each assisted the other two generously at the time of marriage.

The situation had been complicated by the self-determination of some of the mothers, in cases where their sons were not yet old enough to make the decisions. The mother of House J refused to

Jie. A homestead. Note the cattle kraal in the centre. Behind is another homestead, and the settlement's ritual grove is in the middle distance.

Turkana. A homestead. Note each wife's pair of shelters, the larger dome (*Ekal*) for day use and the smaller dome for night use. The main entrance is at the left front.

Jie. A ceremonial meat feast in the main kraal of a homestead.
The younger men supervise the cooking.

Jie. The senior elder leading the men of his settlement in prayers to
the high God.

move in 1938 when those houses, which remained in the old settlement, set up a new homestead. She built herself a one-yard homestead and remained there with her young children. The mother of House N refused to secede along with her late husband's other wives; on the other hand the mother of House K refused to remain behind with her late husband's chief wife and went off with the other dissentients. The latter move was rather awkward for her pro-husband, whose loyalties were thus divided between the two rival groups as his own house remained behind.

To summarize the situation, it can be said that because of a combination of unexplained human deaths and unequal incidence of stock disease, ill-feeling and accusations of witchcraft sprung up. Inequalities of marital fortune worsened the issue. Certain cases of inter-personal rivalry were no longer suppressed, and especially there grew up rivalry in the practical leadership of the Family after its residential cleavage. The group had reached a fairly advanced stage of disintegration although its unity was still respected in some ways. In ritual activities particularly it was always referred to as one unit, and that unity was emphasized by excessive attention to detail and procedure in exact formal behaviour. I talked with most of the men many times, and each of them stressed this underlying unity although they did not deny the actual state of interrelations. 'Are not our stock all one?' and, 'Are we not all grandsons of Longoli?' I was asked rhetorically. The ideal of Family unity remained. Indeed, it remained to aggravate the situation by the ever-present comparison of what ought to be with what actually was. It appeared to stimulate the uneasiness of the men's minds and made them feel guilty, and thus more liable to lay the blame upon the others. It will be appreciated that, of the important men in the matter, perhaps none were entirely innocent of malpractice.

Two other points arise out of this case. The first is that the main cleavage, the cases of inter-personal rivalry and jealousy, and the outstanding case of friendship, were not specifically correlated with affiliation amongst the house-lines. It is important to emphasize this, since it bears out the contention that mature houses are fully independent and not necessarily bound by considerations of membership of a common house-line. House-lines are not balanced, oppositional segments of the one Family. Indeed, the structural proximity of houses of a single house-line may only cause greater dissension when there are varying fortunes of wealth, marriage, etc. Men of different house-lines do not feel so closely bound together and may therefore be more tolerant of one another. Secondly, it will be noticed that inter-house rivalry is largely defined in terms of the inter-personal rivalry of the heads of those houses. The senior brother sets the pattern for his juniors, and also for his and their sons. Purely inter-personal considerations enter into the structural circumstances and the conditions of wealth, marriages, deaths and so on.

In the time of the 'fathers', this Family is described as a highly integrated group in which relations and co-operation were close and generally cordial—although nostalgic memory is as prejudiced in Jieland as elsewhere. Nevertheless, these men often spoke of the not-so-distant days when they were young men as a time when the Family was a real unit of amicable mutual assistance. They themselves see the present situation as a direct result of the now independent houses. Jie expect, even though sadly, a deterioration of relations between close agnates, and contrast this with an ideal of a single on-going unity of purpose and development. This particular Family has reached a stage of actual physical division which reflects extremely bitter relations. Such residential cleavage does not usually occur,[1] nor do relations necessarily reach such a dramatic level. But the general pattern remains the same, and above all the general tendencies towards the disintegration of the Family. The personal characters of the actors may affect the actual way in which the basic process is played out, but in principle it remains the same because of the same root causes to be found in the structural basis of the house and the Family. It seems likely, for instance, that Longoli (House D) exacerbated the situation by his rather selfish, uncompromising attitude to other people. He was selfish towards his younger brothers (see p. 67) as well as towards the members of parallel houses, and was often niggardly in his assistance to these latter.

The slackening or deterioration of agnatic relations which showed up so dramatically in the case of the Family of Longoli appears as a milder but nevertheless steady and almost inevitable development in the Family of Kopengamoi (see genealogy in Figure 9). Here there have been no outstanding clashes or bitter rivalries, yet there

[1] Until about thirty years ago—well within the lifetime of older men—such a geographical separation was wellnigh impossible. With fear of raids, people had perforce to live close together for protection. As already remarked, the *pax Britannica* has allowed geographical scatter, and perhaps therefore a more dramatic mode of expressing ill-feeling and bad relations.

is obviously a similar weakening of inter-house relations as expressed
for instance, in the sizes of contributions to bridewealth payments
over the last decade or so. My reliable informant, Logwela, who is
head of one of the houses, went out of his way to maintain co-
operation with his agnates, and did not continually compare his own
fortunes with those of his admittedly more fortunate half-brothers
and cousins. His own house had suffered seriously from rinderpest,
but he has accepted his fortune philosophically. I have already quoted
his remarks concerning his younger brother (see p. 68), and it may
be added that he did not resent openly the fact that his half-brother
had two wives whilst he had but one, and his cousins' plurality of
wives was regarded as their good fortune and not his ill-luck or bad
treatment. When we discussed these matters Logwela often stressed
what he felt to be the need for maintaining the unity of his Family.
Yet his own house was drawing away gradually from that of his
half-brother, Kidemoi, and his full cousin, Nadenya.[1] When Logwela's brother married, Logwela himself insisted that he alone
should hand over the bridewealth cattle to the exclusion of his senior
agnates of the same house-line, much to these men's discomfiture
and somewhat in contradiction to ideal standards of Family unity.
More recently, when Kidemoi's son married, two of his father's
cousins each gave several goats instead of the customary cattle. One
house, under Loyamoi, has removed to a new homestead a few
yards away from the traditional one occupied by the rest of the
Family. Loyamoi has married four times whilst none of his living
cousins has more than two wives, and whilst this has not produced
the bitter reactions evident in the Family of Longoli, it has brought
a noticeable coolness in mutual relations. Though there exists, that
is to say, a greater sense of toleration amongst the men, there is
nevertheless a similar deterioration of intra-Family relations.
Stripped of their details, the two Family histories are basically
similar. Each Family has its individual history. That of the Family
of Longoli shows highly difficult, even bitter relations, but this is
not at all an extreme or isolated case. The Family of Kopengamoi
has had a smoother history of recent years, perhaps a more easy one
than most. It would appear, *prima facie*, that either way the system of
Family relations is likely to break down into two or more independent systems, especially in view of the fact that Jie insist that each

[1] 'Full-cousins' are the sons of full-brothers; 'half-cousins' are the sons of half-
brothers.

99

current Family is descended only from a common grandfather. It would appear, therefore, that the development of the next generation of males will cause essential cleavage.

This is the theoretical pattern of Jie Families—the way the people themselves visualize and describe it. They can give an account of their own Families in terms of their development each from the house of the grandfather, and the independence and gradual separation of the current houses. Beyond the range of a two-generation link with related houses they suggest that relations become too distant to maintain reciprocal rights; therefore it is no longer of significance to remember them, and they are forgotten. I have often attempted to stimulate the memories of my informants when recording their genealogies, especially with reference to the brothers and half-brothers of the grandfather, and their present descendants. I almost always met with failure. As already mentioned, the grandfather's father is occasionally remembered, but this adds nothing to the horizontal range of the effective genealogy. My efforts have sometimes been met with amused surprise. One man said, 'We have forgotten. We do not remember these things. It is all long ago and we are different from them' (i.e. any possible descendants of his grandfather's brother). Another man said, 'Who remembers those names? We forget these people; they are all ancestors long ago. Perhaps my father knew—he never told me. Such things do not matter now.' Above all, to the native it is an irrelevant matter and therefore not worth attention.

The observer is strongly tempted to arrive at the conclusion that there is a constant process of fission and dissociation going on, wherein each Family divides up as its core reaches beyond an optimum range of a three-generation descent group. Indeed the Jie imply this by their insistence upon the disappearance of relationships beyond that three-generation range. Yet with the exception of a few cases, a known, remembered final cleavage does not occur. Everything appears to be set for progressive disintegration and fission; but it does not normally happen. We shall now examine actual data, genealogical and other, to discover a possible explanation of what does happen.

The Problem of Family Development

The problem of the history of the Jie Family resolves itself into the fact that a pattern of disintegration does not occur in order to maintain the necessary balance of the contemporary group at a three-generation range, despite the undeniable fact that the growth of a new male generation must equally necessarily upset that balance. If there were a continual process of cleavage in a Family and a hiving off of certain branches to form new and independent groups, at least two results would follow. Firstly, some Families would be undergoing that actual process at the present time, or have just completed a cycle; and secondly, there would tend to be a large and increasing number of Families, unless many were simultaneously dying out. Now, although there are memories of cases when Families have split up, they are few and always involve some unusual and disastrous circumstances. It may appear that the Family of Longoli, discussed above, is likely to split. It cannot be determined at present. The men themselves, though on such poor terms, always assert their formal unity, and I discovered no major occasion when reciprocal rights had absolutely broken down. In any event there is not a vestige of any evidence that such a fissiparous process occurred in the previous generation. I have investigated as many cases as possible of the histories of the fathers of the present senior adult generation in Jieland and have been able to find only a few cases of Family fission. In such cases as could be found, there is a well-remembered story of severe losses of the Family herds due to disease or raids, or of unexplained human deaths leading to general fear and to accusations of witchcraft. A more or less dramatic schism followed; and in these cases the names of the secessionists are remembered, and they or their descendants can be identified today. Such cleavages, as far as my information goes, have usually led to at least one of the parties moving away to another settlement, there to construct a new homestead and to begin a new life. One case occurred in Kaputon settlement, following a highly successful raid by the Dodoth which unfortunately caught a concentration of the Family's cattle at the homestead, and also caused the deaths of several people. The Family, poverty stricken and appalled, divided into three parts, each of which moved to different settlements some three generations ago. Memories of it are still clear, for I was given my first account of it by a middle-aged man who said that it happened at the time of his father's grandfather. His father, an extremely old man of about eighty years, supported this dating of the event; and the story of one of the other branches confirmed the history. It is significant that the men of these three branches sometimes refer to the whole group as 'one Family' and that though now living miles apart, they often attend each other's weddings, initiations and similar events of note. The men today say that their 'great-grandfathers' (whose names they cannot recollect) split up not because of ill-feeling but because of poverty and in the movement to their own maternal kin or affines for help and even subsistence.

Another instance of such cleavage occurred in a complicated situation of witchcraft concerning the death of a wife of one of the men. Several people are supposed to have died as a result of the machinations of this woman's people in various houses of the Family. There was a partial scatter of the group which has never wholly reunited. This occurred in the generation of the 'fathers' of the present senior adults, and today there are two descendent Families of which their members say, 'The Families are different now. Our stock are different.'[1]

Such cases are uncommon, but they are quite well remembered and no attempt is made to hide the facts, both by the present descendants of the original participants or by other Jie. To a large extent the factors responsible for cleavage appear to have been accidental and adventitious, unconnected with the essential relationship structure of the Jie Family. It may well be the fact that the already strained agnatic relations could not withstand the additional pressure from external sources, but it was the latter which caused the actual cleavage at the time. One can gather evidence concerning other Families where similarly difficult situations have been weathered without a final cleavage. Whilst noting these instances of past cleavages, we must therefore look elsewhere for a general principle regulating the histories and development of Jie Families.

Another factor which throws considerable doubt on any frequent and constant process of fission is that the number of Families in a clan is always small, yet a clan contains all men who are agnatically related and who must necessarily follow a set ritual course, performed at one set place (the ritual grove of the settlement where the clan lives). Clan membership does not exclude the few cases of seceding groups mentioned above. No agnates ever belong to other clans, and men do not, in fact cannot, forfeit membership by the physical and social act of moving away. Yet there is no Jie clan which contains more than eight Families, and there are one or two

[1] The Jie word *egela* is here and elsewhere translated literally as 'different'. A freer version might be 'separate', or 'independent'.

clans which are composed each of a single Family. On the average about four Families make up a clan. Jie always insist that new clans are never formed and that all present clans are age-old. Had a process of cleavage been going on for many generations it might be expected that in some clans at least there would by now be a multitude of Families. An important element here is the probability (and in the light of available evidence it can unfortunately be put no higher) that the Jie population has been largely stationary during the generations preceding the European advent. Briefly, the evidence may be summarized as follows. The people speak of their numbers remaining 'about the same', and will specifically deny any particular increases before modern times. It is certain that during the latter half of the nineteenth century the small settled area shrunk slightly. Men have shown me old homestead sites beyond the limits of present-day settlement, where, they said, their 'grandfathers' used to live. The Jie were a warlike tribe, surrounded by hostile and more powerful neighbours. Warfare—i.e. raiding and counter-raiding— was more or less incessant. It is probable that on balance the Jie suffered more than their neighbours over the years[1]. In addition to warfare there were recurrent famine years due to the failure of the rains. A serious food shortage occurs about once a decade, and less frequently there have been severe famines, both of which cause varying losses of life and also a weakening of general physical condition and resistance to disease. Occasionally these bad years coincide with stock epidemics; this was particularly the case with the severe rinderpest epidemic in the 1890's.[2] When recording genealogies I was often told, in reference to the people of a generation ago, that some died in war and others 'when there was no food'. It is also likely that deaths by epidemics would have occurred. Old-established Jie homesteads are not notably hygienic, and the cramped sleeping-quarters would have certainly caused infections to be passed on. Cases are known where one after another of a Family have died of

[1] It seems to be current theory amongst some observers that the warfare of the old days was not as blood-thirsty and important as Africans would have us believe. This is likely to be true of the part of East Africa under review; but it would be incorrect to go completely over to the contrary view and deny that inter-tribal warfare had any demographic effects at all. In both Jieland and Turkanaland I have recorded very many specific instances where population has been reduced by, for example, the deaths of some or many of the young men of a Family, by the decimation of the whole population of several homesteads, and by the severe losses in stock and thus in economic resources and ability to marry and carry on former social activities.

[2] Cf. Turpin, *Uganda Journal*, xii, 1948, pp. 161-5.

what would seem to have been contagious diseases such as tuberculosis and influenza (turning to pneumonia).[1] The relatively small numbers of the 'fathers' generation is always in contrast with the number of their sons alive today. Doubtless some of this is due to the mere forgetting of insignificant men, but certainly not all. Unless the pattern of marital and family relations have altered greatly then, one way or another, there are likely to have been many deaths to account for the difference between survivors of the 'fathers' and probable births.

Such stability of population could have affected Family structure in several ways. The deaths of young people and the failure of lines of descent even to maintain themselves, let alone to multiply, might have caused the extinction of some Families. Other groups might have been comparatively fortunate and continued to prosper and develop, even possibly to the extent of multiplying into independent branches. Or there might have been, by and large, a broadly similar effect on most Families, reducing their strength continually and roughly maintaining them at the same size through successive generations. This latter result would appear to be most probable.

I cannot produce data of a Family that has died out. Probably, unless it had very recently occurred, the Jie would not consider it significant history. The whole problem of historical memory in Jieland, and in many other pre-literate societies, is a complex one and cannot adequately be discussed here. One is inclined, *a priori*, to say that, for the Jie, history only begins two generations ago, or even more recently. Beyond that there are only vague legends concerning an undated and relatively unimportant past, and which relate not to events concerning individuals but only to the tribe as a whole, or large parts of it. On the other hand, the memory of Family cleavage such as that already described resulting from the disastrous Dodoth raid, calls for some modification of too simple an explanation. Where it is of interest or value to living descendants, therefore, history *may* be remembered even beyond the limits of genealogical reckoning. Nevertheless, I think that this is rare, for the Jie still live in a conservative society where the past is not felt to be of especial significance, and in which there has so far been little effect from the

---

[1] These are the cases when native notions turn to witchcraft as a cause. It is interesting that nowadays the normal procedure is to move to a new homestead to avoid the evil influence, and the abandonment of unhealthy quarters makes an end of the train of deaths.

modern outside world of European influence. For instance, I have never been able to obtain clear accounts of the catastrophic rinderpest epidemics of the end of the nineteenth century, stories of which usually figure so largely in tribal memory in Eastern Africa; nor could I obtain satisfactory accounts of the first European arrivals, or of the Swahili and Arab ivory traders, and so on. Although the Jie were so friendly towards me and my researches, I could not collect really adequate life-histories of the older people. 'We have forgotten It is all long ago. It does not matter.' Those were the typical comments made in reply to my efforts even by friendly old men. The explanation would seem to be that Jie social structure is a 'timeless structure' which contains no historical high-lights. There have been few, if any, significant points of structural differentiation or cleavage in most Families and clans; there are no large kinship groups which serve as pegs on which to hang historical facts or to act as stimulants to memory. In the particular case of attempting to discover evidence of Families which have died out, there is an additional factor involved, for, *ipso facto*, there are no descendants for whom the event might have significance and who remain to tell the tale. For other Jie the matter would have been of less concern and therefore only briefly remembered. It is possible that prolonged residence in the area might produce more evidence picked up by chance remarks. That sort of possibility, however, is a defect in any sociological investigation, and is not very important in the long run. If a factor is of significance for the understanding of a society under review it should surely emerge during intensive field-research.

There are a few cases where a Family has been reduced to a single house, and such a house is sometimes small in numbers and poor in stock, and may therefore not survive for long. In one case it is certain that a Family will not last beyond the present generation. Lotemel and his aged mother are the sole survivors of their Family. He is forty-five to fifty years old and has lost his only wife. He has only two or three cattle and no goats or sheep, and lives largely on the charity of his neighbours. He has no sisters or daughters who might bring in new stock by marriage. Since he cannot be expected to help his kinsmen and friends by contributing stock, he rarely gets any animals as a share of their inpayments. On the other hand, I did not discover a single case even in the most prosperous and numerous clans which would bear an interpretation of relatively uninterrupted growth and cleavage.

Thus, although it is probable that some Families have died out, demographic evidence does not point decisively in any direction; it does not explain the relatively small number of Families in existence today, nor the apparent disappearance of all the brothers and cousins of a grandfather.

The problem remains that the typical Family is a three-generation descent group (plus wives) composed, in the living generation, of a number of independent groups (houses) whose interrelations deteriorate by reason of their structural opposition and structurally nurtured rivalry to the point almost of separation. The explanation appears to lie in some sort of compensatory and complimentary process of fusion and re-amalgamation. That is the hypothesis which is now to be put forward in what follows. Briefly the theory is, that whilst there is a continual tendency towards fission in the Family, it seldom reaches its logical conclusion because of the simultaneous process of fusion whereby the various branches of the group are brought into a new balance to maintain the continuum. It will be suggested that such fusion occurs as a result of the forgetting or neglecting of former genealogical links and the fictional forging of new ones to conform to the ideal pattern of the Family as the Jie conceive of it. This process is part conscious and part unconscious. To reduce it to the simplest terms—far simpler than ever appear in actual life—the lineal descendants of a grandfather's brothers and cousins are called *kaipopai* (s. *lokapa*) a term very like the English 'cousin' in its broad classificatory range. In time the actual nature of genealogical links between such 'cousins' is forgotten, partly deliberately; and by *a posteriori* reasoning on all sides the men assume them to be closer than in fact they are. It is but a short and easy step for all the men to take the most prominent man of the grandfathers-generation (often the only one at all well remembered) as the founding ancestor of the re-amalgamated group. Agnates who are 'cousins' maintain amongst themselves a system of reciprocal relations, significantly expressed in rights over domestic animals. The actual sociological continuum amongst a relatively small and stable number of such men is re-interpreted in the light of a convenient ideal fiction. What matter are the concrete interrelations; genealogical presentation is only a rationalized symbol of that structured system.

Before presenting the evidence upon which this theory is founded, a methodological point must be raised. If there is a process of forgetting or of verbal re-interpretation it is extremely difficult to demonstrate because, of course, the evidence is largely lost in so far as the process is successful and complete at any one time. The external observer is largely presented with a *fait accompli* which is not easy to investigate, however suspicious it might appear. If the process is complete, then the fictional bonds are regarded as the only true ones—others never existed. Fortunately the process goes on more or less continuously under the observer's eyes, and it is sometimes possible to discover something about genuine genealogical connections before they are completely submerged. Indeed, as will be seen, men are sometimes willing to acknowledge discrepancies between real and assumed bonds, although they then invariably say, and believe, that the latter are the important ones. And from a purely sociological viewpoint we must agree, for the fiction fits the social reality better than the truth. Obviously, the longer the observer lives with the people and becomes intimate with the details of many of the Families, the better his evidence becomes. Unfortunately my own data were gathered during some eight months in Jieland, spread over a period of about thirteen months altogether. For the rest, therefore, I can rely only on a body of circumstantial evidence, which may be convincing enough if it is large enough and if it all points to one general conclusion. In the evidence that follows I cannot claim to cover all or even most Jie Families; but for all Families that I knew at all well the data agree convincingly. Nevertheless, I do not claim to prove that this process of fusion and re-amalgamation occurs, but only to assert that, in the light of what evidence can be offered, it is the most probable explanation. In what follows an attempt will be made to distinguish between facts as they were recorded in the field, and my own observations, inferences and conclusions drawn from them. This applies to any scientific record, and nowhere more than in such an instance as this. It will be recognized that only an approximation to the truth can be offered, and some doubts will remain unresolved both for the writer and for the reader. Nevertheless, it is felt worthwhile to attempt to illustrate the hypothesis, since some explanation is certainly called for concerning the logical inadequacy of the ideal pattern as described by the people. It is also thought to be worthwhile since, if the hypothesis is tenable, it may throw light on important social processes, for Jie is not the only society where genealogies are fictionalized and where the kinship system is not what it appears to be on the surface. In some societies the divergence involves only individuals or a small group who are attempting to affect and alter their position in the total structure. For instance, a commoner may attempt to attach himself to an aristocratic line.[1] A more generalized example of the process has been recently described in the case of Nuer local communities, where maternal links may be reckoned as paternal links in order to fit a person or group into the prevailing agnatic structure.[2] In Jieland something of a more universal nature is involved, since genealogical fictions and antecedent re-amalgamation run right through the foundations of the whole agnatic structure, inevitably affecting all Families at all times. Indeed, it is an integral part of the structure and a basic principle of the social organization of agnatic relations.

Fusion and Re-Amalgamation

The Family of Kopengamoi. As a first example of re-amalgamation I give a brief account of my investigations into the structure of this group in the field, since that procedure may illustrate the way in which my evidence was accumulated. The genealogy in Figure 9 was given to me by Nadenya, the present head of the Family, an old man of about seventy years (House B). It was cross-checked with Logwela, the head of another house, a man of about fifty years (House E). Nadenya said that he could not remember his grandfather's name, although he asserted the common descent from that man. Logwela gave the grandfather's name as Kopengamoi, and his account of the four house-lines agreed with that of Nadenya. Some time later Logwela was describing to me the composition of his clan. He told me that his Family is called *Lorekali* and was to be distinguished from the rest of the clan which is called *Awi-agitor*. These 'sub-clans' were the result of a split in the clan many generations ago, 'long, long, ago, before our grandfather was born'. This information was readily substantiated by members of each division although the cleavage is of little significance today. Now, if the event had happened many generations ago—specifically before two generations ago—what had happened to the Families and constituent houses since? In fact, Lorekali consisted of only one Family all of whom claim descent from the original dessentient group, as Logwela told me when we discussed the situation. He agreed therefore that he and his parallel agnates could not have descended from a single

[1] Cf. Culwick, A. T. and G. M., *Ubena of the Rivers*, London, 1935, p. 180.
[2] Evans-Pritchard, E. E., *Kinship and Marriage among the Nuer*, 1951, chapter 1.

grandparent. Indeed, he added that he could not remember the name of his father's father, and he doubted if any of his cousins could remember theirs. 'We are not children now. It is all long ago. We forget those names,' he said. I reminded him that previously he had given me the name Kopengamoi as that of their founding grand-

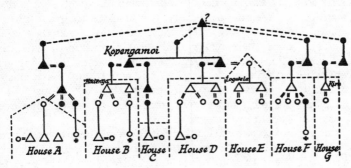

FIGURE 9

THE FAMILY OF KOPENGAMOI

= INDICATES MARRIAGE

⧣ INDICATES UNMARRIED MOTHER

Total membership of Family—87 persons

A detailed analysis of six of the above houses is given in the Appendix to Chapter 3.

The genealogy of this group is given in some detail in order to illustrate the internal articulation of an actual Family. The founding-brothers of each house are shown, together with all wives and unmarried mothers who have formed separate yards. Children only are omitted.

father, and he replied that Kopengamoi had actually been the father of Nadenya.[1] Kopengamoi had been an important man in his time, had lived to a great age and had been famous as a ritual leader. He was, in addition, the father of the present head of the Family. Today no other man of Kopengamoi's generation in that Family is well remembered by his descendants. 'We say he is our grandfather,' explained Logwela. 'We are all "cousins". We live near together. We give each other cattle. Our herds are like one herd; our wives

---

[1] I had not detected this similarity of names, as Nadenya had originally given me his father's personal name, whilst Logwela had used the more common hero-name. In any case a son may sometimes have the same name as his father.

were all married from one herd. We are one Family (*eowe*) and different from other people. Kopengamoi is like our grandfather, for he was a big man long ago; we remember. I do not know the name of my father's father. That is how we say it is.' Afterwards I talked to Kire (House G), and he said that his real grandfather was 'a little different' from the grandfather of Nadenya and Logwela; but 'it does not matter now. We are one Family. It is as if we are grandsons (of one man).' Under pressure, then, these men agree that they could not actually trace their real genealogical connections. The four separate house-lines are really based on four separate lines of agnatic descent whose original links are lost but which must have existed more than two generations ago. It appears that only Houses B, C, D and E are genuinely descendent from one grandfather, but even that may not be wholly correct.

It is important to emphasize that for the men themselves the real links are unimportant. The actualities of the contemporary relations are what matter and they are adequately, indeed accurately, reflected in the fictional genealogy. On a later occasion I heard the group being described, at a ritual feast, as 'the children of one grandfather. We are all grandsons. There is one Family.' That is meaningful both to the men themselves and to the rest of their community. By a paradox the real genealogical links are no longer truthful in indigenous conceptions.

A similar case to this is the Family of Lokong (Figure 6). This Family is composed of the descendants of one of the three groups constituted by the disastrous Dodoth raid, previously described,[1] which occurred more than two generations ago. The remaining old man of the 'father's' generation admitted that he was not literally the half-brother of the three others of that generation. 'We only say so because we are one Family,' he told me. One of his sons said, 'Our fathers were different. We [i.e. the men of his own generation] are not grandsons [of one man]. It does not matter. It is like Lokong being our grandfather. He was a big man long ago. We do not forget his name. He is still our grandfather and we are cousins. There is only one Family. Look! Are we not all together? Are not our cattle like one herd?'[2]

---

[1] See p. 101.

[2] The group occupied a single homestead, separate from their neighbours. Their cattle were usually herded and watered together, and also the typical reciprocal stock rights as between agnates, members of one Family, were strongly maintained.

FAMILY AND PROPERTY IN JIELAND

The Family of Lothikiria. In this group one old man of his generation remains alive today, and a new adult generation has grown up
in which the older men are between forty and fifty years old. I was
able to record the Family genealogy from adult men of two succes-

(*a*) The version of Ibokwel and Langilang:

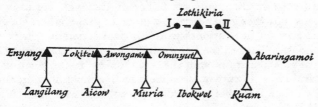

(*b*) The version of Owunyut:

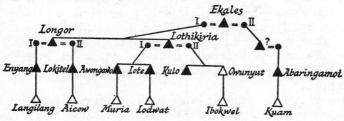

FIGURE 10

THE FAMILY OF LOTHIKIRIA

In both versions only the eldest sons in the most junior generation are given. Owunyut
was about 65 years old, Langilang was about 50 and Ibokwel was 40-45.

In version (*a*) Ibokwel and Langilang gave their cousin, Lodwat, as a younger son of
Awongawo. Owunyut in version (*b*) said that Lodwat is the son of Awongawo's
younger full-brother, Lote. This man died at an early age, and Lodwat himself,
although remembering his true father's name, has come to think of Awongawo as
his father and not merely the former head of his house. Awongawo had not long
been dead. Structurally the error is of no consequence. This is a simple case of
structural amnesia.

sive generations and by comparing the two the rationalization of the
process of re-amalgamation becomes apparent.

These two versions are given in Figure 10. Diagram (*a*) is the
version of Ibokwel, who was about forty years old and had long
since passed the stage of irresponsible youth. He assumes a good
deal of the responsibilities of his father's house, since the old man

is not only infirm but he has been totally blind for many years. Ibokwel related his account back to his grandfather, Lothikiria; and in this was supported by the senior man of his generation, Langilang. It is a simple genealogy, showing two house-lines descended from the two wives of Lothikiria, for there were only two houses in their 'father's' generation. Afterwards I obtained the genealogy given in Diagram (*b*) from Owunyut, the father of Ibokwel. He took the Family back a further generation to a different grandfather. He gave a different account of relationships in his own generation, with five separate houses. Thus in the latest generation there has been a clear case of re-amalgamation and the consequent re-formulation of genealogical links. Owunyut is unlikely to live much longer, and it is probable therefore that genealogy (*b*) will die with him. I confronted Ibokwel with his father's version, and he replied as follows: 'My father is an old man. He knows more than we do. If he says this [i.e. if this is his version] it is right; my words are wrong. We are still one Family. Do you understand that? My father told you that. There is only one people, one [herd of] stock. I remember the name of Lothikiria; he is our grandfather. Who knows other grandfathers? Only Lothikiria remains. He is our big man [i.e. founding ancestor].'

It may be noted that the version of Ibokwel and Langilang does not even conform to the facts of the present situation. Had Owunyut in fact been a full-brother of the other three men (Enyang, Lokitel and Awongawo) there would still be a single unified house pending his death. Yet the sons of the other three 'fathers' formed separate houses and it was well recognized that their cattle and goats constituted independent herds, even to the extent of quite separate kraals and bush camps. This is not necessarily inconvenient, since the genealogy is only a heuristic scheme, a kind of Family charter based on *a posteriori* rationalization. Once Owunyut dies the genealogy will be 'correct' and no one will be able to prove otherwise. Owunyut's genealogical memory, or any other version, cannot affect present actualities, and it merely sets up a more complicated scheme. Ibokwel and Langilang gave a version which is the simplest genealogical account possible and which will soon fit the facts perfectly. Note that the house-line Abaringamoi-Kuam is made quite separate in both versions. This seems to accord with a practical recognition that the line is rather more distantly related or less successfully integrated with the rest of the group.

Jie Women.

Turkana. Unmarried girls. Note the ostrich egg beading on pinafores, and the quantity of beads worn.

Turkana. Young man. Note the mudded headdress, and ivory ball fixed to his lower lip.

Turkana men. A histrionic dispute over bridewealth before a wedding.

The Family of Mamukine. In this case no specific claim is made by any of the men that they are descendants of a single grandfather; but significantly enough they say—in the words of one of them—'We are one people, one kin. The stock are different from other people's stock—one herd only. All right! There is one Family; we are all cousins.' When I suggested that the descendants of perhaps three grandfathers were represented amongst the living members of the group, my informant said, 'Who knows! our grandfathers are different? Ee! it is like one grandfather. Our father's fathers are one. Perhaps they were full-brothers; I forget. It does not matter. There is only one people now.' The ideal theory is observed even in the breach.

This group of seventy-four people has had an unfortunate history, for it was seriously affected by the believed results of prolonged witchcraft from outside and by the fears and accusations involved. One house broke away some ten or more years ago and built a new homestead about a hundred yards off. The residential cleavage was emphasized because the head of the seceding house was one of the few Christians in Jieland and he had a Karamajong wife—both matters of some suspicion to the rest of the group. To some extent this situation may account for the present dissociation of the various descent lines in the group. Nevertheless, my informants asserted that the people continue to think of themselves as 'one Family'. Their neighbours speak of them as such also. The men continue normal agnatic relations in so far as reciprocal stock rights are concerned.

Structural Amnesia[1]

Illustrations have been given of the process of the merging of separate grandfathers into single putative ancestor, termed 'grandfather'. This means that only one of these ancestors is remembered by their descendants. It cannot of course be demonstrated for all Families even though it may be strongly suspected for many; but some men when pressed will admit that the names of some grandfathers have been lost. I have already quoted some of my informants' remarks on that score. For one reason or another one particular ancestor is remembered and is put into the ideal role of founder. In the case of the Family of Lothikiria (Figure 10) that man's name

---

[1] I borrow this useful phrase from Barnes, J. A., 'The collection of genealogies', *Rhodes-Livingstone Journal*, v, 1947, pp. 52-3.

is remembered because, *inter alia*, he was the father of Owunyut, now a very old man and the last of his generation. It is probable that Owunyut has been responsible unconsciously for the creation of this myth since he often talks of his own father and his life but seldom if at all of the fathers of his cousins. According to Owunyut, his father also lived to a great age, well beyond the time of the death of his brothers. In other cases the remembered name is that of the youngest of a range of cousins who, for that simple reason, lived longest.

Some further examples of structural amnesia will be given to illustrate how the process occurs. These examples refer to relatively recent Family histories, and therefore did not then wholly affect the basic structure of the groups involved. It is plausible, however, that they will become part of putative genealogical reckoning in subsequent generations. Almost every Family that I knew at all well contained an example of this process. The very fact that an external observer could detect them fairly easily meant that they had not yet run the full course of amnesia.

In a house founded by two full-brothers, the eldest had for many years been a chronic invalid and seldom left the homestead. His junior, Lotiowi, younger by a year or two, took upon himself all the duties and responsibilities of the head of the house, organizing all pastoral arrangements, supervising stock transactions and attending to all essential ritual. He is a self-assertive type of man and takes a leading part in settlement and even district ceremonies, though not yet ranked as a senior elder. Early in 1951 the elder man died. His two widows were both about or past the menopause. They remained in the homestead with the two wives of Lotiowi. There was, of course, no question of the break-up of the house. By the time I left Jieland some six months later there were already signs that the memory of the dead man was beginning to be forgotten. On ritual occasions I heard the house called 'the people of Lotiowi's homestead', and he himself spoke of 'my four wives' and 'my children'. When I was engaged on a garden survey in the settlement, one of the widows placed herself for me as 'Lotiowi's wife', although strictly speaking, there is no institution of wife inheritance, and in any case Lotiowi had not even become pro-husband.

There were two half-brothers, the only sons of their father, and both called Locoto, the elder of whom died as a fairly young man. Until his death he had promised to become a prominent war-leader and therefore to achieve high reputation and status. In fact, I only learnt about his former existence in connection with military history, and some months after I had recorded the genealogy of the group according to his namesake whom I knew fairly well. The younger Locoto has lived on to the present day, some thirty-five years later, married three times and has several children. He is such a relatively agile old man that he has become prominent in ritual affairs when his contemporaries have become comparatively inactive owing to old age; and he has also a considerable personality, being widely known throughout the tribe. In so far as both the Family and outsiders are concerned he has almost completely supplanted the memory and position of his elder namesake, although the latter left a widow (now an old woman) and has children still surviving. Some at least of these children are the physical off-spring of the younger Locoto, who became pro-husband to the widow—though now it is difficult if not impossible to be sure which children. All of them, however, regard the man who still lives as their father; so much so indeed that instead of establishing an independent house as they are properly entitled to do, they have been, and remain, content to become part of their pro-father's house alongside the latter's real sons. Today the Family consists in practice of a single house subdivided into the three yards of the younger Locoto's wives and the one yard of the widow of the elder Locoto.

Apalopua has lived to an old, if undistinguished age. He is, by virtue of sheer seniority, the ritual head of his settlement, although he is usually content to leave affairs to the care of more energetic elders. His paternal cousin died many years ago leaving two sons who were then boys. These men cannot remember their father as a living person and had some difficulty in recalling his name for me. Their house and their stock are quite separate from those of Apalopua and his sons, to the point of separate kraals in the joint homestead. For all practical purposes these men, now about thirty-five years old, refer to Apalopua as their father. They know he is not, and are well aware of their independence; yet he is a conventionally respected elder and they are willing, within limits, to defer to his seniority and influence. Their children are now being brought up to consider Apalopua as their grandfather, not necessarily as a conscious policy, but because he is almost equivalent to one; and of course he is well within the range of classificatory grandfather. Their real grandfather is unknown to them. There is no compelling reason why they should learn differently as they grow up, for his name is never mentioned. His former existence is now quite irrelevant to actual circumstances and relations.

Actual adoption of males is uncommon, but it does occur occasionally, and in so far as it is successfully accomplished it is a form of structural amnesia, though rather different from the examples hitherto given. An adoptee is taken into a yard of the house of this 'father', but is given an inferior status, being regarded as junior to all his 'brothers'.

A process in some ways comparable to adoption is the absorption of foreign groups into the Family. In one case, by reason of long residence in the Family of Longoli, and an especially firm friendship with Longoli (grandson of the founder), Etuko and his half-brother Nangiro have by now become accepted as established members. For some reason, not now entirely clear, Etuko's father, Lokiru, moved to this Family's homestead many years ago, leaving his own settlement and district entirely. Lokiru and Longoli's father, Cowno, were bond-friends and on excellent terms. Lokiru brought his own stock and co-operated with Cowno and other members of the Family. Etuko was born in the homestead and has never lived anywhere else. Today he has a wife and children and is pro-husband to his father's junior widow—that is, he has a well-established social position. He has always been a close friend of Longoli and, when I knew them, they were inseparable companions. Etuko has always supported Longoli in the Family quarrels and rivalries (see pp. 93-8), and he has become a fully accepted member of the group. Indeed, it was only through a member of the rival faction in the Family that I learnt that strictly accurately he was not even their clansman. Etuko himself was exceedingly unwilling to admit to his real genealogical connections, the details of which were by this time naturally rather obscure, and he could not be persuaded to discuss the matter. Longoli said, 'Long ago he was different—now he is like us. His Family is our Family.' Etuko strictly conforms to the system of reciprocal rights and was a generous contributor to Longoli's bride-wealth payments; and Longoli returned the compliment when Etuko married. I could not discover any active connection between Etuko and the people of his father's former settlement. By the passage of time and the cultivation and adoption of standard intra-Family relations, he has become a full member of the clan and Family of his upbringing, even to the extent of joining unreservedly in all the ritual, as, theoretically, only a person born into the clan should do.

The final step of creating fictional genealogical links has not yet been achieved though the stage seems set for it, since no one denies his actual membership of the Family. Were his intrusion resented, it could probably be challenged fairly easily on ritual grounds, since he is by birth affiliated elsewhere. The elders of the clan (belonging to other Families) accept him as a fellow clansman, for 'he is of the children of Longoli now'.

Structural amnesia operates in two general ways, which are, however, often complementary and concurrent. There is first the forgetting of certain men, and secondly the especial remembering and consequent aggrandizement of other men. A man tends to be forgotten if he died young, if he left a few children or today has few surviving descendants, if he was chronically withdrawn from normal social life or if his life and character was relatively empty of especial significance. A man tends to be remembered and that memory enhanced for quite positive reasons: old age is especially important and common, particularly where it is combined with survival beyond the time of all or most of a man's contemporaries; the last survivor of a generation, whatever his age, is likely to be better remembered than the rest. Important social status is often a cause of a man being especially remembered—successful war leadership, ritual seniority and general success and prominence in ceremonial affairs, outstanding wealth of cattle the founder of a numerous or wealthy branch of the Family, and the purely accidental role of father of a prominent man of the present generation.

The Dynamics of the Extended Family

With the foregoing concrete documentation it is possible to see more clearly the process of Family development in Jieland and what the social mechanism is. Firstly, we examined the fissiparous development of the single house, which is the paradigm of the history of the Family. Then it was seen that logically it was plausible that this process should lead to decisive cleavages within the group as a result of structural tensions, translated into inter-personal antagonism, rivalry and jealousies and accompanied by a slackening of reciprocal obligations and interests. It was noted, however, that although there were a few cases of former Families which had split up (and those are well remembered by the Jie), it was impossible to find evidence that this had often, let alone generally, happened. Almost all Families insist on their descent from a common grandfather, yet no trace could usually be found of clansmen who were the known descendants of that grandfather's brothers and cousins who should formerly have constituted a common Family. The problem also arose as to why, at least in a fair number of cases, there was not common descent claimed from a great-grandfather as a new generation of adults grew up. The hypothesis offered here is that there is a complementary and simultaneous process of re-amalgamation with a subsidiary process of structural amnesia whereby certain ancestors are neglected and eventually omitted.

The typical dynamic system is seen in the light of this evidence to be one such that a Family today consists of all the male agnatic descendants (with their wives) of a Family of indefinite number of generations ago. By fictional genealogical reckoning centrifugal tendencies are checked by centripetal development. The line of descent is always being drawn together and new links forged to bind together constituent sub-groups which tend to move away. Apart from infrequent and atypical cleavage, the only agnates who are lost are the sisters and daughters who marry and leave, and they are replaced, as it were, in each generation by the wives who are married and come in.

This hypothesis is only explanatory in that it deals largely in categories of final products. To speak of the forging of fictional links and the continuous re-binding of the groups together is to see the system from the outside as a series of completed stages. But the genealogical fictions are in themselves relatively unimportant; it is the realities out of which they emerge that are primarily significant. For purposes of exposition the evidence has been largely presented in the genealogical form, since by that method each instance could be most easily summarized. However, the remarks of all my informants invariably related these genealogical results to the pattern of actual social life and to actual working relations. Simply stated, the process of Jie thought may be paraphrased as follows: all Families are the descendants of one man, the grandfather; we are manifestly one Family because of the relations that exist between us; therefore we are, or can say we are, descendants of one grandfather. This indigenous theory is based directly on the moral ideal of reciprocal rights in domestic animals resulting from joint inheritance of a single herd of the grandfather, two generations ago. Facts are re-interpreted to fit the theory, but they are not themselves altered in actuality. Those facts are actual social relations.

The question remains—what stabilizes actual relations when they appear to be on the point of breaking down? The answer is that, although structurally defined opposition consistently diminishes the strength of agnatic ties, there comes a time when they reach a stage where they are not close enough to engender further opposition and rivalry, but where they have not yet broken down altogether. The tension relaxes and mainly disappears. A new relationship structure develops wherein the original tensions are resolved and a new balance is established. The moral ideal of agnatic solidarity has not yet been irrevocably denied and is sufficiently strong and sufficiently valuable to create a fresh equilibrium. It would of course be false to speak as if a new equilibrium normally does become established, although in some cases, where new structural tendencies are not released by the deaths of existing houses over a long period, there may be a temporary balance during much of that time. Structural tensions are normally ever present as old houses develop and as new houses come into being; but any particular set of relations within the system can become temporarily stabilized before a new stage of Family development begins.

An attempt must be made to translate this into terms of actual life and relations. It was not easy to discover evidence of fictional genealogical reckoning, and it is no less difficult to discover data concerning the development of those real relations which lie behind the fictions. It has been seen that opposition and rivalry occur over matters of stock rights and stock transactions, because principally the working group called a Family is built up on reciprocal rights, and, broadly speaking, self-interest clashes with agnatic obligations. It has been seen further that the chief occasions on which these sentiments are exhibited are connected with marriage and the transfer of bridewealth. This is because bridewealth is by far the major transaction involving the use of stock and the invoking of rights; and also because through marriage the individual house develops its strength and independence and in general follows the ideal path as conceived by the Jie. In this development houses tend to move apart and varying fortunes of their separate herds assist the process. Acknowledgment of obligations weaken in protest against supposed (and often actual) violations of rights. The stage is reached when two or more houses become almost independent of one another to the extent that they could become more or less completely autonomous if forced and relations could fail. At this point opposition and antagonism dies down, for each house is no longer a rival of the others. On the whole, a man of one house, for instance, might be able to obtain sufficient stock for bridewealth from the herd of his own house and from his range of external relations—maternal kin, affines, bond-friends, etc. Nevertheless, a compromise is reached with the formerly rival house such that each can still be of value to the other without either exposing their futures to the risk of undue retardation. The time has come when tribute can now be safely given to the ideal of the common herd and the common ancestor. Thus eventually two houses, which stand to each other in terms of half-brothers or paternal cousins, settle down to a new practical relationship. One no longer expects one's cousin to put joint development before the strong interests of his own house, nor to give up stock for one's own bridewealth in prejudice of his own plans of development. At the death of the old, all-embracing house, contributions usually begin at about four to six cattle per new house; and they eventually settle down to a uniform one or two cattle—no more is expected on either side. This gradual falling away of contributions (and of corresponding distributed shares) can be traced through the successive bridewealth transactions of a Family. Where houses have been established for a fairly long time as independent units an analysis of their bridewealth figures almost always shows a steady figure of one or two head of cattle (or sometimes an equivalent number of goats) as the size of agnatic contributions and shares.

With the element of opposition largely gone, a new and valuable relationship works to the mutual advantage of both parties. Members of one house feel that they can afford to take a genuine interest in the other's development, to voice friendly approval and disapproval, to give both material and moral support and to co-operate both in day-to-day matters and at times of life's social crises. This is the general norm of inter-house relations in an established Family group.

In order to point up the issues involved here, the general picture has, perhaps, been slightly overdrawn, for in fact the rivalry and antagonism may never reach dramatic proportions. Not all newly mature houses are in violent opposition to one another. This does occur in many cases; it has been illustrated by a brief account of the Family of Longoli,[1] since in such a case the issues are more clearly revealed. The Jie are, however, well aware of the dangers involved in inter-house relations, and therefore the ultimate compromise solution may be reached relatively quickly and smoothly by a diplo-

[1] See pp. 93-8.

matic recognition of the ambitions and tendencies of closely related houses. The change-over can then be made without the latent opposition breaking out on the surface; but most Families have stories of quarrels between half-brothers and cousins in the past which are now patched up in mutual toleration. Wherever I have investigated newly independent houses (i.e. where an old house had recently died out), there were almost always signs of tension whilst adjustments were being effected. The general pattern is also often modified by particular inter-personal friendships and animosities between men of different houses. A man's closest friend is often one of his cousins with whom he is of an age and has shared a common upbringing and common life and leisure in the bush camps as young men. Because of such friendships, examples of which have already been given, two houses may remain in closer relations than would otherwise have been the case. Then differences and tensions are partly overcome by mutual affection and esteem.

Indeed, the Jie are not normally hostile, suspicious people, but are temperamentally friendly and tolerant towards others. There is a philosophic acceptance of the fact that half-brothers and cousins are likely to clash, and therefore allowances are made, and a mental pre-adjustment effected. The opposition, tensions and rivalries previously described are structurally defined tendencies in Jie society and need not break out in highly emotional form; but whether they do break out like that, or if they remain in a less intense form, they are that part of close agnatic relations which produce the inevitable relaxation of ties to the point of useful, mutual adjustment of reciprocal rights, and lead therefore to the gradual creation of a new relationship.

This account of the development of agnatic relations applies to those houses which have come out of a former unitary house of the preceding generation. It is largely the history of the house-line. With other houses inside the same Family, development is slightly different. Before an old house dies it is likely to have reached some stability in its relations with parallel houses and this pattern can fairly easily be inherited and continued by the newly independent houses. Thus the 'fathers' had established a *modus vivendi* with the houses of their half-brothers and cousins which their sons may follow. Therefore, *vis-à-vis* other house-lines in the Family, generally speaking, relations continue through successive generations fairly steadily and enduringly. This fact is given formal (if fictional) recognition by the continual re-creation of genealogical links such that house-lines never move further away in a structural sense. A clear example of this is afforded by the two genealogies given in connection with the Family of Lothikiria (see Figure 10). Because of the myth of common descent and the concretely reciprocal rights in each other's stock which is conceived of as a kind of joint ownership, there is no difficulty in the fictionalizing of genealogical links to fit the ideal pattern. To re-quote one of my informants: 'We are all "cousins". We live together and give each other cattle. Our herds are like one herd; our wives were married from one herd. We are one Family, different from other Families. Kopengamoi [the putative grandfather] is like our grandfather; he was a big man long ago and we remember.' The pseudo-genealogy is completed, that is to say, by relating it to the focal point of some recent ancestor who for one reason or another is especially remembered and respected. At bottom it is really quite irrelevant whether the group of men are descended from one grandfather or not—that is only the myth. What really matters is that a useful system is kept in being; the fiction merely gives it a rationalized justification and explanation. The fictional genealogy is a formal method of stating actual relations in conventional terminology.

The system of mutual rights and obligations amongst a group of herd-owners is inherently valuable to the participants. It affords a man a role and a status in a fixed group in his society and gives him a body of reliable supporters, friends and sympathizers. The system differs from all other kinds of important relations each member has in that it creates a corporate unit which is in fact also a residential and day-to-day co-operative group. Once the moral contradiction between the way a man ought to act towards his agnates and the way he wants to act are resolved in mutual toleration, relations may become enduring and their content is largely inheritable by the men's sons in the succeeding generation.

It appears that the system has grown up in a society where population size has been fairly static. As generation followed generation there was, by and large, only a restricted number of allied houses and close agnates. It was unlikely to have been difficult to maintain such a small-scale system and to re-incorporate it in formal terms. Most Families, even today, have only about fifty people—perhaps about ten adult males divided amongst three or four houses. It appears likely that the Jie population is now increasing rapidly. In

1919 military officers carried out a census of Jieland and gave a population figure of about 10,000 people. The East African Native Census, 1948, gave a figure of 18,211. This is an increase of over 80 per cent in thirty years. Even if it is assumed that the earlier census was an underestimate, there has still been most probably a considerable increase during the present generation which has grown up in modern times.[1] It may well be that during the next generation traditional Families will become unwieldy in their larger numbers. A useful working-group may be obtained following Family cleavages, though not necessarily affecting the ideal myth. Had such cleavages been allowed to occur in the past, there would have resulted a large number of smaller, splinter groups which could not have afforded the security, mutual assistance and general value of the traditional Families.

[1] See my paper 'The Population of Karamoja', *Uganda Journal*, xvii, 1953.

CHAPTER FIVE

FAMILY AND PROPERTY IN TURKANALAND

(a) THE NUCLEAR FAMILY

Structure and Pastoral Organization

In Turkanaland the basic family group which emerges in actual life as a legally independent, stock-owning, more or less self-sufficient unit will here be called the nuclear family. This may be described in a preliminary way as a man and his wives and children. A daughter leaves it when she marries and she then joins her husband's nuclear family. Sons remain within the group together with their wives and children, though they tend increasingly to achieve a considerable degree of autonomy together with physical and economic separation. The Turkana refer to this group by the general word *awi*, which means literally 'a homestead' in the physical sense of thorn fences, huts, kraals, etc. By extension, *awi* also means the people who normally occupy the homesteads of an independent man and who join in the care and use of the domestic stock kraaled there.

Polygyny is not only the ideal but also the common practice (see Appendix to Chapter 8). At the same time married sons do not become entirely independent of their father until his death. The Turkana nuclear family therefore has elements both of a 'polygynous family' and of a 'patrilineal expanded family'. My use of the term 'nuclear' is different from the usage by Murdoch[1] and others. It is to be used in this present account to express in a convenient, shorthand way the basic position of the group in Turkana society and in structural contrast with the 'extended family'. It is the smallest, independent, corporate kin group and is specifically identified by its ownership and use of a herd of domestic stock. The smaller groups contained within it are not legally independent and are only sub-

[1] Murdoch, G. P., *Social Structure*, New York, 1949, chapter 1.

sections in the structure of its internal organization. A number of nuclear families are linked together by a web of genealogically defined, social bonds to form the more amorphous group, the extended family. The use of 'compound', 'composite', 'polygynous', etc., would not, I think, express this structural position of the group, though perhaps satisfactory enough as descriptive terms. Further, except in cases where a man has only one wife and no married sons, there is no specific unit composed of a man, a wife and their children. This 'elementary family' as such does not exist in Turkana society within the nuclear family. Sub-sections are 'yards', composed each of a wife and her children, which in a structural sense stand apart from the husband-father.

Although Turkana speak of there being one *awi*, yet, except amongst the poorest people, few nuclear families occupy a single, physical homestead, for, as we have already seen, ecological and pastoral conditions normally necessitate at least two homesteads.[1] From an external and also an economic point of view these two homesteads are similar. Both are constructed on the same pattern with similar materials (thorn and bush wood); each is more or less self-sufficient economically, the inhabitants living on the products of the animals kraaled there, plus wild fruits gathered locally; each, if possible contains a wife of the head of the nuclear family or of one of his sons or of some other dependant, and she supervises the domestic and feminine side of life and work in the homestead, e.g. milking and watering the animals, fetching drinking-water, collecting and preparing, building and repairing, etc.

The 'chief-homestead', *awi napolon*, is that in which, at any one time, the head of the family is living. A 'secondary-homestead' is called *awi abor*.[2] The composition of these has been briefly described earlier,[3] and all that need be stated here is that the labour force of the family must be distributed between the homesteads, so that if possible an adult male and a wife live in each, together with youths, boys, and girls, to carry out the necessary routine work. In this it is by no means possible for brothers to keep together, nor for them to live with their mother. A shortage of womenfolk may require that an adolescent girl live apart from her mother. Except in the case of

---

[1] These are the usual minimum arrangements. A wealthy family may have three or even four homesteads. In what follows, for convenience of exposition, it will generally be assumed that a nuclear family has two homesteads, and in fact this is the most usual state of affairs.

[2] Literally this means 'the rearward homestead'.   [3] See pp. 28 and 40-1.

an elderly man who has several wives and many children, most families are perennially short of labour, though it may be pointed out that, on the whole, work for either sex is not particularly heavy. Examples of the size and distribution of some families' labour forces are given in the Appendix to this Chapter.

It is not possible to make a neat distinction between a main homestead and the cattle camp as amongst many pastoralists. The chief-homestead at any time is the centre of the family's life and organization, and here nearly all important social and ritual activities connected with the whole family are undertaken, under the direction of the family head. From the pastoral and economic viewpoint a secondary-homestead often moves and lives in a completely different geographical region from that of the chief-homestead.[1] Although the family head exercises ultimate control over movements and activities, yet he is commonly too far away to do more than lay down general policy. His representative, the senior adult man at the homestead, not only takes day-to-day decisions but decides when to move and where, his decision being based on his own judgment of the state of water and pastures and of future prospects. As will be seen later, an adult son assumes a good deal of independence in his control over the secondary-homestead, even to the point of direct disagreement with his father as to the general region in which that homestead is to operate. Despite a certain amount of visiting, a man may not see his cattle for months at a stretch, co-wives may not meet, nor sons be with their mother and brothers; for in the dry season a cattle homestead may be two or more days' journey away across rough country.

Though physically and economically divided, a nuclear family remains nevertheless a distinct and corporate group. This unity stems directly from the head of the family who legally owns the stock. As we shall see later, a man inherits his own herds of animals through his 'house' after his father's death, and these herds become quite distinct from all others, not excluding those of his brothers who also inherited from the one father. He is able to control and move them as he chooses and to herd them where he desires and as he sees fit. He assumes the sole use of them both for narrow economic and wider social purposes, and they are recognized by all people as 'his stock'. Through him, wives and children share this ownership and use, and together the group is distinguished from all similar groups, however nearly related, as the owner of certain herds.

[1] See Figure 4 and pp. 45-8.

FAMILY AND PROPERTY IN TURKANALAND

In actual life the nuclear family often does not exist alone as such, but is associated in the same homesteads with parts or wholes of other families. So far we have defined the nuclear family in purely structural and legal terms with direct reference to stock-ownership, and Turkana do the same. In practice, however, a Turkana would also include people who, for the time being, join in the pastoral and economic activities of the group, and whose stock (if any) are not distinguished externally. A man welcomes additions to his family's labour force, and adult men are especially acceptable. A man with his nuclear family cannot achieve complete independence until he has sufficient làbour to manage all the duties of nomadic, pastoral life. Consequently a young man or one of early middle-age, with perhaps only one wife, attempts to attract young male relations to help. Occasionally a poor, unrelated man, even a complete pauper, may become permanently attached to a family, acting as herdsman in return for food and shelter. Such a person becomes almost 'one of the family'.

If they possess stock of their own, such associates keep them in the relevant homestead of their adopted family. For many practical purposes—herding, watering, movements, even kraaling sometimes —their stock are merged into the herds of the family. Nevertheless, to some extent economically, but especially socially and legally, these stock are quite distinct from the herds proper of the family, and this is clearly recognized and acknowledged by the people involved. Later a man may wish to strike out independently, or before that time may shift his allegiance to some other man. In either case his animals go with him, together with all their offspring and all accretions by gifts, etc. Economically there is a good deal of give-and-take over the consumption of milk and blood, and even of meat, yet it is accepted that an associate has prime rights to the produce of his own animals.

Sometimes, though not in the majority of cases, two independent men ally together in pastoral and friendly co-operation. A pair of full-brothers, close agnates, brothers-in-law or bond-friends may co-operate in this way. The men, heads of their own nuclear families, occupy a joint chief-homestead and maintain a joint secondary-homestead. In all such cases there are separate kraals for each type of animal for each family. In addition it is a strict rule that each family has its own main gateway through which, and only through which, its stock are driven, irrespective of joint herding during

127

the day.[1] This segregation in the homestead directly reflects the independence of the herds and of their respective owner. Turkana speak loosely of the larger *de facto* group as *awi*, though always restricting the full meaning of that word to the independent stock-owning unit proper, i.e. the nuclear family. They put it: 'One *awi*, one herd of stock. Other *ngawie*, other stock are different.'[2]

Internal Organization

The internal organization of a nuclear family in Turkanaland closely resembles that of a Jie house as already described. It is sufficient here, then, to make only a few salient remarks.

The family is divided into 'yards' on the basis of maternal affiliation.[3] The family head stands, as it were, outside the yards, being the focal point genealogically and sociologically at which they are united into the single corporate group. To each wife as the founder of a yard are allocated female animals (cows, camels, ewes and goats), perhaps a few male animals, and two or three donkeys for pack purposes. Allocations are made directly by the family head in accordance with the proportionate requirements of each wife for the staple food—milk. Only the chief wife has an allocation beyond her needs, and in this case the term 'allocation' is scarcely applicable. Being the first wife, say Turkana, she has at first domestic use and control of all her husband's stock; when another wife joins the family she is allocated animals from the total herds which were hitherto undifferentiated. The bulk of the stock, including most of the male animals, are retained by the chief wife. 'They are not really her stock,' said one informant. 'She holds them for her husband, for the big man [i.e. the family head]'; neither has she unrestricted claim

---

[1] The significance of the separate gateway (*ekidor*) is referred to in connection with the internal structure of an extended family (cf. p. 153). An example of a joint homestead is given in *Survey of the Turkana*, Diagram C, p. 77. It is exceedingly rare that more than two independent men share a common homestead.

[2] Examples of various types of groups who occupy pairs of homesteads are given in the Appendix to this chapter.

[3] The *ekal* of a Turkana wife is literally a day-hut—a half-dome of intertwined bushwood and leafage. Associated with this is a smaller night-hut and the space around. It might be better to translate *ekal* here as 'hut'; since, however, we are to contrast Turkana kinship structure with that of the Jie, I prefer to use a common terminology applicable to both. In Jieland, *ekal* specifically refers to an enclosed yard and not a hut of any kind; but, as Turkana pointed out to me, the Jie yard and the Turkana day-hut are similar in function. Each is the centre of the wife's domestic life and activity, and her private domain in a homestead; each is the material and domestic focus of the sub-group formed by the wife and her children.

on their milk. Indeed, the chief wife's real allocation is similar to that of junior wives, the rest of 'her animals' being a 'residual herd' of which she has only the use when they are not required for other purposes. As each new wife joins the family, whether a junior wife or a son's wife, this residual herd provides all or most of her allocation. In poorer families the residual herd disappears, and in all but the wealthiest families it is reduced to a small size. Examples of the internal distribution of cattle and camels are given in Figure 11.

FIGURE 11

THE INTERNAL DISTRIBUTION OF CATTLE AND CAMELS IN A NUCLEAR FAMILY

(*a*) The nuclear family of Imana—an exceptionally wealthy man:

	cattle	camels
chief wife (with 9 children)	100	43
2nd wife (with 3 children)	10	7
3rd wife (with 1 child)	10	5
4th wife (childless)	5	2
In addition,		
eldest daughter (*c.* 17 years old) . . .	4	...
two other grown daughters (2 each) . .	4	...
Totals . .	133	57

(*b*) The nuclear family of Lodeki—an 'average family':

chief wife (with 4 children)	18	5
2nd wife (with 2 children)	9	4
Sister (concubine)	4	1
Totals . .	31	10

(*c*) The nuclear family of Imuru—a poor man:

chief wife (with 2 children)	9	...
2nd wife (childless)	2	...
Total . .	11	...

Note.—I was not able to collect comparable figures for the distribution of goats and sheep. Their numbers are generally too large for the Turkana to deal with them quantitatively in this way, and I never found all the wives of a man at the goat homestead so that I could cross-check satisfactorily. Nevertheless, I was repeatedly told that allocations of goats and sheep are made in an identical manner to that of cattle and camels. This is borne out at the time of inheritance when each yard takes its former allocation as its own herds. There does not appear to be any difficulty in the matter of the possession of goats and sheep.

This scheme is complicated by a degree of sub-allocation within each yard. Adolescent daughters are often allocated one or two female animals from their mother's herd or from the residual herd. In so far as the number of milch animals and the supply of milk allows, each member has his own beasts from which he has prime right to milk. For much of the year milk is relatively scarce and the whole supply is pooled for the primary benefit of the younger children; nevertheless, the idea persists of certain animals 'belonging' to individuals. In view of later analysis, I think it is not insignificant that the individual should be afforded this explicit recognition inside his own yard. Right through the fabric of relationships and values of Turkana society runs an outstanding respect for the individuality of each person which is not entirely submerged by the needs of co-operation and corporate action, and which is expressed in the wide dispersion of houses and of the whole extended family.

These allocations are modified in practice by three overriding necessities. Firstly, over the year the supply of milk is not constant nor sufficient to supply all requirements. As milk yield decreases in the dry season, wives must pool their supplies in order that at least the children are fed as long as possible. It would be a grave violation of the needs and moral rights of the young, and of the corporate unity of the nuclear family, if one wife were unable to feed her children whilst a co-wife had enough to feed older persons. Normally the cordiality of relations between co-wives is sufficient to ensure this co-operation, but ultimately it is the responsibility of the family head, who, as always standing outside the differentiation of yards, represents and acts for the interests of the family as a whole.

Secondly, because of the conditions of pastoral organization a wife and her children do not always live together, nor can they always live with all their yard's stock. For example, a wife living at the goat homestead in the plains may be many miles away from her cattle. Frequently all the wives of a family live together at the cattle homestead in wet-season pastures, and then the pattern of the allocation of cattle does exactly determine the distribution and use of the milk supply. At other times a practical compromise is effected. A wife has the milk of the stock of her own yard which are kraaled at the homestead where she is living, and milk from animals of absent wives is shared equally amongst the people present. An adolescent daughter or an adult son will claim much or all of their absent mother's milk.

Because of the superior and prolonged lactic qualities of the camel, wives often take their own female camels with them wherever they live.

These are practical, commonplace arrangements and call for no especial comment. On the other hand it is worthwhile to emphasize that despite the suppression of the yard-allocation system, the moral idea of it persists, and invariably, when conditions permit, wives attempt to bring it into operation again so far as is possible. Membership of a yard does not only mean a specific maternal link, a genealogical principle; it means the attachment of sub-groups to parts of the family herd. Allocation comes to be on organizational principle expressing the separateness and individuality of the yards.

Thirdly, in the supply of the other staple animal foods—blood and meat—the yard principle is almost entirely ignored. Seldom is more than one animal bled each day in a homestead. The provision of meat directly affects the size of the herds, and only the family head can authorize slaughter. The provision of blood and meat is therefore made on a communal basis under the direction of the family head. In the same way, only he may authorize the disposal of stock (usually sheep and goats) for barter purposes, either with itinerant traders or when expeditions are made to alien centres.

In these modifications of the scheme of allocations, as indeed in the making of the allocations in the first place, the authority of the family head is paramount. He is the stock-owner and he represents the family as a unit. In all things concerning the control and use of stock he has prime authority, and normally he does not yeild that to anyone unless perhaps he is an old man lapsing towards senility. There is, however, a definite moral idea of the use of the herds for the common benefit of the family as a whole under the autocracy of the family head. The notion of the importance and solidarity of the nuclear family produces the commonly quoted remark, 'A man does not own stock; a [nuclear] family owns it.'

The non-economic uses of domestic animals in Turkanaland are similar to those amongst the Jie. Once a man's sons reach adulthood —from initiation onwards—they begin to require stock for all these purposes and thus come into competition with one another and with their father. For that most important use of stock in bridewealth, the sons' demands are regulated by a seniority system essentially similar to that of a Jie house. Whereas in the latter institution, involving the range of sons of a number of full-brothers, modifications of the strict order of birth are common, in the Turkana nuclear family such modifications are not usual amongst the narrower range of sons of one man. Nevertheless, the formal principle remains, and also the concept of equalizing the fortunes and progress of the various yards. As in the Jie house, the composition of a bridewealth payment (and also the distribution of one received for a daughter) largely ignores the allocations of stock to the yards.[1]

The Development and Dispersal of the Nuclear Family

In such a relatively small group as the nuclear family where most physical and social needs are satisfied from the family herds, it is perhaps inevitable that tensions should arise concerning the regulation and apportionment of the use of the stock. Most of the Turkana food, clothing and material apparatus are obtained from the herds. Animals provide the only significant source of wealth and store of value. All important social relations are expressed in one way or another in terms of reciprocal rights in stock and through reciprocal obligations to assist one another in stock affairs. There can be little doubt about this for an external observer; and the people themselves express it explicitly as well as implicitly in their activities, ideas and values.

It may be said at once that there is little difficulty raised in the economic sphere over the use and disposal of animals. For one thing there is a genuine and conscious attempt to equalize the distribution of the economic products of the herds; and in any event, whatever the faults of the mechanics of this process, it is tempered by a high degree of communalism in distribution. Few Turkana, for instance, would deny milk to a member of another yard if supplies differed to any great extent; it is virtually impossible not to share meat or blood or the products of barter. As we have seen, a wife and her children are normally separated from at least some of the stock allocated to them, and at the same are time allowed to use the products of the stock of other yards. Broadly speaking, people have the use of the animals which are kraaled at the homestead where they are living at the time. Indeed, to some extent this communalism goes beyond the individual family or the individual homestead to the immediate (primary) neighbourhood or even further.[2]

Difficulties and tensions arise over the use and disposal of scarce

---

[1] See the relevant section on the Jie house, p. 63 ff.
[2] Information on this matter is given in *Survey of the Turkana*, pp. 111-14.

resources of stock in social transactions. In what follows here we shall principally be concerned with the use of stock in bridewealth and in the allocation to sons achieving autonomy as heads of their own family homestead. This is not to deny the presence and contribution of other elements, but conditions will be described mainly in terms of the chief factors at work, and the ones moreover that Turkana themselves emphasize.

The first type of tension which arises in the development of a nuclear family occurs between father and sons. As sons reach adulthood they become fully aware of and drawn towards the traditional course of individual development. Briefly, this course is a process beginning with a first marriage and culminating in independence as head of a nuclear family and owner of stock. The first desire of an adult son is therefore for stock with which to marry. Such a desire, of course, necessarily conflicts with the desire of the father himself to marry again, since his own individual development is furthered by the addition of another wife and also by the increase in his field of affinal relations. As the father is legal owner and controller of the herds, he is in a strong position. He is permanently given a good deal of respect, and his sons grow up under his authority, and therefore it is not easy to challenge his decisions. In general, the desires of the father are paramount and he may continue to use stock for his own immediate purposes rather than for his sons. The whole of traditional structure and traditional moral values are on his side. Bridewealth payments are heavy in relation to the sizes of herds and are a real strain on family resources. It is not usual that both father and son can take stock from the family herds at the same time, for care must be taken not to deplete the herds below minimum economic requirements. However wealthy a nuclear family is, bridewealth demands are roughly proportionate to the ability to give,[1] and thus the degree of strain is somewhat similar for all conditions of families.

A son must accede to his father's desires and decisions; but he need not and often does not accede entirely gracefully. The idea of competition between father and son is begun, and it continues to grow. It grows slowly, especially at first, for men are brought up and culturally conditioned to the fact that they must give way to their father for many years. Immediately after initiation (at about the age of eighteen) and the recognized assumption of adult status,

[1] See Chapter 8.

133

privileges and ambitions, a son does not expect to marry straight away, even though he might perhaps like to. Men with living fathers seldom marry before the age of twenty-five and frequently later. 'Young men like to court the girls, go to dances and to play [i.e. enjoy themselves freely],' say Turkana. Typically, adult sons live at the secondary-homestead, relatively out of touch with important family affairs, centred as these are at the chief-homestead where the father lives. Neither is it very long ago since young adult men spent a large proportion of their time in raiding, roaming the countryside and engaging in age-set activities generally. This was the practice only a generation ago, and the tradition of relatively irresponsible youth persists. Another mitigating factor lies in the whole marital structure of the society. Since men tend to marry fairly late they are likely to be middle-aged or elderly by the time that their sons are wanting to marry and therefore competition for bridewealth stock may be correspondingly less as fathers desire less and less to marry again. Nevertheless, a son does begin to chafe at his father's restrictions in this matter, to the point of resentment against his father's use of stock which denies him the possibility of his own first marriage. When a father does eventually agree to his son's demands, he himself feels a certain resentment because it marks the end of his own marriage prospects; further, it marks the definite beginning or specific recognition of his approaching old age and of the dimunition of his authority and of the tight unity of his nuclear family. A father is well aware that his son's marriage is but the prelude to the eventual autonomy of that son. Tension and the idea of competition between father and son does not necessarily reach a serious level, or at least not for many years. Elderly men, as they have told me, do genuinely recognize and respect their sons' desires to marry. The situation is regarded as more or less inevitable and therefore to a large extent must be gracefully accepted. Commonly, affection between father and son is enough to prevent the father persisting in too autocratic an attitude. It would be incorrect if I imply that father and son live normally in a state of hostility, even if suppressed below the surface of everyday relations. Affection between the men, and the common bonds established within the unitary nuclear family, permit the marriages of sons as alternatives to new marriage by the father. A new wife is brought into the group, more children may be born and new affinal links are established. Thirdly, in the case of an eldest son, at least, there is a valid reason why his marriage should not be too long delayed, and having once begun the process of sons' marriages it is difficult to revert back again to the old primacy by the father. An eldest son ought to marry fairly early in order to provide at least one settled line of succession to the father at his death. Turkana say that only a married man can properly inherit the father's position as head of the group and take over the herds. If a man dies and leaves only unmarried sons, the continuity of the group is believed to be threatened. People say that it would be necessary for some near agnate (the deceased's brother, for instance) to intervene, and that man's prime loyalty lies elsewhere, in his own nuclear family. There would be a possibility of the two sets of herds becoming mixed up, and that might negate the whole conception of the independence of the nuclear family as a man has established it during his lifetime. As will be seen later, there is a considerable distinction between even full-brothers, let alone other agnates, and their herds; for the whole trend of individual development in this society is towards the complete independence of a man and his own family. The continued independence and specific indentity of a man's family is ensured by the existence of at least one married son. In actual fact this danger may be overcome even where there is no married son to inherit; but the general attitude, the desire to make sure, persists in the minds of elderly Turkana. I do not wish to over-emphasize this point, for it may be ignored by fathers; often, how-ever, it is at least a contributory factor in the situation here discussed. Fourthly, as sons reach adulthood, they reach a stage also where their attachment to the allocated stock of their yards increasingly approaches a conception of ownership, even though remaining within the orbit of the father's over-all ownership and family unit. It tends to become increasingly difficult for a father to alienate the herds of a yard for his own marriage. Again at this point this factor must not be overemphasized; but it may be noted as a further strand in the web of relations between father and son, and another modi-fying agent. This factor lies rather at the level of moral attitudes and sentiments than at the level of legal rights and relations.

In addition to all this, there is the purely economic aspect to be considered. A family can scarcely afford a marriage each year, but, after the expenditure of stock in one bridewealth, must pause to rebuild its resources even though assisted, now more, now less, by the income received at the marriage of daughters. The question of marriage is doubtless perennially in the minds of the men of the family, but it cannot constantly come to a head in the course of actual events. The problem of marriage may also be postponed by poor wet seasons when most men prefer to await more favourable times. Unless the family head lives to a great age, or unless there is a high income of stock from daughter's marriages, there is often little cause to strain against the leash of his authority. Economic facts are against sons, and this is generally recognized and accepted philosophically. On the whole, Turkana men do not live to a great age, and even if a man has several sons of adult status it is unlikely that more than one or two of them can hope for marriage in his lifetime, however understanding and unselfish he may be (cf. Figure 12).

For these reasons it is maintained here that, although tension and opposition between father and son is produced as a direct result of structural roles, yet it does not necessarily attain to a high degree of significance in the matter of marriages. On the other hand, as previously emphasized, the marriage of an adult son is only the first step in his course of development; it merely sets him on the path towards autonomy and independence. For the moment, a married son continues uninterruptedly as a subordinate member of the nuclear family, subject still to his father's authority. Nevertheless, a son aims at a partial dissociation from his father and his natal family; he aims, that is, at his own autonomy, his share of the family herds with which to live and move apart from his father, in his own homestead with his own wife and children. Immediately after marriage he cannot even attempt this, for in order to become autonomous he must have both sufficient animals to provide the economic basis of separation and enough dependants to carry out the normal and necessary labour requirements of nomadic, pastoral life. Conventionally, as the Turkana always put it, he must wait until he has at least one son of an age to begin herding work, i.e. about five or six years old. This is not only a matter of labour supply but permits a decent interval between marriage and the assumption of autonomy in breaking away from the family head.[1] A son of working age is, in fact, not an absolute necessity in many cases, nor even perhaps the normal method followed. Secession from his father's family and homesteads may follow the line not of individual separa-

---

[1] For example, see the case of Lopola, whose labour distribution is given in the Appendix to this chapter. He had been able to achieve autonomy about seven years after his marriage, when his first son was old enough to herd the small flock of goats and sheep. Lopola himself herded the cattle.

tion, but of the withdrawal of his yard, in part or whole—that is, it involves not only the married son but some or all of his brothers and sisters, who together provide an adequate labour force under their senior.

This aim is of course a direct threat to the solidarity of the nuclear family; it is also not only a threat to the authority of the family head but to a considerable extent to the interests of members of other yards. It must be made quite clear, however, that secession by a married son during the lifetime of his father does not permit complete independence, for the bonds of paternal authority persist. Chiefly, succession provides a new economic and pastoral unit within the framework of the nuclear family. The married son has his own homestead, where live his wife and her children and any other dependants, together with herds allotted to him by his father. Pastoral and nomadic organization are the responsibility of the son, who is now head of his own homestead-unit. But in matters of the disposal and distribution of stock the head of the whole nuclear family retains his authority. To distinguish this state of affairs from true independence, I propose to refer to it as 'autonomy' in this present account; and the new autonomous sub-group will be referred to as a 'homestead-unit' to distinguish it from normal chief- and secondary-homesteads, and from the all-embracing nuclear family. Turkana term all these units by the one word, *awi*.

Let us return for a moment to the newly married son. Turkana recognize the tension that is inherent if not necessarily active in the relationship between a man and his married son, and therefore it is universally insisted that the son shall not live in the same homestead as his father. I never found a case where this rule was not strictly followed. Thus a married son invariably lives, with his wife, at the secondary-homestead, as its head. Straight away then he achieves a certain autonomy. His own wife and not his father's takes charge of domestic affairs; he himself takes on the control of the pastoral organization of the homestead. Of course, he was probably head of this secondary-homestead already, but now together with his own wife he assumes an increased authority. At this stage many fathers, probably wisely, leave their sons a fairly free hand. In any case, as previously pointed out, if the secondary-homestead is a long distance away, the father must perforce recognize his inability to direct its activity; an overbearing father can be circumvented without great difficulty, and a married son feels able to do so. It is, for instance, a not uncommon occurrence that such a son decides to herd the family cattle in different mountain pastures to those previously conventionally used by his father. Most fathers accept this without much protest and acknowledge their sons' rights to arrange things as they see fit. Such a change of pastures is quite often drastic, involving a major alteration in the pastoral routine formerly established. A son may prefer to live in the same neighbourhood as his wife's kinsmen, or with a bond-friend perhaps; or his own judgment and experience lead him to the opinion that alternative pastures would be preferable.[1]

Later, as his wife bears children, as his full-brothers reach adulthood and as his father's authority imperceptibly but steadily slackens, a married son definitely begins to consider greater autonomy. Primarily, of course, the possibility is limited by the size of the family herds. A relatively small herd cannot be divided amongst two separate homesteads and remain economically adequate. A married son may, therefore, for the time being anyway, be constrained from further autonomy. Another limiting factor already mentioned concerns the labour supply that the son can muster. The actual step may be deferred also by the father's and by half-brothers' intransigent opposition; but sooner or later such attitudes will be overcome, if only through the mere fact that everyone concerned well recognize the inevitability of the whole process. In the last resort a son may more or less take the law into his own hands and move off on his own, taking with him his yard's allocated stock. As far as I could ascertain, fathers do not attempt to persist in their refusals to allow sons to move off. In any case the new conditions may be welcomed, since they allow a wider spread of the family herds and a reduction of the risks of stock losses due to starvation following the failure of pastures in one area,[2] to disease and (not so long ago) to raiding. Through the son's secession the nuclear family is able to encompass an additional secondary-homestead. It also allows expression to the developing ambitions of a younger son who can now become head of the old secondary-homestead.

---

[1] It has already been pointed out that this type of pastoral decision contains a large element of personal opinion and choice. The adult son's decision to change to different pastures does not necessarily mean that conditions have changed, much less that his father's former decision was at fault.

[2] Due to the vagaries of Turkanaland's rainfall, in most years one or more regions are liable to have a more or less serious failure of pastures. Mountain grasslands no more than fifty miles apart may receive appreciably different rainfall in the same year.

Except in the wealthiest families it is unlikely that the seceding son can take with him a full complement of stock sufficient to accommodate the usual two homesteads of an independent man. Normal sized herds do not allow of such division. Very often not enough stock can be spared from the nuclear family's herds even to maintain a single autonomous homestead. At first, then, several possibilities are open to the married son. He may join with a man in a similar position to himself, and the two together establish a joint homestead in mutual co-operation and assistance. The second man may be a married half-brother, so that the two together—or more precisely their two yards—can claim a sufficiently large portion of the family herds. In other cases the second man may be a married son of another nuclear family of the extended family group; or he may be the wife's brother, sister's husband, or a bond-friend. In all such cases a new autonomous joint homestead is set up, economically and pastorally separate from the homesteads and nomadic routine of the nuclear family of each man. For example, an autonomous son, Maiyen, was able to take only about fifty goats and sheep and three camels. He established a joint homestead with his wife's brother, who was in a similar position, and neither man controlled any cattle at all.

Another course is for the seceding son to attach himself to one of the homesteads of his wife's father. By doing this he both exercises his rights of autonomy from his father and expresses and makes use of the exceedingly important affinal ties. Thus, for instance, in the Naitera valley, Lomon came to live with his wife's father's brother, Lokoyen,[1] bringing with him only a handful of cattle and goats. His wife built an annexe to Lokoyen's chief-homestead and she and Lomon depended to a considerable extent on milk, blood and meat from Lokoyen. In the dry season Lomon's few cattle were kraaled at Lokoyen's cattle homestead. Another course again is for the married son to secede with only one variety of stock, leaving the rest of his house's entitlement with the family herds. In such a case he takes stock of other yards as well as of his own. Thus Moiya, in the Oropoi basin, was able to secede with some twenty-five cattle, leaving his father's cattle homestead with about thirty head. Moiya actually took the allocation of his own yard and of the next most senior yard, the eldest son of which, though not yet married agreed to join him. In another case, Lobuin was able to move off with a flock of about

---

[1] Lokoyen had for many years been pro-husband to the mother of Lomon's wife, and for all practical purposes counted as wife's father to Lomon.

one hundred goats and sheep and one female camel, leaving his father nearly two hundred goats and sheep, all the cattle and the rest of the camels. Lobuin's married half-brother took charge of the father's secondary homestead. It is obvious that in the large majority of cases secession means privation for the son, his wife and dependants. Turkana recognize this but accept it as a necessary evil, the price of valued autonomy. Whenever possible, however straightened his immediate circumstances, a son chooses the course of autonomy.

Despite the willingness to accept a good deal of privation, and the various schemes to temper that necessity by co-operation outside the nuclear family, unless a family is exceptionally wealthy it is unlikely that the size of herds and of available labour supply will be sufficient to allow several sons to secede. In the case of the nuclear family of Towot (see Appendix to Chapter 6) this was possible, and at his death there were four autonomous sons, each with his own homestead-unit. This was a case of both great wealth and also unusual longevity of the family head. It is more usual that only the eldest son of all can achieve autonomy during the father's lifetime, and for that he is temporarily allowed to take not only the stock attached to his own yard but that of other yards also. The remaining one or two yards must remain with the father by force of economic necessity; further internal cleavage is out of the question. A limiting factor here results from the former position of the family head in his father's nuclear family. Unless he had been amongst the eldest one or two sons it is unlikely that he would have married before he was thirty years old. Therefore in his old age even his own eldest son would scarcely have had time to have achieved autonomy. This seems to be a common occurrence. Few Turkana men indeed live beyond about sixty years of age, and many die earlier, for the severity of nomadic life in Turkanaland is not conducive to ripe old age. At the same time, few sons achieve autonomy before the age of about thirty.[1] Many men therefore die even before a first son secedes.

The ideal pattern, as described by the Turkana in a general way, is that a father lives to see his nuclear family increasingly dispersed through the secession of one son after another. Undoubtedly this represents the tendency, but which, limited by economic necessity and relatively early death, is scarcely the usual event in actual life. In Figure 12 are given some figures of the numbers of elderly men,

[1] An eldest son usually does not marry before about the age of twenty-five and subsequent sons tend to marry rather later than this.

FIGURE 12

SOME STATISTICS RELATING TO THE NUCLEAR
FAMILIES OF ELDERLY MEN IN FIVE
NEIGHBOURHOODS

Neighbour-hood	Total Families	Family heads over 50 years old	'Old' Families with no married sons	Number of married sons	Number of autonomous sons
A	24	11	7	7	2
B	8	3	3	0	0
C	13	8	6	3	3*
D	5	3	1	2	1
E	8	5	4	1	0
	58	30	21	13	6

* In this case two of the autonomous sons were sons by different mothers of the same father.

A primary neighbourhood is a temporary, discrete cluster of home-steads usually not more than five in number. A secondary neighbourhood is a group of primary neighbourhoods which occupy a fairly distinct area and whose inhabitants, for the time being, engage in face-to-face relations. All of these neighbourhoods described here were secondary neighbour-hoods.

A—in the Oropoi basin, north-western Turkanaland, wet season 1949. An unusually large community of twenty-seven cattle and camel home-steads of average and above average wealth. My data refer to seventeen of these homesteads only.[1]

B—near Kanamut, western Turkanaland, dry season 1949. An average-sized plains community of six goat and camel homesteads of average or above average in wealth.

C—at Logiriama, Tarac river, western Turkanaland, early wet season 1950. A community of eight goat and camel homesteads of about average wealth.

D—near Loicer Nggamatak, central Turkanaland, dry season 1950. A small community of four goat and camel homesteads of average or below average wealth.

E—near Karibur, north-eastern Turkanaland, dry season 1948. An Average-sized plains community of seven goat and camel homesteads. Seven of the families were below average in wealth, and the eighth was above average.[2]

[1] A sketch-map of this neighbourhood is given in *Survey of the Turkana*, p. 112.
[2] *Ibid.*, p. 110.

married sons and autonomous sons in five neighbourhoods. Of thirty family heads over the age of about fifty, twenty-one had at the time no married son; and of a total of thirteen married sons only six were autonomous, two of whom were half-brothers. That is, of thirty nuclear families whose heads were over fifty years old, only five contained autonomous homestead-units.

This small sample gives, I believe, a fair picture of the circumstances of nuclear families whose heads are elderly men and which are therefore in relatively advanced stages of growth. It can be seen that the degree of dispersion of families is not usually very great. On the other hand the potentiality exists and by the time of their father's old age at least the eldest son will be looking forward to the ideal of autonomy. As we shall see later, the death of the father and the end of the legal unity of the group is very often the signal for considerable dispersion as each yard and each adult son seeks to gain independence.

Two points must be made in connection with all this. Firstly, the seceding son takes with him all or at least most of his yard's allocation of stock. This is the first significant occasion on which the yard emerges as something more than a convenient division of the nuclear family. Yard identity begins from the time when an independent man marries a second wife,[1] but as we have previously seen it is of little importance in anything other than internal domestic economy and the distribution of the milk supply, and in this latter respect pastoral necessities demand the submergence of yard exclusiveness. As the sons of a man reach adulthood and begin to marry and to look towards the ideal of autonomy, they tend increasingly to think along yard lines and towards the division of the herds amongst the yards. With the autonomy of the first son of a yard, that sub-group becomes distinguished once and for all as a stock-holding unit, even though submitting still to the overriding authority and ownership of the father. Usually a seceding son takes with him one or more of his younger brothers, and he himself becomes head not only of an autonomous homestead-unit but also head of an active yard with its own stock. Ideally, say some Turkana, the whole yard should break away with its eldest son, and even the mother should leave her husband to live with her children. Secession then is a fairly simple matter of the appropriation of the yard's allocation. In a few cases

---

[1] In a nuclear family whose head has only one wife, yard and family are more or less coterminous groups for practical purposes.

this does happen, but only where there are two or three other wives to remain with the family head to attend to his needs and supervise domestic activities. That is to say, the family head must be a wealthy man with more than the average number of wives. In any case, say other Turkana, the mother and at least her youngest son ought to remain behind in one or other of the family homesteads. The former account may be the cultural ideal[1] and this latter a rationalization of inevitable practical necessities. A woman must normally stay with her husband, who also requires the services of some of his sons in herding and supervisory work.

Secondly, and this must be emphasized, in every case of secession a son does not achieve full independence from his father, nor therefore from his half-brothers. To the family head remains ultimate authority over both humans and stock, notwithstanding the gradual and continuous reduction of his power in certain matters, chiefly pastoral and economic. Wherever the stock are kraaled—at the chief-homestead, a secondary-homestead or at an autonomous son's homestead—the father continues, at least in all major matters, the authority residing in his legal ownership. He has yielded to one or more of his sons a free hand in pastoral and economic spheres; he is not necessarily consulted over the alienation of small numbers of stock, such as are involved in gifts, ritual obligations and feasts. Where, however, the question arises of the alienation of large numbers of animals, the father must be consulted. Not least of the sanctions operative here is the vigilant, not to say even jealous, watch kept by less fortunate half-brothers who are determined that the man's autonomy shall not deprive them of their rights and privileges. The family head, similarly, alone can give permission for the marriage of a daughter, even though she be living with her autonomous brother. There is no real chance of the brother secretly marrying her off, for not only is it extremely unlikely that her suitor and his kinsmen would agree to this, but the whole of the extended family, let alone the father and half-brothers, would descend on him in fury and indignation. Such an attempt—really unthinkable to Turkana—would imply an act of attempted secession from his extended family. Receipt and distribution of bridewealth is the concern primarily of the family head, as too is the proper per-

---

[1] This is also the cultural ideal amongst the Masai. Cf. Fosbrooke, H. A., 'An administrative survey of the Masai social system', *Tanganyika Notes and Records*, No. 26, December 1948, p. 43.

formance of relevant parts of the marriage ceremonies. Again, if the autonomous son, or one of his dependants, becomes involved in a dispute, management of the affair should be left to the family head, especially if there is any question of serious compensation.

In brief, any matter which significantly affects the existence and future development of the family herds should remain under the authority of the family head. Some of the sanctions and practical considerations behind this situation have already been mentioned. Another sanction lies in the family head's ritual and supernatural powers over his children. For instance, he makes a wedding legally binding by his handing over the bridewealth, or alternatively by his receipt of it; but he also makes the union ritually binding by his essential participation in the lengthy process of marriage which transcends material and legal considerations.[1] Without his participation, that is without his full agreement to the marriage and all that entails, it is believed that the union would neither be stable nor fruitful—as great an affliction on son or daughter as Turkana can imagine. Besides this, however, Turkana believe that the family head, like all people in positions of authority, respect and high seniority, has the automatic support of the High God, *Akuj*,[2] and that therefore recalcitrant sons go in danger of supernatural retribution. In fact, I have never heard of a father who either ultimately refused to undertake ritual obligations in his son's interests or who sought specifically the active support of the High God; rather, in my own experience, the threat is used, or a rebellious son is reminded of his ritual dependence. Some informants have told me that they have known cases of open conflict, but I have not been able to check such accounts. Turkana have not a high regard for supernatural forces in the normal way and therefore these weapons in the father's hands might well prove illusory. They would seem to be secondary sanctions only and chiefly important as conventional rationalizations of traditional authority.

In any case, personal relations and the personalities of the men involved modify the situation considerably. By the time that even one son has achieved autonomy a father must be an old man, to some extent therefore relatively willing to allow his son a free hand

[1] See section on 'Marriage' in Chapter 8.
[2] Such supernatural support also appertains to the head of a house or of a whole extended family, to an age-set leader, war-leader and above all to a diviner. It is a privilege and power accruing to authority roles.

and to be influenced strongly by his son's opinions. Conversely, a son may be inclined to submit easily to his resolute old father. The wife-mother may act as a successful intermediary. As I have emphasized before, affections between father and son are commonly strong enough to produce co-operation in the face of tensions due to family structure, the difference in generation and the difficulties of scarce resources (i.e. the insufficiency of family herds to meet all demands).

In all these matters there is no external agency to regulate intra-family relations. This is part of the significance of the independence of a nuclear family. Although a nuclear family is part of the wider 'house' and of the extended family, it is in no way part of those groups in an over-all authoritarian structure. This will emerge more clearly in later analysis of the extended family and agnatic relations in general. Near agnates, especially brothers of the family head, might intervene as friendly arbiters where relations between father and adult son (or between half-brothers of the one nuclear family) are strained, but such intervention might too easily create dangerous dissension in the whole extended family. In any case a family head is jealous of his independence and unlikely to welcome what he would probably consider interference in his own affairs.

This individuality and independence of related agnatic kinsmen and families affords the clue to the fundamental sanction of the continued unity of a nuclear family. That sanction rests on the moral idea of the nature of the nuclear family and, exactly co-ordinate with it, of the ownership and use of stock. The whole structure of the group emerges out of the close physical, social and emotional bonds amongst a man, his wives and children, This independence of a man and his family causes an intensification of the internal integrity of the group in contrast, and this integrity is firmly welded to the ownership and use of the herds, without which the greater part of physical and social life would be impossible in this hard, semi-desert country, and which are embedded in the value system of the people.

It is intended to suggest the basic nature of the group, together with its inviolate unity, by the use of the term 'nuclear'. Thus, from the larger structural viewpoint the geographical dispersal of the family, as sons achieve autonomy, does not affect the status or, essentially, the composition of the group. There is a gradual change in the internal constitution, but this need not be too greatly emphasized, since by ecological necessity the nuclear family is typically never a single residential unit.

To summarize the argument thus far: the Turkana nuclear family is an independent, stock-owning group, composed of a man, his wives and unmarried daughters, his sons, and their wives and children. As head of the group and as legal owner of the herds, the man has ultimate authority over both people and stock. In contrast, and in pursuance of the ideal that the stock also belong to the family as a whole, allocation of animals is made to constituent yards —each a wife and her children—but certain reservations are made in the interests of the total group and the continuity of the herds. As with all important Turkana social relationships, family relations are closely bound up with stock and rights over them. Marriage is by far the most important occasion for the large-scale use of stock, and rights here are strictly regulated according to seniority. Primary tension emerges between father and son in competitive situations where the son gradually but inevitably decreases his father's power. On the whole, fathers no less than sons accept the ineluctable course whereby sons move gradually towards greater autonomy. However, whilst his father remains alive the son cannot altogether escape his authority, most particularly concerning affairs relating to the herds, both alienation and receipt of animals. Therefore whilst an adult married son may achieve a certain autonomy and establish his own homestead-unit, the essential moral and legal unity of the nuclear family persists until the father dies. This group is the stock-owning unit amongst the Turkana, and ownership is exercised and administered by the father in the name of his whole family. Fundamentally, a son cannot freely own and use stock whilst his father is alive.

APPENDIX

HOMESTEAD ORGANIZATION

The chief-homesteads of these eight men made up two adjacent primary neighbourhoods in the middle of the dry season 1948-49.

Head of Family	Chief-homestead	Secondary-homestead
	Nuclear Family plus Dependants	
IMANA (about 50 years old)	*Herdsmen:—* camels—sons 2 and 4 of wife 1. goats and ewes—son 3 of wife 1. young stock—Imana and young children. *Others:—*Imana, wife 1, wife 3, daughters 2 and 3 of wife 1.	Cattle Homestead I *Herdsmen:—* cattle—Karamajong pauper. sheep—young brother of wife 2. calves—son 1 of wife 2. *Others:—*wife 2, daughter 1 of wife 1, half-sister. Cattle Homestead II *Herdsmen:—* cattle—son 1 of wife 1. calves—herded with those of adjacent homestead. *Others:—*wife 4.
	Nuclear Family plus Dependants	
EGERU (about 40 years old)	*Herdsmen:—* camels—herded with those of Imana (see above). Egeru himself often went out with the herd. goats and ewes—young brother of wife 2. young stock—young children. *Others:—*Egeru (part time), wife 1, wife 3, daughter 1 of wife 1.	*Herdsmen:—* cattle—unmarried half-brother. sheep—younger half-brother, son 1 of wife 2. calves—son 1 of wife 1. *Others:—*Egeru (part time), wife 2.
	Nuclear Family plus House of Father's Junior Widow, plus Dependants	
ATHERKWUN (about 55 years old)	*Herdsmen:—* camels—sons 1 and 2 of wife 1. goats and ewes—sons 1 and 2 of wife 2. young stock—young children. *Others:—*Atherkwun, wife 1, wife 2, father's junior widow.	Cattle Homestead I *Herdsmen:—* cattle—brother of wife 1, young half-brother 2. sheep—young half-brother 3. calves—son 3 of wife 2. *Others:—*wife 3, concubine of brother-in-law, daughter 1 of wife 2. Cattle Homestead II *Herdsmen:—* cattle—younger unmarried half-brother 1.

Head of Family	Chief-homestead	Secondary-homestead
		calves—daughters.
		Others:—daughters 1 and 2 of wife 1, two half-sisters.

Joint Homesteads between Brothers-in-law

ATHAGAL (about 35 years old) CILA (about 40 years old)	*Herdsmen:*— goats and sheep—son 1 of wife 1 of Cila, son 1 of wife 1 of Athagal. young stock—young children. *Others:*—Cila and his wives 1 and 2, wife 1 of Athagal.	*Herdsmen:*— cattle—son 1 of wife 2 of Cila (Cila's eldest son). calves—son 2 of wife 2 of Cila, son 2 of wife 1 of Athagal. *Others:*—Athagal and his wife 2.

Autonomous Homestead-unit

LOPOLA (about 35 years old)	*Herdsmen:*— cattle—Lopola, and son 2. goats and sheep—son 1. young stock—wife.	No other homestead. This man had only recently become autonomous of his aged father and of his elder half-brother, and his herd was small.

Compound Family

AICOW (about 40 years old)	*Herdsmen:*— camels—young unmarried half-. brother. goats and sheep—son 1. young stock—young children. *Others:*—Aicow, wife, father's widow.	*Herdsmen:*— cattle—sister's son (Aicow's sister was a concubine and thus he was legal father to her son). calves—daughters 1 and 2, two half-sisters.
LONGOMO (about 35 years old)	*Herdsmen:*— goats and sheep—wife's half-brother, own half-brother. kids and lambs—younger half-brother. *Others:*—Longomo (part time), wife, father's widow.	*Herdsmen:*— cattle—younger unmarried brother. camels—younger half-brother, Longomo (part time). *Others:*—concubine.

Nuclear Family

LONGOR (about 55 years old)	*Herdsmen:*— camels—son 2 of wife 1. goats and sheep—son 1 of wife 2. young stock—young children. *Others:*—Longor, wife 1, wife 2, wife 4.	*Herdsmen:*— cattle—son 1 of wife 1. calves—daughters. *Others:*—Wife 3, daughter 1 of wife 1, daughter 1 of wife 2.

N.B. Very young children (i.e. under the age of at least five years) and old women are omitted here since they did not form part of the normal labour of the families. From the age of about four, boys would go out with an older brother, but this was more for the company than for serious work.

Apart from the particular cases noted above, the adult men, heads of families, frequently went out to the pastures during part of the day, and in this area the men had to be ready to go off to drive away or kill marauding hyena. (In some pasturelands, at least one adult man has to be with a group of grazing herds in order to protect them from wild animals.)

In addition to their normal domestic and watering tasks, both wives and girls often lent a hand in looking after young stock, and even occasionally the main herds also.

CHAPTER SIX

FAMILY AND PROPERTY IN TURKANALAND

(b) THE EXTENDED FAMILY

Introduction

As amongst the Jie, the extended family in Turkanaland is based upon a shallow agnatic descent group whose senior males usually have a common grandfather; but occasionally the founder-ancestor is a great-grandfather and not infrequently only a father. The wives of the male members are specially included, whilst sisters and daughters leave at marriage. Unlike Jie, however, the Turkana extended family is neither a residential nor an economic and pastoral grouping. Over the years members move in different nomadic courses and not even the conventional wet- and dry-season pastures are the same for most of them. At times, some of them may be fairly near together, at other times they are likely to be many miles apart, scarcely cognizant of each other's movements and activities. Not only does membership of the extended family afford little restriction upon the pastoral organization of the Turkana, but, as we shall see later, the type of intra-family relations that exist serve largely to keep close agnates geographically apart from each other by reason of the social and psychological tensions that are so often involved, and because geographical separation emphasizes legal independence. It is a common occurrence that on such occasions as marriage or funerals, close agnates come from their own homesteads as much as thirty or forty miles away.

There are two distinct but interrelated organizational principles operative in the internal structure of the Turkana extended family. One concerns *awi*—'family'—the other concerns *ekal*—'house'.

Awi is literally the Turkana word for a physical homestead. By extension it also means any kind of 'family'—that is, for present purposes, an agnatic group descended from one man, but always including the wives of the men involved. Within the extended family

150

there are three grades of *ngawie*, or 'families'. First, there are the *nuclear families* of the current senior adult men, each consisting of a man, his wives, sons and their wives and children, and unmarried daughters. Secondly, there are *compound families* based on the deceased fathers of the present senior adults, each consisting of the group of nuclear families of the sons of the founder. Thirdly, there is the *grand family* based on the grandfather of the present senior adults and consisting of the group of compound families of the sons of the founder. At each level, only living people comprise the group, but the point of demarcation, or the position of the founder, makes the family more or less inclusive.

Ekal is literally the word for a wife's day-hut and occasionally also the area around each hut. By extension it also means any kind of 'house'—that is, an agnatic group descended from one woman, but always including the wives of the men involved. Within the extended family there are three grades of *ngkalie* or 'house'. First, there are *yards*, consisting of each wife of the head of a nuclear family together with her children. Secondly, there are *houses* proper, consisting each of a set of full-brothers whose father is dead, together with their wives and children, their mother, if she is alive, and their unmarried sisters. Thirdly, there are *house-lines*, consisting each of the agnatic descendants of a grandmother together with their wives, or based (in other words) upon a set of deceased full-brothers. The dominant element involved in the concept of a 'house' is the grouping together of full-brothers and their descendants.

The theoretical pattern of the extended family subdivided into ascending orders of houses and families is given diagrammatically in Figure 13. It will be seen that whereas any 'house' is a section of the inclusive 'family' of the next senior generation, a 'family' is a section of the inclusive house of the same generation. This is a direct result of the dynamics of family development in the society; for a house proper is the unit of inheritance—that is, the domestic stock are inherited from a father by sets of his sons as determined by maternal affiliation and not primarily by individual sons. However, the house becomes divided up as each brother eventually achieves independence with his own nuclear family and his own share of the common herd. In turn each nuclear family is internally differentiated into yards, which do not, however, include the family head, for they are new divisions of a succeeding generation and will in turn become houses proper at his death.

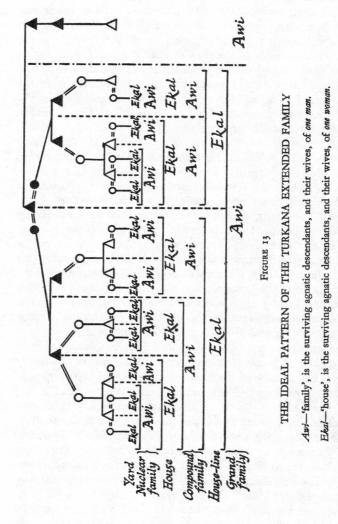

FIGURE 13

THE IDEAL PATTERN OF THE TURKANA EXTENDED FAMILY

Awi—'family', is the surviving agnatic descendants, and their wives, of *one man*.

Ekal—'house', is the surviving agnatic descendants, and their wives, of *one woman*.

Ideally the *extended family* is also a grand-family, but as it emerges in actual maintained social relations the extended family may not wholly coincide with a specific genealogical unit. One or more houses or families may be excluded by prolonged geographical separation. If the grand-family of the grandfather's brother is involved, not all of its members will be included in the field of actual relations.

FAMILY AND PROPERTY IN TURKANALAND

Either type of subordinate section, at whatever level, is termed a 'gateway', *ekidor*, of the larger inclusive group. *Ekidor* means literally the gateway to a homestead through which stock are driven to and from the kraals. It obtains its extended meaning by reason of the fact that if two parallel sections—'family' or 'house'—inhabit the same homestead, each has its own gateway through which, and only which, its herds are driven. It is a practical measure to prevent the mingling of separate herds and becomes a symbol of independence.

It is important to note that the terminology used here has a specific reference to the current senior adult males of the extended family. They themselves are founders and heads of existing nuclear families, the smallest independent groups. Yards are subordinate groups which may attain a degree of autonomy but which cannot realize independence whilst the head of the nuclear family is alive. Thus a house posits that its senior male members' father is dead. Similarly the compound family is a grouping of such houses.

Ideally the extended family comprises a grand family; Turkana always speak of their own agnatic groups as 'the children of a grand-father'. In practice the precise boundaries are not necessarily clearly marked, nor do they always correspond with the formal limits of any set genealogical group. The effective extended family may comprise only a single house, or it may comprise a grand family, or the whole or part of any genealogical section. This is the group within which active relations, rights and obligations persist, although outside it there may exist other people related by known agnatic ties. The extended family is a pragmatically defined group which can only be discovered by a knowledge of existing relations at a given time. Its internal structure is articulated at levels of 'houses' and 'families', but these, like the whole group, seldom engage in corporate activities.

It is convenient at this point to give some illustrations of the few corporate activities which do occur in connection with the extended family and its sub-sections. Mortuary ceremonies provide some clear examples because they necessitate the assembly of otherwise widely dispersed members.[1] Immediately after any person dies (except a

[1] Mortuary ceremonies arranged on the same principles as in Turkanaland are of minor importance in Jieland, where perhaps the close, residential groups necessitate less reaffirmation of kinship bonds at times of death. There can be no doubt of the emotional and social value of these ceremonies to the Turkana, and they provide a ritual sanction for the assembly of the group at these times when there must be a re-alignment of relationships.

small baby), all the members of his (or her) house should assemble to perform a purificatory ceremony (*tokronore*) to rid them and their herds of the taint of death. When the head of a nuclear family dies the whole extended family is involved in *tokronore*. Other kin, friends and neighbours, including married sisters and daughters, come to condole with the living, but they take no part in funeral mourning. The ceremonial feast, as with all Turkana feasts, is a public one, and no man can be denied; but the extended family retire alone into the homestead for the actual ritual performance. The following wet season—or sometimes two or three wet seasons later —there is a second ceremony (*topunyare*) at the homestead of the deceased's eldest son. This is strictly compulsory on all family heads and all other males not essentially required for herding-work at the time, whilst most of the womenfolk assemble also. In addition, all the cattle of the component nuclear families (not goats or camels) must be assembled and ritually kraaled and herded as a single herd. Until this ceremony is completed there is an absolute ban on the use of stock for social purposes, e.g. marriage, ritual, gifts, etc. The absence of a man and his herd of cattle is a symbol of his forfeiture of formal membership of the extended family. Turkana say that in the event of quarrels and a general deterioration of relations men will refuse to attend the ceremony, thereby making known that they no longer consider themselves members of the group nor feel themselves bound by obligations in reference to kinship. I know of no actual examples, though I have recorded an occasion when this sort of secession was threatened, much to the concern of the rest of the group, who made considerable efforts, successfully as it happened, to persuade the recalcitrant man to participate. It appeared that he was in fact aiming at the settlement of a grievance in this manner. More commonly, however, men do not attend because they live too far away, and because active, practical relations have atrophied, or because genealogical links have become so indirect and attenuated that ritual interdependence and mutual rights, interests and affections have ceased to matter.

Other instances of corporate action may be mentioned briefly. At any time that a person is seriously ill or in ritual danger the threat is not confined to him (or her) alone, nor yet even only to his nuclear family, but is thought to extend to all members of his house. If certain ritual is prescribed by a diviner, almost invariably it is prescribed for the whole house, both to make it efficacious for the sufferer and ward off contagion. A wife whose property has been damaged or destroyed by fire must be ritually protected against the potential danger to herself, and in company with members of her house she is anointed with the stomach contents of a bull-calf.

If a man is to marry, he himself is almost entirely responsible for the collection of the bridewealth from his range of kinsman; but only the head of the house can ceremonially hand over the animals to the bride's people and he must lead much of the ritual performance involved. He and other agnates should join in the ritual to affirm the marriage and make it prosper. To make the ritual slaughter of any animal efficacious ideally requires the participation of the head of the house. Compensation payment requires that an offender collects animals from his kin and friends and the injured party shares them with his associates. Yet both men require the assistance of their family heads to make the transaction binding and successful. At funeral ceremonies the head of the extended family and other members arrange and participate in the ritual side of the event, but the inheritance discussions concern only the sons of the dead man. In each case, and many others besides, the actual use and disposal of stock are the concern primarily, if not wholly, of the chief participants. The various sections and the total extended family, with the seniormost men as leaders, emerge in corporate activity only in connection with the social milieu of the event in hand, with its ritual success and spiritual significance. A man has no right to interfere into the disposition and use of an agnate's stock—that is the criterion of independence. He has, however, rights to participate in, even to lead, the accompanying ceremonial activities. In so far as we are investigating the connections between kinship and property rights, the corporate nature of agnatic groups is of secondary importance.

These kinds of ceremonial activities mainly occur at the critical times of social life and individual development. They occur relatively infrequently. For the rest of the time agnatic relations tend to be dormant, being re-activated as occasion demands. In ordinary daily life, most or even all adult men of the group maintain an independence of each other, co-operating and living with temporary neighbours and intermittently with other kinsfolk. At these times, quantitatively by far the larger portion of life, the various agnatic groups remain something of a mental scheme, a standard of action rather than action itself. In conclusion, I repeat that the extended family is not a fixed genealogical unit but must be defined pragmatically in each case. The lines of definition, as Turkana themselves give them, are primarily drawn by the limits of co-operation and assistance in stock transactions such as bridewealth, compensation payments, etc. A secondary but nevertheless, by implication, critical criterion is participation in the assembly at the second funeral ceremony of an independent member of the group.

The Metamorphosis of the Nuclear Family—Inheritance

With the death of the father the authoritarian unity of his nuclear family ceases, and it breaks down into a number of independent groups. These groups together still comprise the 'family', *awi*, of the father, but this, in the terminology used in the present account, is a 'compound family'. The constituent groups are of two kinds: firstly there are the 'houses', each comprising a set of full-brothers with their wives and children—these are the primary units of inheritance; secondly there are, or in due course will be, the nuclear families of each independent son.

The principles of inheritance are similar to those already described when dealing with the Jie house. At the father's death, each yard becomes an independent house and takes its former allocation of stock as its own herds. This provokes little difficulty, for however mixed up the various allocations have been for pastoral and economic purposes, everyone is well aware of the precise attachment of each animal. It must be emphasized that problems of inheritance do not necessarily or even perhaps usually become important as determinants of future relations. It is in the succeeding years that the pattern of agnatic relations is established in the loose association of the new compound family. Sometimes, however, the distribution of the 'residual herd' may raise difficulties. Basically this should be divided up (as in Jieland) so that shares decrease inversely to the seniority of the houses. A straightforward case occurred at the death of Towot, a wealthy old man. There were four emergent houses, and five married sons amongst the three seniormost.[1] The residual herd had about fifteen large stock and a small flock of goats and sheep. Only small shares were taken by these three houses; the bulk of the animals went to the junior house, whose senior man was only seventeen years old and still uninitiated. In Turkana law the rights

[1] There were two married sons in the senior house, two in the second and one in the third.

of the junior house were quite clear. A different situation arose at the death of Lokrien. Discussion continued for many days, centring chiefly on the claim of the senior man of the second house, who, as yet unmarried, demanded a large share of the 'residual herd', a portion of which the senior man of the senior house had formerly taken when he achieved autonomy in the lifetime of their father. This demand was based on the fact that the man was the most senior, unmarried son; he claimed the stock in order that he might marry at the earliest opportunity. He was opposed not only by the eldest son and his full-brothers (another of whom was married) but also by the men of the third house who were unmarried and now claimed the privileges of their junior status. So severe was the disagreement that a fight occurred at one stage, though this was quickly stopped by other members of the extended family who were present. Eventually the senior house surrendered a few, but not all, of the animals demanded by the second house, but the junior house took the larger share of the 'residual herd'. Relations became so strained, however, that the men of the most senior house left before the end of the prescribed month, threatening not to make any contribution to the bridewealth of their half-brother.[1]

There is a certain amount of scope for dispute also in the details of the division of the 'residual herd' even when the principles of settlement have been agreed on, for that herd may sometimes contain especially valuable animals, such as milch cattle or camels, fine bulls or rams, and so on. No general rule can be given for such circumstances, for eventual agreement appears to be reached through a procession of bargaining between the half-brothers. It should be noted that in this, as in all disputes about inheritance, discussion invariably takes place on an inter-house basis. The final distribution and use of stock inside any one house is entirely a matter to be settled between the full-brothers, being no concern of the men of other houses.

At the father's death his sons must immediately assemble at the old chief-homestead for the first mortuary ceremony,[2] which is preceded by the inheritance discussions. The ideal of continued solidarity is expressed and practical discussions are also held

---

[1] Some two years later the senior man of the second house did marry, and he obtained two cattle from the senior house, that is, rather fewer than is the normal contribution in such cases.

[2] See p. 154.

concerning the immediate reorganization of the group. Turkana are aware of the newly released tendencies for the compound family to split up, and they accept the fact that sometimes half-brothers might attempt to avoid the inheritance discussions by remaining absent and hoping, by a *fait accompli*, to hold on to more than their fair share of the stock. Ideally not only all the members of the group come together—and they should remain at or near the father's homestead for at least one month—but also all the stock should be driven in. In this way, not only are inheritance discussions completed at one time but the actual physical distribution of the animals can be made. As one informant put it, 'Words are all right, we want animals as well. Who knows if a half-brother will remember the words afterwards. It is good to see the stock and to take them straight away.' This grand assembly of stock can, however, only occur when the father dies in an area where it is practicable for all varieties of animals to live. When Epeyo died in the wet season, though he was living at his goat homestead, there were available grasslands near by for the family cattle. Consequently all of both the humans and stock were able to assemble. The eldest son came with his goats from some fifteen miles to the south, and his cattle were brought in by his younger brother from his brother-in-law's homestead elsewhere. The eldest son of Epeyo's second wife drove in all his stock, which had been kraaled in a single homestead about ten miles to the north. The remainder of the cattle herd had been only about five miles away and it was allowed to remain there, it being considered near enough for practical purposes. This assembly caused little difficulty. On the other hand, when Lokrien died in the dry season, his chief-homestead was at least twenty miles from the nearest grasslands and his cattle homestead was rather more distant. His eldest (autonomous) son had some cattle at an affine's homestead equally far away. At that time the cattle could not be shifted, and moreover youths and boys had to be left with them for herding and watering work. All the adult members of Lokrien's family assembled and brought with them the goat and camel herds. Ritual and social requirements had perforce to be subservient to pastoral necessities. Afterwards goats were killed for the absent herdsmen at their respective homesteads, where the necessary ritual anointing was carried out.

Other members of the extended family have no claim whatsoever upon the stock of the dead man, though they assemble for the mortuary ceremonies. Here again we can see the identity and independence of the (deceased) man's family and his herds clearly expressed.

The House

Ideally a set of full-brothers maintains a strong sense of corporate unity and loyalty which is in part at least expressed and thereby strengthened in the structural opposition to parallel sets of half-brothers, with whom they comprise the compound family. The eldest brother becomes head of the house. It is he who represents the group at inheritance discussions and who specifically takes over the house's portion of the herds. He may already be married, and may even have become already autonomous. In such a case he is joined by the rest of the house (including the mother) at his homestead. In any event there is a general and strong tendency for a new house to establish its own independent homestead as soon as possible; but at least until the time of the marriage of the eldest brother the empirical norm is that a house remains allied to one or more of its fellows which may already be headed by a married man. This does not affect the true status of the house, but does, however, temporarily limit the full-brothers' exercise of all their potential rights. In such cases the marriage of the eldest brother is speeded up, for in addition to this desire to independence the senior man is now controller of the house's herds and he himself can therefore initiate bridewealth negotiations. Here, however, legal property-owning independence is markedly tempered by the need for assistance from the other houses, for it is unlikely that at this stage a man can afford to marry without contributions of stock from his half-brothers. His desire for marriage at this early stage must therefore be regulated by common consideration of the whole range of sons of the dead father.

Sooner or later, however, a house leaves its fellows and establishes its own homesteads and its own pastoral-nomadic routine and becomes economically self-sufficient. This act, for the Turkana, is the supreme expression of a genuine legal independence. At this time the house is a quasi-nuclear family—a single stock-owning unit, with the conventional two homesteads under the authority of its head. This man, the eldest brother, is for the time being allowed prime authority by virtue of the status of birth, but he only exercises that power in the name of the whole group of brothers of which he is but one. At first the energies of the brothers are chiefly directed at the goal of separation from their half-brothers; but no sooner has this been achieved than the unity of the house begins to be threatened as each successive brother first seeks to marry and thereafter to become independent himself. Whereas the son of a living father could only achieve a degree of autonomy, a younger brother aims quite consciously at complete independence from his elder brother. A nuclear family has an inviolate unity; a house has not that degree of unity because, unlike the nuclear family, it is not compulsorily kept together by the single authority of one man over his dependants by virtue both of paternity and his ownership of the herds. A house is an association of equals—subject to a certain reservation on account of seniority—and there appear to be no overriding reasons why they should make efforts to retain their unity, whilst there is a strong cultural convention amongst the Turkana which sets great store on individualism. The house is, as it were, but a holding unit, a temporary stage between the individual ownership of a man and that of each of his sons. Ultimately, in Turkana conceptions, property in animals is held only by a single man, who confers his ownership upon his nuclear family—his wives and children. In the end a man owes no legal property obligations to his full-brothers and half-brothers, although he accepts a certain fluid liability in respect both of near kinship and reciprocity. The whole structure of the house, and indeed of the compound family and the extended family, can be traced to this conception of ownership amongst the Turkana. Having accepted this axiom of individualism, the cleavages in agnatic kin groups can readily be understood.

At first younger brothers are content to follow the lead of the eldest, and to a considerable degree they are willing to accept his authority. On the other hand the younger brothers do not forfeit their rights in the herds, most especially in the matter of bridewealth. It is a strict rule that marriage occurs in order of seniority, and therefore the eldest cannot refuse the claims of his juniors in order, himself, to marry a second time. That is, he has not the power that a man has over his sons. Because of his position as the eldest, he formally holds the stock in the name of the whole house; and therefore his agreement to his brother's marriage must be obtained, and in fact only he can properly hand over the bridewealth to the bride's kinsmen. He cannot refuse the stock to his brother without real justification, such as the inadequacy of the herds, and even here he acts only as spokesman of common opinion. He merely operates as a focus of action in connection with the use of the herds and in general with all things affecting the group. The herds of the house are looked upon as the joint property of all the brothers, in which, subject to seniority, each has equal rights. The authority of the eldest brother comes in reality from his superior seniority and not from his ownership of the herds. This seniority affords him a certain control and confers upon him certain ritual prerogatives which allow him to represent the total group.

Nevertheless, this does not mean that there is always complete accord between full-brothers in this matter. Although the senior cannot marry a second time, yet his estimate of the adequacy of the herds for marriage may not agree with that of his junior who is waiting to marry. The latter is always, perhaps not unnaturally, more willing to deplete the herds and suffer economic privation thereafter than is the senior. His junior's marriage will also materially affect the size and frequency of gifts and in general the use of stock by the senior. It is a question of the optimum use of relatively scarce resources, in which the two men's valuations do not coincide. At this stage the seeds of contention are first sown. They do not necessarily always continue to grow, of course. It is nevertheless a critical point in the development of fraternal relations, and the situation is repeated each time the question of the marriage of an unmarried brother crops up. Each successive time it occurs it becomes more complicated, since the eldest brother's attitudes tend to a certain extent to be reinforced by those of his juniors who are already married. Each married brother not only tends to be against depletion of the herds in general, but himself wishes to detach a portion of them with a view to achieving his own independence as head of a nuclear family.

Immediately following the marriage of a younger brother the unity of the house is not affected, but the stage begins to be set for the next step, just as it is with a married man in a nuclear family. A process is begun whose recognized goal is ultimate and complete independence. This is achieved by geographical separation and division of the herds. Such separation is an expression of and the practical means towards a man's independence, together with the administration of his own share of the herds over which he obtains prime control. He is no longer subject to superior authority in the use and disposal of his stock. One informant summed it up: 'Your father is not like your brother. Your father possessed all the stock, absolutely; your brother possesses only his own.'

At first, however, it is not possible for the younger man to move away, for sheer economic reasons. Because of his marriage, the house's herds will have been depleted and there are unlikely to be sufficient stock to allow of division which would provide a working herd for his homestead. In any case he is probably not yet able to obtain sufficient labour for the needs of a separate nuclear family. Conventionally, as in the case of a married son, Turkana say that a married brother should wait until his oldest son can begin to herd goats. This means a matter of at least five to six years after marriage before a man can hope to establish his own nuclear family in its own homesteads; but of course no man need invariably depend only upon his own children for labour. He can attract younger, unmarried men (his junior brothers, cousins or other kinsmen); or he may ally himself with some other man in the same situation so that the two together produce an adequate labour supply, or he may ally himself to a kinsman already independent through whose assistance he can obtain his own independence of his full-brothers. In this connection his close affinal kin and to a lesser degree his close maternal kin are important.

This aim of a younger brother to achieve his full independence may cause difficulties, and tension may arise which will leave its mark on future fraternal relationships. The independence of the younger man necessitates a division of the herds and reduces the authority and wealth potential of the elder. Thereafter the younger man will control his own portion of the animals and will make his own decisions regarding the use and disposal of them, the degree to which he assists his brothers and the shares he allows them of the in-payments which he receives. He does not ignore the conventional standards of mutual assistance between brothers, but there is a range in the numbers of stock that may be given or demanded, within which a good deal of play is possible. In any case, rights between brothers are now largely directed by the conception of reciprocity and not merely outright obligation. The eldest brother is most particularly concerned, for it is to his direct interest in many ways to maintain the unity of the house of which he is head. His chances of marrying again are higher so long as the herds are undivided. Once a younger brother moves away he cannot be compelled to give more animals than he feels he can afford—almost always rather less than the older brother would have hitherto been able to take. The herds are now providing for two homestead-units and the demands upon animal resources are therefore greater; the surplus left for bridewealth and other external social transactions is smaller. Whilst both brothers appreciate this, the younger (the secessionist) feels the loss is less important than the achievement of his new status. The separation of the younger man also affects the labour supply of the elder's homesteads, for the former is likely to take one or more younger brothers and sisters, and possibly also the mother.[1] The senior man may find some difficulty in maintaining his former homesteads and his standard of living. At any rate his position in many ways is likely to be less favourable, and for that reason he may oppose the movement of his juniors or delay it as long as he can. The procrastination and obstructionism of an eldest brother are almost proverbial amongst the Turkana; they are, at the very least, a source of irritation to younger men, and they are potential causes of deeper and more durable friction which can develop into rivalry and antagonism. Practically from the time of marriage of the younger brother, fraternal unity and affection tend to fall away before an increasing tension. Each man realizes the inevitability of physical and legal separation—the elder wishes to delay it, whilst the younger desires to accelerate it.

The dispersal of a house is a lengthy process, especially if there are several brothers and the herds are about average size. Even under favourable conditions a brother cannot expect to move away for a year or two at least, and, if the herds are successively depleted by marriages of more junior men, secession becomes even more difficult. The opposition of the elder man is added to by those who still remain unmarried. If a house consists of only two brothers, a cleavage is relatively simple in due course, the only question that remains is exactly when and in what manner it should occur. If the house is larger, secession is delayed and often takes the form of a dichotomous cleavage and the parts are headed by the eldest and second brothers respectively, younger brothers and sisters attaching themselves to one or the other. The division of the herds may occasion some trouble, for the situation may be less clear cut than it is between houses at the time of inheritance. To take the simple case of a house of only two brothers, who are of course at this stage both married with children: each man's wife has an allocation of stock which is regarded as the nucleus of her husband's herd. The 'residual' herd is reduced to a minimum and even disappears altogether by an

---

[1] The mother should always live with her youngest son; if he is in the mountains at the secondary-homestead, she usually remains at the corresponding chief-homestead.

equal division. Each in-payment is formally divided up roughly equally,[1] e.g. a sister's bridewealth. When the younger brother secedes there remains little difficulty, for each has equal rights and here seniority scarcely counts, except in so far as the older man may have more children and therefore a greater claim on their behalf. Where there are other younger brothers, the 'residual herd' will have been retained, and in this, man for man, they have more or less equal rights. Seniority does not affect this particular issue, for it is held that the order of marriage by that ranking will continue and therefore the most senior unmarried man will be the first to claim contributions from all his other brothers.

There are also certain ecological factors operating in the dispersion of the house which do not necessarily relate to the quality of fraternal relations. Owing to the poverty of vegetation and the vagaries of rainfall there is both an optimum size to the herds to be maintained at a single homestead and the number of homesteads that can exist together in a neighbourhood. Overcrowding of stock only leads to the speedy exhaustion of pasture resources and a larger number of nomadic movements. Further, it is easier to move a single home-stead and a comparatively small herd than a group or a large herd. An important factor in the Turkana pastoral system is the flexibility of nomadic routines, and this comes directly from the principles of individual movement according to personal choice and opinion. Turkana dislike to cede their freedom of action for the doubtful value of membership of a fixed group. Thus local groupings of homesteads are almost always impermanent. A man does not wish to become tied to any territorial group, and a nomadic band based on agnatic kinship is but one possible form of this. Personal susceptibilities apart, as they see it, the total herds of a group of related men are best cared for by their dispersal over the country, each unit taking advantage of local conditions and the whole not jeopardized by any single calamity. Disease, though not rife in Turkanaland, is always a potential danger, but at least dispersed herds are unlikely to be affected simultaneously. Only a generation ago the dangers of raiding existed, and that has left its mark still on the present system of dispersal. Disastrous dry seasons are a permanent threat, and inadequacy of vegetation in local regions kills off stock nearly every

[1] It is not easy to balance a cow against a bull-camel nor a number of fat goats against a poor ox. There must be a good deal of give and take on all sides through bargain and compromise.

year. If herds are kept in different regions this danger can at least be mitigated. To summarize remarks of informants on this question: poverty of pastures will not allow large congregations of people and herds without causing too large a number of movements; on the other hand it is preferable to maintain the highest mobility and pastoral flexibility by having small, easily manageable units without fixed ties to each other in the choice of pastures. This must be set against the background that there are no specific rights in pasture-land anywhere, a principle which, I believe, was originally brought from another country with a different environment.[1]

Another factor leading to the dispersion of a house is the principle that where tensions exist between individuals, for whatever reason, it is best to relieve them by geographical separation, when, if they do not gradually die down, they will at least necessarily be reduced. To take examples outside the present point under discussion, if two co-wives habitually quarrel, one of them will go to live in the other homestead of the same nuclear family; at another level, if two men quarrel and bad relations persist, then one or both will shift his homestead elsewhere. Such practical arrangements are not difficult in Turkanaland, where on the one hand each family maintains at least two homesteads, and on the other where mobility is high. In a situation such as the division of the herds of a house, the order of secondary marriages and the extent of obligations of assistance, potential sources of difficulty are plentiful. However altruistic brothers may be towards each other, there are genuine problems which are reducible to the question of the distribution of scarce resources. In ordinary life men are frequently inclined to be selfish, unappreciative of the needs and desires of others and jealous of their superior fortunes. There are, as we have seen, certain mechanisms for the control of conflict and for the equitable apportionment of stock amongst various users and uses; they are not wholly efficient, and even if they were improved it is extremely doubtful if they could be made entirely satisfactory unless demands are reduced to the level of practical supply. Without .considering possible ideal arrange-ments, it can be appreciated that the Turkana are presented with a difficult situation in which tensions and rivalries are almost bound to occur. If brothers continue to live close together, those tensions are likely to be exacerbated; it is better, and the native will say this, that brothers live apart when there is less chance of trouble being per-

---

[1] I.e. from the Jie country. I shall refer to this point in Chapter 9.

petuated. After the problem of the divisions of herds has been settled in whatever way, each brother goes his own way, being his own master, and primarily dependent upon his own efforts and achievements.[1]

Despite the indigenous mechanisms to reduce tensions between brothers, there are cases where such men become no less than enemies between whom co-operation almost or completely ceases. Usually, it would seem, the greatest animosity lies between a brother and one or more of his juniors—as between successive juniors there appears to be less antagonism. The demands and finally the secession of each junior brother appear as threats to the authority, wealth and development of the eldest, who may strongly oppose the final break in each case, and attempt afterwards to maintain a degree of authority unacceptable to and unenforceable upon the others. In some extreme, but nevertheless not entirely rare, cases tensions develop to the state of producing fratricide. Almost every informant with whom I discussed the general situation could tell me of at least one case of fratricide that he knew of, and always as far as I could gather, the offender was the eldest brother.[2] In one such case, Pedo, the eldest brother, had been bitterly opposed to the secession of the second brother, Angole, who had in fact 'taken the law into his own hands' and simply seized what he believed to be his share of the stock. With him went the third brother, the mother and at least one sister. Some time later this sister married and Pedo demanded what the others considered to be an unduly large share of the bridewealth, and he backed this up with the threat of a ritual invocation to the High God to punish them. Angole would not meet his full demand, and in this was supported by his younger brother, who, as yet unmarried, was apparently hoping to use most of the in-payment for his own bridewealth. Following severe quarrelling, Pedo killed both of his brothers and seized the whole of the stock as sole owner, for there were no other children of his mother left.[3] In another case, the

[1] There are clearly also specific psychological factors involved in this situation which cannot be dealt with in this account.

[2] It was not easy to obtain details of occurrences of fratricide, for people were unwilling to disclose to a European what they knew the Government regarded as indictable murder. The normal suspicions of the Turkana were more than ever acute concerning such matters.

[3] Unfortunately I failed to enquire what happened to Angole's wife and children. Pedo was regarded with a certain awe by his neighbours as a very fierce person. When I knew him, many years after these events, he was a wealthy and locally influential man. It is clear that not the whole of the causes of the antagonism and final quarrel were due only to him.

eldest brother demanded what was considered an unduly large share of the bridewealth of his junior's daughter. In the subsequent quarrel the junior man was killed, and afterwards his stock were taken by the murderer. In these cases there was of course no possibility of judicial action against the murderer, for in the indigenous legal system it was no one's concern to initiate action. In the case of Pedo, there were not even half-brothers; but in any case, as informants told me, it was purely an affair of the house. Normally a victim of murder would be avenged by his closest kinsmen, his full-brothers even possibly against his other close agnates, but in fratricide the victim is left without a champion.

In such extreme cases it would seem—for I have not personal, first-hand records in any instance—that although fratricide was the final result of severe and prolonged tension, rivalry and antagonism, yet the immediate cause is a bitter quarrel when murder is done in the heat of the moment. There is no evidence of a deliberate plan by a man to get rid of his brother. It cannot be said that fratricide is an institutionalized procedure amongst the Turkana, for the people themselves regard it as exceptional and evil.[1] Nevertheless, the fact that it does occasionally occur illustrates the extreme to which antagonism may reach; and it will be remembered that ideally the house is supposed to be the group of greatest unity. It is suggested that the very closeness of the relationship between full-brothers, coupled with the difficulty of the division and use of stock, is the principal cause. Murder is rare in Turkanaland in any case, but I have not been able to record a case of a man who killed his half-brother or paternal cousin. As we have seen, the problem of inheritance is not usually very great, and thereafter half-brothers can be as independent of one another as they wish. In the second case of fratricide noted above, both of the brothers must have been about middle-age at the time, for the younger had a daughter of marriageable age. This supported my informants' evidence, which presented a picture of antagonism over many years. It has been mentioned already that where a house's herds are relatively poor it may be many

---

[1] Whatever the relationship between the two men, murder is wholly condemned in Turkanaland. An expression of this attitude is that homicide is believed to prevent rain falling—perhaps the greatest disaster the Turkana can conceive of. Internecine fighting with intent to kill is virtually absent in this largely untouched society, and there is no reason to believe any other values held in previous generations, since this is a common sentiment throughout the tribes of the Karamojong Cluster. It was not, of course, considered murder to kill a member of another tribe.

years before brothers can achieve their independence; that is what had happened in this case.

I wish to reiterate, however, that fratricide is not the norm of intra-house relations nor has it any kind of moral, or even amoral, approval. The ideal remains that full-brothers are united in mutual interests and affection, and that ideal is more commonly reached than is the stage where fratricide might possibly occur. The norm in practice is of a range of warmth of affection, but nevertheless of mutual accommodation and continuing mutual interests and reciprocal assistance in many ways, including the giving of animals. Turkana men are brought up to the idea that younger brothers will eventually seek their independence and to some extent therefore elder brothers are prepared for the course of events. The dispersion of a house is not necessarily the result of, nor need it always create, bad relations between brothers. It is not uncommon that two or more full-brothers keep together for some years after they could have separated and gone their own ways. In such a case the younger man may make a token move to a new homestead a short distance away from the old one controlled by his elder. In this way he begins his own independent nuclear family and takes his portion of the herds. Later, after a normal pastoral move, the two brothers may build a joint homestead, but now each has his own sector with his own gateway (*ekidor*) and kraals for his stock. As Turkana put it, each nuclear family becomes an *ekidor* of the total house.[1] It is significant that the symbol of independence is the movement away from the old homestead, and it cannot be brought about by mere spatial reorganization of the old homestead.

On the other hand, my impression (supported by several well-known cases) is that where two full-brothers remain together for many years it is because of the dominance of one over the other by strength of character and force of will. Only a very few elderly men continue to live with or near to their full-brothers, and no one considers it necessarily laudable to do so.

Eventually, then, whatever the precise nature of relations between the brothers, a house breaks down into a number of independent nuclear families. Each brother has prime control over his own herds and is not legally subject to the authority or demands of the others. On the other hand, reciprocal rights between full-brothers are the strongest known to the Turkana. Whatever the degree of affection

[1] Cf. p. 153.

between brothers, they continue to depend on each other for very considerable assistance in stock affairs, for of all his stock-associates a man's brothers are the most important. Nevertheless, full-brothers, at this stage, are fundamentally stock-associates[1] and not co-members of a highly corporate group wherein rights and obligations are legally defined and prescribed. Further, a man's legitimate successors are his own sons and not his brothers, as we saw in the discussion of inheritance.

Magico-religious factors are not particularly important for the Turkana, being usually only secondary factors in social relationships.[2] The ritual interdependence of brothers is primarily a reflection of the basic kinship and property relations, though at any one time it may be important both for an individual and for the house as a group. A man should not normally undertake an important ceremony without the presence and co-operation of his full-brothers, and ritual leadership is allowed to the eldest. A man in danger of severe illness or ritual impurity (almost similar conditions) also puts his brothers and their families in danger, and communal action is required. Where geographical distance or unfriendly relations make such co-operation difficult, however, these requirements are often ignored, at least temporarily. On a slightly different level, it is chiefly a matter of respect and an expression of unity that the eldest brother should ceremonially hand over the bridewealth when a man of the house marries, for it can be, and sometimes is, done without him. Fundamentally the head of a nuclear family can use and dispose of his stock as he desires, irrespective of the wishes and feelings of any other man, including his full-brothers. The house normally begins as a quasi-nuclear family on the death of the father, communally owning and using herds in distinct independence of those of half-brothers. It gradually ceases to be a residential, economic and pastoral unit, and exists specifically as a complex of fraternal relations, chief elements of which are reciprocal rights over stock.

The Compound Family

In this account so far we have considered the basic nuclear family, and following its breakdown we have isolated the house in order to see the nature of its unity and development and therefore the nature of stock-ownership. But the house is not isolated in this way in real

---

[1] See Chapter 7.
[2] Cf. *Survey of the Turkana*, chapter 20, pp. 229-30, and *passim*.

life, for in the first place it exists within the system of the compound family, the structural successor to the father's nuclear family; and secondly, both house and compound family are contained within the wider sphere of the total extended family. Continuing this diachronic study, I intend in this section to examine the constitution and internal relations of the compound family, and then the whole agnatic complex will be brought together in a study of the extended family.

First we must return to the death of the father and the breakdown of the old nuclear family. Until this time there was compulsory co-operation and assistance in stock affairs, and, apart from the relatively few cases of autonomous sons, there was a unity of purpose in the pastoral, economic and nomadic life. All this was maintained through the superior authority of the father. Now there is no longer any overriding authority and the legal necessities of unity are gone. Relations between half-brothers turn on a different factor—the mutual convenience and moral idea of co-operation between independent groups. For the moment we may regard each house as a single, unitary group which has inherited certain herds.

The immediate pattern of the new compound family follows from the state of development which the old nuclear family had reached. If the father was wealthy and died in his old age, the eldest son of each house might already be married and therefore it is possible for each group to go its own way, to establish its own homesteads and herds and pastoral routine, and in short to become self-sufficient groups headed by fully adult men. For instance, at Epeyo's death, Loporoboi and Lopola, the senior sons of the two houses, were already autonomous. After the final division of the herds each man returned to his former homestead together with the whole of his stock, and accompanied by his brothers and sisters. This was the most straightforward case that I recorded, and there was a minimum of reorganization. The old chief-homestead and secondary-homestead were 'wound up' and the new compound family emerged as a fairly cohesive group of two integrated houses.[1]

More usually, however, it is not the case that each house has a married son, and soon may not even contain an adult man at all. Two possibilities are open here. One is that immature houses (not headed by a married man) remain attached to a more senior house

[1] This case occurred near the end of my field-work in Turkanaland and therefore I was unable to record the subsequent development of relations between the two houses.

which is itself self-sufficient. If there are no married sons at all—and that has been seen to be not uncommon[1]—the eldest, if at all possible, marries as soon as the post-mortuary taboos are lifted. A common pattern of the early compound family is that in which the old homestead and pastoral organization are retained under the leadership of the eldest son. For instance, at about the age of thirty Longomo had been married only a year or so when his father died, leaving three widows and a number of children, some very young. At the normal inheritance discussions the division of the herds was formally settled, but no physical alteration occurred. Longomo took the role of leadership left by his father. His oldest half-brother, Ekale, was barely twenty and the eldest son of the third widow was about fourteen years old. Neither half-brother nor their mothers[2] objected to this arrangement. The whole compound family remained as a quasi-nuclear family. To continue the account of this group, for convenience sake here—Ekale was old enough, supported by his mother, to look after the interests of his house and its herds. The family was no more than of average wealth, and Ekale, scarcely yet ready for marriage by Turkana evaluations, refused to permit his herds to be used for the second marriage of Longomo, beyond the limits of conventional assistance. This was a constant source of contention, which, however, did not reach serious dimensions. Longomo's herds were not at that time large enough for him to marry again, and in any case Ekale rightly considered that he himself had, in due course, prior right to marriage. Informants pointed out to me that the herds of Ekale's house were quite separate from those of Longomo's house, despite the fact that for convenience they were herded and kraaled together and Longomo had taken charge of pastoral organization. That is to say, the identity of the houses was not submerged because of the economic and pastoral unity which remained as a matter of convenience.

The second possibility of compound family organization is that some or all of the houses seek or merely accept the guardianship of a kinsman of the father. If a man dies and leaves only small children, his oldest full-brother may become guardian to them until at least the first son comes to an age to marry. This full-brother has no claim on the dead man's herd and should only take temporary charge of them for the children. Informants have told me stories of rapacious

---

[1] Cf. Figure 12 and relevant text.
[2] Longomo became pro-husband to the junior widow.

171

brothers who steal their young nephews' stock whilst those youths are largely unaware of what is happening or unable to prevent it. Certainly this is morally condemned by Turkana as a violation of legal rights, but in any case such injustice does not occur in perhaps the majority of cases. Sometimes the youths and boys with their mothers are content to become dependent sections of the nuclear family of the dead man's brother, and accept rights in it as if born to it. This frequently occurs when a man dies at an early age, particularly if he has not yet achieved his own full independence. The young widows accept their husband's brother as pro-husband and he becomes indistinguishable from the true father. The herds had not been divided and the women and children all owe their status to the expenditure of stock of the unified house. The compound family becomes submerged into the house and nuclear family of the guardian. The dead man's yards fit into the scheme of seniority, and they retain the allocation of stock formerly made to them. Such a realistic compromise, arising out of the moral unity of the house, is not usual if the dead man had already become independent. Where division within the house has been made, it is difficult to bring about a satisfactory reunion. This kind of arrangement is rare if the dead man's sons are approaching manhood, when they are more aware of their status and rights and the possibilities offered them. In such cases the sons, encouraged by their mothers, seek the guardianship of their mother's brothers. The compound family may split up, each house going to its maternal kin, or sometimes the houses follow the leadership of the eldest and of the senior widow and they accept the protection of her brother. It is said that maternal kin are more trustworthy at this time than are the dead man's agnates. I discovered no case where a maternal uncle had misappropriated his nephew's stock.

Some actual examples will demonstrate the sorts of solutions that are reached. Lobenyo died at the age of about thirty-five, leaving a young widow and three children, the eldest of whom was about seven years old. Lobenyo had not become fully independent. His eldest brother, Eregai, about forty years old, had two wives and several children. He became pro-husband to the widow, who with her children came to comprise a yard in his nuclear family, retaining and using their former allocation of stock.

When Lokimat died his eldest son was about eighteen years and the second son of the senior yard was about sixteen years old. They went with their mother to live in her brother's homestead, and took her allocation of stock plus a lesser portion of the 'residual herd'. The second widow's eldest son, Lopenamoi, was no more than ten years old, and she still a young woman. She accepted her husband's younger full-brother, Lokoyen, as pro-husband and with her children went to live at his homestead, taking the remainder of Lokimat's herds. These stock remained attached to the group—legally now a house—and some ten years later Lopenamoi married from the herd and received a generous contribution from his guardian. There was apparently no question of the complete absorption of either the widow and children or their stock into Lokoyen's nuclear family, though it seems that he was able to borrow fairly freely when he himself married earlier. Lokoyen made no special protest against the action of Lokimat's senior wife and her sons. Some fifteen years after Lokimat died, Lokoyen said to me: 'Were they not a separate house? They went to our affines and drove their stock away. It was their words [i.e. their affair], they owned the stock. They took them from their father, Lokimat. His stock were separate from mine—two [nuclear] families. We were full-brothers but we were separate. Lopenamoi was the head of his house also in exactly the same way.'

A long and heated discussion followed the death of Ebu, who had left two widows and several children, the eldest of whom was a youth of about seventeen. The widows and this son wished to remain with Ebu's homesteads and herds and to continue to maintain the established pastoral routine. Ebu's younger brother, Lotome, held that the youth was too young to act as head of the new compound family. He suggested that they should all go to live with him. He also claimed the right to become pro-husband to the widows, but both refused, and the youth insisted on maintaining his family's independence. At the post-mortuary discussions the rest of the extended family was divided in opinion, although the literal rights of the widows and the youth were generally admitted, for Ebu had been head of his own independent nuclear family for eight or nine years. Some agnates, however, felt that for purely practical reasons at least Lotome ought to become guardian of the group. One widow openly said that not only did she not want Lotome as pro-husband but also that she believed he would misappropriate his dead brother's stock. Eventually they had their own way and Lotome could do nothing about it.

It may be clear that compound families begin life under a variety of forms, or they may even be entirely absorbed into another nuclear family. In most cases the compound family persists as a distinct group and commonly it exists at first merely as a continuance of the old nuclear family but with a changed internal structure. Whatever the solution reached short of absorption, there is a gradual and, as Turkana see it, inevitable tendency towards geographical and pastoral separation as each constituent house comes to exercise its legal independence and to establish its own homesteads and nomadic routines. From the time of settlement of inheritance each house has been an independent stock-owning unit and as soon as possible it asserts its status by physical separation. This cleavage is not necessarily the result of unfriendly, let alone hostile, relations between half-brothers, though in some cases it is. The factors behind the urge towards independence have already been mentioned in the previous section in relation to the cleavage within a house, and they need not be repeated again here in what is a similar situation. They may be summed up briefly by saying that the system of stock-ownership stimulates structural cleavage in an environment where the inhabitants aim at dispersion of population and herds.

Relations within the compound family largely become inter-house relations, with the senior brothers of each house as the chief actors. It has been seen how the property-owning system produces house identity and a notion of separation; each house feels that its future development is bound up in its own herds. In the case of marriage, each group of brothers realizes that the major portion of bridewealth must come from its herds, whilst conversely the major portions of in-payments remain with the house, e.g. a sister's bridewealth. There are of course other factors affecting the situation and supporting the general lines of cleavage. From the beginning each house has relations with its own maternal kin, and such relations are scarcely extended to their half-brothers. This is an important factor, particularly before the senior brother has married, for until that time the affection and predispositions of the mother may be a strong influence tending to draw her sons towards her brothers and away from their own close agnates. Almost invariably if one house breaks away before its head marries, it is in order to join maternal kin—usually the mother's eldest brother. In any case men do look to their maternal kin for assistance and general support, and to that extent they find an exclusion from half-brothers. Another category of external relations is with affines, and these again are largely confined to the limits of the house. As soon as the head of the house marries, his new affinal relations are likely to become of great significance to his house and to his house's relations in the compound family. The most common way perhaps in which a house first establishes its independence from the rest of the compound family is through pastoral alliance with these near affines. The house, led by the senior brother, goes to live near the homestead of his wife's father, or maintains a joint homestead with his wife's brother or some similar convenient arrangement whereby the set of brothers can obtain assistance. The wife's kin can frequently be relied upon to lend a milch animal or two if milk is short, or to give an occasional goat for meat. Labour supply is pooled, and herding and watering facilitated —this is a chief attraction of the arrangement for the wife's kinsmen, for labour is usually a scarce commodity of Turkanaland. So close are affinal ties, however, that even without material profit the wife's kin welcome her husband and his brothers.

The development of a house has already been described and it was seen how each group breaks down into a number of independent nuclear families. House unity becomes a more exiguous thing. Younger brothers, in addition to exercising control over their own separate herds, also begin to develop individually their own system of relations with their half-brothers. Relations within the compound family gradually become those between nuclear families—principally family heads, all the sons of the dead father. This is not to suggest that the initial distinction between houses is entirely lost, for on the whole a man continues to feel closer to and to exercise greater rights against his full-brothers than he does in respect of his half-brothers. Apart from special and individual friendships that cut across structural divisions, a man and his full-brothers retain a greater unity than is to be found within the compound family as a whole. This is, of course, not a matter of residential association nor of economic or day-to-day co-operation—such things vary from time to time according to the nature of nomadic movements; in general, relations either in house or compound family are not dependent on these factors, though they may be important at any one time. Where the closeness of relations can most easily be estimated is in the relative strengths of reciprocal rights over stock; and in this connection full-brothers normally remain more important than half-brothers.

On the other hand, as the herds of the houses are split up with the successive establishment of nuclear families, so each individual owner must treat with each other owner and family head concerning the exercise of rights and the acceptance of obligations. Although the scale of reciprocal rights is initially determined by house affiliation, the exercise of them is maintained between individual family heads and not within or between houses as such. The relations of a man with his half-brothers become increasingly independent of the relations between them and his full-brothers. Thus a younger brother does not maintain relations and rights and obligations via his senior, the head of his house, nor can that senior man compel his junior to give more or less generously to half-brothers. The point of significance is that a house no longer exists as a stock-owning group, nor really as a group which can emerge in social action against or in cooperation with other groups. Both houses and the compound family have by this time essentially the same constitutional values, but in different degrees. Both are principally complexes of agnatic relations chiefly expressed in rights over stock, rather than corporate groups. We shall return to this point in consideration of the general nature and development of agnatic relations within the extended family as a whole.

Because constituent nuclear families are independent stock-owning units, there is no longer any question of compulsory rights within the compound family. The former seniority ranking and prescribed order of marriage has no authoritative value; yet the idea of such a ranking and of a 'proper' order of marriage persists. Although a man cannot be compelled to wait his turn for marriage, the moral rule remains in men's minds. At first it is extremely difficult to break the rule, for that would put a man in danger of excommunication from his closest agnates, those from whom he normally expects to receive large contributions to his bridewealth. Seldom if ever can a man afford to marry without his half-brothers' support, for in any case bridewealth demands are based on the assumption of their assistance. At first, then, marriages continue according to the old ruling, for a man dare not contravene it; and at this early stage the system works fairly satisfactorily. Gradually, however, it begins to conflict with the desires and ambitions of independent men, who come to resent the egalitarian restrictions imposed upon them. A man wishes to save his stock against his second marriage rather than give generously to a half-brother who is himself taking a second wife. An older man may wish to marry a second or third time rather than wait for the first marriage of a very much younger half-brother.[1] The conception of equality which lies behind the moral rule and which has been inherited from the former nuclear family of the father is not only irksome but may be increasingly belied by the diverse fortunes of the various nuclear families. Wealthier, more successful or more lucky men do not wish to be restricted to the level of their poorer half-brothers, nor to see their herds dissipated upon these others; on the other hand the less wealthy, less fortunate members attempt to stress and prolong the acceptance of the moral rule which operates to their benefit. Even if discrepancies of wealth are small,[2] men quite definitely resent the automatic notion of obligations to half-brothers and indeed to their full-brothers also. The whole conception of continuing equality is contradictory to the diversity of individual development, and in the face of increasing difficulty and tension the rule is gradually abandoned though not without a good deal of trouble. By the time that men reach middle age, a variety of marital fortunes exist within both the houses and the whole compound family. This situation demands a change in attitude to these close agnatic relationships on the widest scale. The right of sons in a nuclear family are directed by superior authority, and obligations cannot be avoided. In the early compound family, though the legal force of compulsion is gone between half-brothers yet there persists the notion of egalitarian development and of a structure of almost automatic rights principally through the continuance of the seniority ranking of the order of marriage. In a sense, a man *had* to give stock to his half-brother's bridewealth irrespective of his own predisposition, and he *had* to wait his turn before he himself could assemble bridewealth. Finally, however, that delicate system breaks down as first one and then another member of the compound family refuses to fall into line. At this time a man is faced with a situation which he must accept as philosophically as possible, and he endeavours to build up reciprocal rights based on the closeness of kinship between himself and each of his brothers individually. The old system is untenable, and even though he should desire to perpetuate it he cannot coerce his co-members of the com-

[1] Because of widespread polygamy and the tendency for a man to make second and third marriages during at least middle age, the age-range of his sons may stretch over twenty to thirty years.

[2] In previous generations wide discrepancies of wealth could occur as a result of both the profits and losses of raiding. Still, today, famine, disease and different abilities of husbandry affect the wealth and fortunes of closely related men.

pound family, for they are each the head of an independent nuclear family. A man can but make it worthwhile for each brother to maintain rights and a certain co-operation with him. In other words, men have to change their attitudes to the nature of fraternal relations. No longer are brothers willing to be bound by any fixed ruling covering the compound family as a corporate group, and relations become relatively fluid between a man and each of his co-members severally. No longer can a member regulate his obligations to another in terms of an all-inclusive and comparatively automatic system of rights and rightful behaviour, but he must establish a *modus vivendi* wherein each can be of assistance to the other without claiming to control his external activities. Assistance comes to depend in a large measure upon reciprocity. You give to your brother as he gives to you; but you make no attempt to interfere with the way in which he uses or disposes of his stock, when he marries or how often, to whom else he makes gifts, and so on. Both parties agree that the very closeness of kinship predisposes generous assistance and mutual interests and privilege; but ultimately that depends upon continued reciprocity and toleration, for the size and frequency of complementary assistance is not a fixed standard as between every pair of brothers, even within a single compound family.

There is then a process of adaptation and readjustment of attitudes and practical relations, and it may take some time before the compound family emerges as a new, stable unit. During the process, interrelations may become strained and some antagonism may develop between those who seek to establish the new system and those who tend to hold on to the old. Rivalry and even hostility may arise between certain pairs of brothers. In general, however, the adjustment and mutual accommodation occurs fairly easily, if only because each man is simultaneously concerned with establishing his own full independence (and that of his nuclear family with him) and with developing his own particular field of social relations with his kinsfolk and friends. Each man increasingly feels himself to be drawn gradually further apart from his brothers. In all this it is to be remembered that each man with his nuclear family is moving in an individual nomadic routine, differing from that of each of the rest of the compound family. At times the homesteads of such a family may be scattered over a wide territory[1] and these close agnates may not

---

[1] Examples of the dispersion of compound families are given in the Appendix to this chapter.

see one another for periods of several months; and even less frequently do they all, or nearly all, come together for some common purpose. If two of these men are unfriendly to 'each other they can and do keep out of each other's way in the course of nomadic movements. Both full-brothers and half-brothers in pairs, but rarely more, make pastoral alliances and share one or both homesteads jointly. Such alliances are often short-lived, and none that I learnt of were entirely permanent. Imana and Eguru were two friendly brothers who maintained close and cordial relations, and at times, for mutual convenience, they shared a joint chief-homestead and pooled their herdsmen. During over two years of first-hand observation and according to their own account over a much longer period, they never shared secondary-homesteads. At no time were their herds of cattle kraaled at a joint homestead. Yet this was certainly not a case of ill-feeling or even mere neutrality of sentiments, but mutual recognition of differing desires, needs and opinions, and of each other's legal status.

In conclusion, I would go so far as to say that obvious ill-feeling between brothers is not the usual state of affairs, though a certain coolness or apathy is not uncommon. There is a general attitude of 'live and let live' about the whole system of relations. Underneath there may be a basic antagonism and rivalry, but it rarely comes to the surface, at least not to the extent of threatening the structure of family relations. One informant said cynically: 'Your brother only comes to visit when he wants something. You give it to him and he immediately goes off to his homestead.' As an afterthought he added frankly: 'He is your brother and you ought to help. Do not you, another time, go to beg from him in the same way? That is how it is between brothers among the Turkana.' Antagonism is one of the factors leading to and involved in separation and independence, but when this latter is established firmly, it can remain dormant or will even die out altogether.

The Pattern of the Extended Family

Internal relations within the extended family are principally those between the heads of independent nuclear families. However, relations beyond the compound family have a rather different emphasis from those inside it, as described in the previous section. Only heads of nuclear families of a single compound family have been formerly united in an authoritarian group—i.e. a nuclear family of the preceding generation. It has been shown how the change-over occurred from enforced, egalitarian association, tempered by consideration of seniority, to the free and fluid relations between close kinsmen which are given value through a system of reciprocal rights. Agnates of different compound families have never been co-members of any authoritarian group, for the preceding nuclear families of their various fathers were independent units. They have therefore never been subject to mutual superior constraint in regard to their relations with one another. Cousins of all degrees do not have the same problems of re-adjustment which prove so difficult between brothers. They inherit, as it were, the pattern of relations previously established between their fathers in the previous generation. There is not in general, therefore, the same sort of tension between cousins as there is between brothers. Relations commence on a basis of reciprocal rights, which have already reached a level of stability. The common source of inheritance is relatively remote and the individual's history of personal development to independence only indirectly connected with that of his cousin. It is more or less fortuitous whether a man's cousin lives near to him at certain times of the year, whether or not they tend to use common pastures; but it is likely that they are geographically separated more often than not. Although the frequency of social intercourse permitted by such separation has its effect upon the strength and cordiality of relations, basically, between cousins, the important factor is the mutuality of stock rights accepted on either side. The notion of reciprocity is little affected by considerations of personal development. On the other hand, because of the relative indirectness of the kinship tie, reciprocal rights are weaker than they are between brothers.

Sections of the extended family—houses, compound, families and house-lines[1]—seldom emerge as corporate groups, and then not in any structural sense of segmental opposition and symmetry. The value of concepts of 'family' and 'house' lies chiefly in the ordering and classification of relations and therefore of rights, obligations and interests. An underlying theme of Turkana social organization is the general difficulty of group activity on any large scale because of ecological conditions which cause a widespread dispersal of population together with diverse and frequent movement. Density of population is low everywhere, and in addition there is the cultural norm of strong individualism in connection with nomadic move-

[1] Vide Figure 13.

ments so that residential relations seldom become important over a period; and there is neither particular need nor opportunity for the frequent assembly of kinsmen. The only entirely corporate groups are nuclear families under the authority of their founders and heads. These are, as we have seen, the basic units of the Turkana agnatic system; they are geographically separate, economically self-sufficient, nomadically self-determinant and legally independent. The heads of nuclear families maintain direct personal relations with other, related, family heads. Such men are regarded as closer or more distant by reason of house/family affiliation, but relations are not thereby organized at the level of nor through the agency of house, compound family or house-line. This affiliation classifies relations between agnates in degrees of intensity which are given practical effect in a corresponding system of rights and obligations. The ideal correlation of agnatic ties and claims against stock can be represented as follows. Full-brothers have the strongest claims against each other, for they have jointly shared a herd inherited directly from their father. Half-brothers base their claims upon the fact of sharing what was a single herd of a generation ago—that of their father. Full-paternal cousins share a herd of a single house of a generation ago—that of their fathers, who formed the house. Half-paternal cousins share a single herd of two generations ago—that of their grandfather. Beyond that stage rights practically cease to exist unless 'you know your cousin very well and you are friends.' The nearer in genealogical and therefore chronological reckoning that the shared herd existed, the stronger are reciprocal rights between contemporary agnates.

The Turkana express this approach to the claims of kinship by quoting house and family affiliation. To take a generalized example—when a man wishes to marry, his primary claims are determined in respect of each agnate by virtue of the scale of the smallest section of the total extended family to which both men belong. A greater claim lies against a member of the suitor's own house than against a member of his compound family but of a different house; and a greater claim lies against the latter than against an agnate of the same house-line but of a different compound family, and so on. This is to state the position in the most formal terms, for it has already been emphasized that relations with, and therefore rights in respect of, each agnate are not fixed but depend finally on the state of inter-personal ties and the acceptance of reciprocal obligations. A man does not necessarily maintain equal rights with, say, each of his full-cousins. In the actual collection of animals a potential bridegroom himself, and he alone, is entirely responsible for seeking out each agnate and begging the appropriate contribution. In every case the common group (or, more correctly here, the common category) is not brought into the corporate action at all; but in each case it exists as a mental scheme of values regulating the attitudes and interests of the man.

It is to be noted, further, that these various groups are not entirely specific within the extended family for all of its members. What is, for instance, a house to one may be a house-line for his deceased brother's son. In the accompanying diagram, three brothers, X, Y

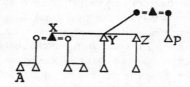

and Z with their nuclear families make up a single house. On X's death his nuclear family breaks down into two houses—it becomes, that is, a new compound family. For A, his house is composed of himself, his full-brother and their nuclear families. Ideally the old house founded by the three brothers persists and will be so regarded by agnate P. For its members, however, relations have reached a new stage of differentiation, affecting men Y and Z and the independent sons of X.

The extended family and its sections do sometimes emerge in corporate action and are not entirely categories of relationships. Some examples of such activity have been given earlier in this chapter. It is to be noted, however, in this matter that where a family or house does so emerge in action it is not directly in connection with the use and disposal of stock but principally in relation to the social arrangement and procedure of some event, and concerning its ritual success and spiritual significance.[1]

The Dynamics of the Extended Family

It is clear that for the Turkana the extended family is not important in their ordinary everyday life. It is not easy for the external observer

[1] See pp. 153-5.

to discover its precise boundaries, or to see it in action when they are known, for not even the people themselves are necessarily entirely sure at any one time. Because of the geographical dispersion of agnates and the natural difficulties of operating constant and active relations over long distances, the group only comes together on the most important occasions of life. A man is not always certain where other agnates are at a given time, though on the whole he knows the rough location of homesteads and can if necessary find them or send messages to them. Considerable delays are almost inevitable, however. For the rest of the time, in default of any more extensive action, the house or perhaps the compound family (or at least large sections of them) may maintain rather more cohesion because of the closer bonds and the ritual imperatives that exist.

A person will usually be well aware of the exact composition of his own house-line and of its internal structure. He may not be fully cognizant of all the details of house-lines descended from his grandmother's co-wives, though the main outlines and the positions of the more important men will be known. Almost certainly he will know comparatively little about the internal structure of families based on his grandfather's brothers, if he knows of them at all, which is not a usual condition.

So far, in this account of Turkana agnatic kinship, for convenience I have adopted the 'ideal' view of the people themselves and assumed that the extended family comprises all the surviving male descendants of a grandfather, together with their wives and children. It is now necessary to turn to a consideration of the family as it emerges in actual life, and as it is demonstrated in maintained social relations. We must henceforth regard the extended family not as a fixed genealogical unit but as a cluster of close agnatic relations, the founder of which may in fact be a father, grandmother, grandfather or even a great-grandparent, not all of whose surviving male descendants necessarily form a *de facto* group. In the following account the largest effective group which emerges in the interrelations based on reciprocal rights and occasionally in certain corporate action will be termed the 'Family'.[1]

The active boundaries of agnatic kinship are not precisely demarcated and they vary from case to case, and from time to time even for a single individual. For any man there is a fundamental core consisting of his compound family, but beyond this the network of

---

[1] This term is used here in order to facilitate comparison with Jie kinship structure.

relations varies. Compound families based on the father's full-brothers are usually included, thus making up the house-line; and frequently, but not invariably, there are included also parallel house-lines from the father's half-brothers. This takes the group back to the grandfather, making what may be called the 'grand-family'; but not always are all his grandsons included. Occasionally, but not typically, some of the descendants of the grandfather's brothers are included, though it is rare for the linking ancestor (great-grand-father) to be remembered by name. Agnatic kinship begins here to reach the stage of dogmatic assertion rather than of genealogical memory, and of theoretical rights rather than active relations.

The limits of the Family are not defined by any ideal considera-tions, but by the state of actual active relations amongst a group of people. Owing to the large-scale migrations that have occurred during the last two generations to newly acquired territories, the nuclear families of a man's grandsons have often become dispersed over a wide area and relations between many of them have been curtailed or entirely severed. Sometimes a man does not know of any genealogically traceable agnates outside his compound family; in another case a paternal cousin is known, but he habitually lives and moves in a region perhaps fifty miles away and it has therefore been impossible to continue active relations. Quite apart from these mass migrations, over the course of years nomadic movements may gradually take a known agnate so far away that, for reasons of sheer distance, relations atrophy for the most part. The moral and social ideas and values behind the kinship relations are unable to withstand geographical and prolonged separation. In quite a practical manner, Turkana say that although such-and-such men properly belong to a single 'family' (*awi*—the agnatic descendants of one male ancestor) and owe obligations to one another by reason of descent and inheri-tance, yet co-operation and interests cannot be maintained against the obstacle of great distance and consequent social separation.

For the Turkana the prime factor relevant to the situation is the possibility of the continuance of useful relations rather than formal genealogical bonds. These latter serve to support and rationalize persisting relations, but they do not in themselves serve to explain why certain sections of the total agnatic field are omitted. The emergence of the effective Family can only be discovered and com-prehended through a survey of existing relations. It is necessary to discover to whom a man goes when he is in need of stock, and of whom he seeks assistance in the critical occasions of life. One must enquire who in turn approaches him to beg stock or to claim shares of in-payments and who feel compelled by both common interests and ritual necessities to come together for important activities. To this end some concrete examples are discussed in what follows.

In those parts of the country fairly recently acquired by the Turkana were many cases where a Family comprised only a single compound family. It was not uncommon that middle-aged or elderly men knew of no other agnatic kinsmen. For example, Lokoyen's Family (cf. Figure 17) was composed of his own nuclear family, that of his half-brother, and his deceased full-brother's compound family. In a few instances Families comprised single houses; sometimes other agnates were vaguely known, but not always. Immediately after the mass migrations it appears to have been common for single nuclear families to exist in isolation from other agnatic kin. This is rare today, however.

The boundaries of the Family do not necessarily coincide with the limits of genealogical knowledge, although these are relatively narrow compared with those in many African societies. The Family of Lobelai illustrates this. Lobelai's eldest son, Ebe, had lived in the region of the middle Turkwel basin (central Turkanaland) about forty years ago. At his death his two widows and four young sons went to live with the brother of the senior widow about forty miles away from Ebe's surviving full-brother, Lokurr. When the sons grew up they left their erstwhile guardian and together migrated westwards to territory recently vacated, or no longer contested, by the Karamajong in the upper Kosibir basin. In 1949-50 the three sons of the senior widow had each an independent nuclear family and herd; a half-brother lived with the youngest of them. Their paternal cousins, the sons of Lokurr, who have remained in roughly the same area as their father, have not been entirely forgotten genealogically, but there has been only meagre contact between the two groups for many years. When Ebe's sons married they did not travel the forty miles or so to obtain contributions of stock from their cousins, nor have they been asked to give stock to their cousins' bridewealths. To some extent they keep in touch regarding major events by news carried by casual travellers. When Ebe's half-brother died in 1949 as a very old man, Ebe's sons did not attend the funeral ceremony; but recognition of the event was made by the formal mourning of a child in each nuclear family of these sons.[1]

Ebe's sons and their nuclear families did not comprise the whole of the effective Family, however, for their father's paternal cousin, Majongalook, had moved independently to the upper Kosibir region and came to live, eventually, near to the homesteads of two of them. Relations between him and them were therefore resumed and maintained on normal lines, and he was accepted as head of an effective Family. In the middle Turkwel area the three remaining compound families also made up a Family. A genealogical summary is given in Figure 14. It will be seen that the Family formed by families A and

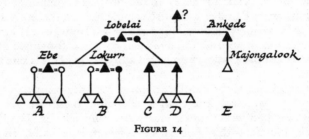

FIGURE 14

THE FAMILY OF LOBELAI

Effective Families are composed of:—
  1. Compound family A and nuclear family E—58 persons.
  2. Compound families B, C and D.

E have an agnatic link through the great-grandfather of Ebe's sons. This usually distant link has been retained in practice because of the geographical proximity of Majongalook and Ebe's sons, who had become isolated from existing closer agnatic kin and who therefore found value in maintaining more remote ties than are usually acceptable.

A rather different situation is illustrated by the Family of Lokwi, a genealogical summary of which is given in Figure 15. Here the effective Family comprised the compound families based on two full-brothers. The chief homesteads of member nuclear families stretched over an area of about thirty miles at the time when details were recorded (wet season 1950) in west-central Turkanaland.

---

[1] A small girl had her head completely shaved and wore no ornaments until her hair grew again. This is the formal behaviour for females on an agnate's death.

Genealogical knowledge, however, extended to a contemporary group descended from the grandfather's brother, although not all its members nor its internal articulation were known to members of the Family of Lokwi. I had recorded the genealogy before witnessing the group engaged in corporate activities, and had obtained some account of this distant line. Later at the wedding of Aleri, the Family head, I was able to see the group in action and to note the contributions and general assistance he obtained from his agnates. The whole of Aleri's house was present and they took active part, for at that time (the wet season) they lived within a few miles of his chief homestead. The heads of the other three houses were also present,

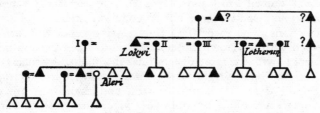

FIGURE 15

THE FAMILY OF LOKWI

Aleri is the head of the effective Family descended from Lokwi and his full-brother, Lotherun. It comprises 9 nuclear families and 3 undivided houses descended from Aleri's deceased full-brothers. (Wives and children are not shown.) There were no longer any practical relations between this group and the descendants of Lokwi's paternal cousin, who formed a separate Family.

The name of the founding grandfather has been forgotten, and the Family was known by the name of his eldest son.

but not all of their brothers and families. These senior men gave Aleri formal support at the handing over of the bridewealth and in the conventional discussions associated with that event, and they took part in all the feasting and dancing. The head of each independent nuclear family within the effective Family, whether he attended the wedding or not, had been visited earlier by Aleri and had given camels and cattle towards the bridewealth, for, as he said, 'We are all one house (ekal), one family (awi) also,' i.e. descendants of one grandmother and one grandfather. No members of the distant agnatic line attended the wedding, neither did they contribute towards the bridewealth. Indeed they were not even visited by Aleri, nor informed of the event, though doubtless news of it reached them in local gossip. Upon specific enquiry I was told: 'Their family is different, a long way off. We know their names [but] their stock are separate now. Long ago our fathers were one [family]; now that is finished. There are two families.' The significance of 'a long way off' in this case was not principally geographical but genealogical. Some of these distant agnates at that time lived no more than about fifteen miles away from Aleri's homestead, rather nearer than two of his half-brothers whose homesteads were about twenty-five miles away. Active relations had lapsed with the stretching of genealogical links; reciprocal stock rights had atrophied as links became more indirect.

As Turkana see it, reciprocal rights tend to fail when the sections of former unified groups move apart, not necessarily wholly or principally in a spatial sense but in common interests, obligations and affections. The men of each successive generation are more concerned with their own closer agnatic and other kinship ties and decreasingly with the more distant links maintained by their fathers. An older man retains rights and interests with his half-cousins; his sons regard them as distant agnates, and their sons are correspondingly even more remote. The wider the smallest common group, the weaker are predispositions to maintain relations. In this particular instance there is no record of severe dissension which might have provoked abrupt dissociation, but only a history of the gradual atrophy of active relations as they became less and less valuable to either side. In general, older men tend to remember distant agnatic links even though they have become empty of practical value. Through the agency of an old man, two separate lines of a former united Family may keep in touch and possibly seek hospitality at convenient times when travelling. With the old man's death the final memory goes. To him it meant at least an echo of a past time of unity; to his sons it has no meaning at all.

The constitution of the effective Family as illustrated in these examples is affected and determined by two factors of distance—geographical and genealogical—both of which bring about a weakening of active relations, with or without the actual erasure of formal links. Geographical dispersion and separation is the more important and the more common factor, and its operation may cause atrophy of agnatic relations before genealogical remoteness comes about. It is the result not only of the large-scale migrations of recent generations but also of what is an almost inevitable process in the achievement, establishment and maintenance of independence by individual men with their nuclear families. It is believe that the majority of Turkana must have been affected by the colonization of newly acquired territories, for this of course concerned not only those who migrated[1] but also those of their kin who remained behind. Certainly, every agnatic group is affected by the tendency to dispersion by its adult members as new nuclear families and homesteads, and new pastoral-nomadic routines are established. In no instance that I have been able to investigate have all the nuclear families of a compound family, and seldom even of a single house, remained permanently together, or at least relatively near to each other. For whatever reason it occurs, this geographical separation tends inevitably to produce a weakening of social bonds, if for no other reason than the difficulties of communication in a primitive society inhabiting an arid country.

Genealogical distance often works in conjunction with geographical separation, but not necessarily so. It cannot be said that more distant agnates tend to live further away than nearer kinsmen; the two factors are not correlated either in conscious intent or in results. On the other hand geographical proximity may tend to support weakening relations. Principally in the matter of genealogical distance it is a question of the people's value system which resides in the scheme of correlating stock rights with the idea of common inheritance and the possession of a common herd. This is embedded in the kinship system from the time of the allocation of stock between the yards of a nuclear family, through the differential inheritance of the father's herd and the subsequent division of the units of inheritance (houses). Each man finds his closest relations and strongest reciprocal rights with his brothers in the compound family, but endeavours also to maintain relations with his cousins; but in their turn his sons find their closest relations in their own compound family which emerges from his own nuclear family, and what were the father's more distant relations tend to weaken and fade out altogether, remaining, if at all, as a mere genealogical memory of little sociological importance.

For the sake of convenience we have been dealing in categories of formal relations between agnatic kin, in terms of house, compound family and house-line. It has, however, been explained that, in so far as property rights are concerned, these Family sections are mainly

[1] It is believed that possibly half of the population took part in these migrations. See p. 7, also p. 260.

categories of the classification of relations and of corresponding rights—such rights being the principal content of the relations. Each head of a nuclear family establishes inter-personal relations with each of his co-members of the Family, and the actual content and operation of these relations depends to a certain important extent upon practical considerations between each pair of men, so that relations and reciprocal rights with one half-brother, for instance, are not necessarily identical with those with another. Relative seniority is no longer of any real importance in the mature compound family (or other section). Considerations of friendliness, or antagonism, are significant in this matter. In such a fluid system of relations within a nomadic society a man is not bound to associate more than absolutely necessary with any kinsmen he dislikes, or who, he feels, has not fulfilled obligations; on the other hand he may, if he wishes, live and move with or near a kinsman with whom he is friendly and who has proved himself generous in the past. The factor of reciprocity has been emphasized *ad nauseam* in this account of the Turkana, and in the actual determination of specific relations it is decisive. The basis of rights and obligations is laid down by the sectional affiliation, so that theoretically (as it were) a man owes greater obligations to a full-brother than to a half-brother. Yet his full-brother may, because of personality or because of the course of the cleavage of the common house, be niggardly in his acceptance of obligations and hard in his claims—in general an unfriendly person. A half-brother may become a man's closest friend and greatest helper. Again, through more or less fortuitous factors a man may frequently come into contact with one cousin in the course of nomadic movements, and never in the normal course of events meet another cousin in everyday life. To some extent this is a result of pre-existing personal inclination, but by no means wholly so.

It is difficult if not impossible to state these kinds of factors in formal, generalized terms, for they are essentially particular and informal in their expression. They are nevertheless of great importance to the proper understanding of inter-personal relations amongst the Turkana, especially in the absence of tight bonds of the membership of close corporate groups. Some examples may help to illustrate the point in question.

During the division and dispersion of his house, Lodieki had come to be on rather unfriendly terms with his elder full-brother, and the two men saw little of each other for they habitually used different pasture areas. Lodieki told me that because of difficult relations he had deliberately left the region in which his brother lived and moved. Lodieki's closest associate was his only half-brother, with whom he shared a chief-homestead now and again, and with whom he was on terms of the greatest friendship. These two men assisted and supported each other in all kinds of ways. At Lodieki's second marriage the half-brother contributed four cattle, against the two cattle and a few goats of his elder full-brother; yet there appeared to be little difference between the wealth of the two men. Lodieki commented simply, of his half-brother, 'We like each other very much.'

In another case, Loreng quarrelled with his elder full-brother over the arrangements and timing of the division of the herds of their house. He eventually moved away to a different pasture area accompanied by his youngest brother. Another full-brother remained with the eldest man, and house relations became arranged on a dichotomous basis of two pairs of brothers—the first and third, and the second and fourth. Loreng had chosen to move near to their mother's brother, from whom he had received assistance at this difficult time. His cattle were for a time kraaled at the uncle's secondary homestead during the dry season. It so happened that a full-cousin of Loreng moved in the same locality and gradually he came to be in frequent contact with Loreng and his younger brother; sometimes they lived in a common primary neighbourhood. When the younger brother sought contributions of stock for his first bridewealth he obtained the same number of cattle from this cousin as from his eldest full-brother, although strictly the latter should have made a large gift at this particular time because of house affiliation and the fact that the groom had not previously married. The cousin's contribution was larger than those of any other close agnate, including two half-brothers. The three men, Loreng, his younger brother and their cousin, tended to form a local agnatic group of no genealogical pattern but based on friendship and local association. Beyond this group, relations with the eldest and third brothers were definitely unfriendly and the cousin tended to support Loreng in this. With the rest of their agnates, relations were relatively normal, except for a half-cousin who had refused to contribute to the bridewealth of Loreng's brother and who was deemed to have cut himself off. Later that same cousin came to seek stock for his own marriage and was refused at first; but he was eventually given some goats by each man on the specific promise of accepting their future claims upon him.[1]

These examples have been chiefly illustrated in terms of bride-wealth contributions, for these are easiest to understand and they afford a ready means of comparison. There are, however, frequent gifts of stock and exchange of calves and other young animals which follow the same lines. A man who needs an ox for ritual purposes, or a fat goat for a feast, tends to seek out some agnate who is friendly and to whom he has given generously in the past. More unfriendly kinsmen are mostly left alone except for the more important occasions such as bridewealth, or a serious depletion of the herds by disease or famine, or payment of compensation.

These brief examples do not give a wholly adequate picture, for they deal only with the high-lights of agnatic relations—the particular hostilities and the notable friendships. But in connection with each individual agnate a man must come to a rough agreement of accepted reciprocity, and each such arrangement tends to be slightly different. Where personal relations have no especially strong element either way, reciprocity comes to be based largely on purely formal, kinship terms; but, *a priori*, one cannot determine its exact nature nor posit that for each man of the same category it will be the same. Personalities, animosities and affections apart, a wealthier agnate tends to be able to give more generously, and from each of his kinsmen he expects and tends to receive a similarly generous return.

---

[1] The 'normal' contribution is roughly one cow or female camel. 'We gave some goats because of our grandfather,' said Loreng; and then, 'He must give stock to us another time or we shall always refuse [in the future] to help him.'

FAMILY AND PROPERTY IN TURKANALAND

APPENDIX

THE GEOGRAPHICAL DISPERSAL OF EXTENDED FAMILIES

Example (a)—The Family of Akurikuri

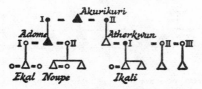

Total membership of the Family—43 persons.

Sketch map of western Turkanaland showing the locations of the homesteads of the Family in February 1949 (dry season).

> Key:—
>   Chief-homesteads (goats and camels)
>   1. Ekal   2. Ngupe   3. Atherkwun
>   also   4. Ikali (autonomous son)
>
>   Secondary-homesteads (cattle)
>   5. Ekal and Ngupe   6. Atherkwun.

The homesteads of other Turkana in this region shown as:—
⊗ chief-homesteads   + secondary-homesteads
   All locations shown are approximate only.

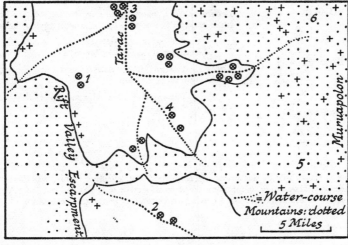

FAMILY AND PROPERTY IN TURKANALAND

Example (b)—The Family of Lokwamothing

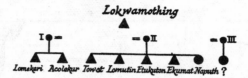

Lokwamothing

HOUSE-LINE I.

Details of this group were not properly known to the members of House-line II from whom the genealogy was recorded. All that were certain were the names of the older sons of the two deceased full-brothers. The approximate, conventional location of the chief-homestead of Lomekeri's eldest son is marked as X on the map, and that of the eldest son of Acolekur as Y.

HOUSE-LINE II.

Details of current senior generation:—

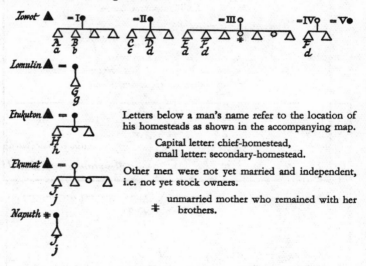

Letters below a man's name refer to the location of his homesteads as shown in the accompanying map.

Capital letter: chief-homestead,
small letter: secondary-homestead.

Other men were not yet married and independent, i.e. not yet stock owners.

‡   unmarried mother who remained with her brothers.

As far as the people of this group are concerned their effective Family was limited to their own House-line, comprising 56 persons. Active relations and reciprocal rights with members of House-line I had lapsed because of geographical distance.

194

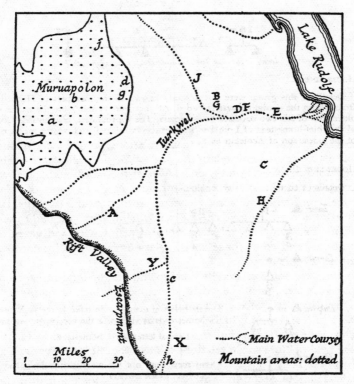

SKETCH MAP OF CENTRAL AND SOUTH-WESTERN
TURKANALAND

Approximate locations of homesteads in March 1950

CHAPTER SEVEN

STOCK-ASSOCIATES

Introduction

In both Jie and Turkana societies each man is the centre of a field of direct, formalized, inter-personal social relations some of which are established by birth—cognatic relations, some by conscious acts of marriage—affinal relations, and some by deliberate pledge—relations between bond-friends. Whilst the emotional and practical content and the moral values inherent in these types of relations differ considerably in some respects, yet they exhibit two vital factors in common which give them essential similarity and mark them off from the fortuitous relations with acquaintances and casual companions, and from those social relations sustained by compulsory ritual co-operation.

Firstly, people related by kinship and bond-friendship are a man's particular friends in the world, the circle in which he finds affection, sympathy, assistance and confidence. They are all people who will help him and whom he helps in return. They provide, moreover, a cluster of relations peculiar to each man not wholly coincident with the field of close social relations of any other person, not even a full-brother. They constitute the range of a man's specifically individual social action. Secondly, with each of these people a man maintains well-recognized, reciprocal rights to claim gifts of domestic animals in certain socially defined circumstances. Thus a particular kind of inter-personal relationship is consciously translated into the right to seek stock in times of need and the roughly corresponding obligation to give stock in times of others' needs. For the Jie and Turkana this is a critical index of social relations, for through the ownership and use of stock a man not only finds the material content of life but also the supreme means whereby he expresses and maintains his social interests and development. Domestic animals are a man's dearest possession and almost the only store of value that he knows;

and without them social life, as understood by these people, would be impossible. Through the use and disposal of stock he is able, in the most definite way, to express his relations towards others. In native conceptions a man who is closely related is *ipso facto* one who gives and is given animals, for this not only expresses mutual confidence and affection but it expresses also a genuine co-operation in each other's life and development.

These people are referred to collectively as *ngitungakan*, 'my people', thus distinguishing them from *ngikolomak*, 'strangers' (who may, however, be acquaintances). In this account I shall refer to them as 'stock-associates', and I shall be chiefly concerned with the connections between these types of close, social relations and the index of reciprocal stock rights.

The occasions on which a man exercises his rights to seek gifts of animals may be briefly summarized by way of introduction. The principal occasion when a man needs stock is at the time of marriage, when he must give bridewealth. In discussing his system of social relations and range of stock-associates a Jie or Turkana invariably refers first to bridewealth, and in that institution are embodied the essentials of the whole complex. The potential bridegroom goes to each of his stock-associates at such a time and begs from them contributions of all kinds of stock for his bridewealth; and the contributions in general reflect the type and closeness of each relationship involved. From his own herd comes about half of the bridewealth, the remainder being made up of contributions from his stock-associates. An average bridewealth consists of about fifty large stock and up to two hundred goats and sheep, and the number of contributors may number up to fifty persons, or even more. In both tribes polygyny is not merely the ideal but the normal practice; therefore it can be understood that bridewealth involves not only large numbers of stock but that assembly and payment and subsequent redistribution amongst the stock-associates of the bride's father is an occurrence involving a man relatively frequently. Marriage is a fundamental institution in most societies, certainly in these two, and its establishment in each particular instance is a heavy material as well as moral burden on the bridegroom, and is therefore pre-eminently an occasion when he exercises to the full his prerogatives against his own stock-associates.

However, marriage is not the only occasion on which stock rights are exercised. Compensation, payable only in stock, is the normal means by which serious injuries and disputes are settled; and in paying compensation an offender seeks the assistance of his stock-associates, who conversely expect shares if a man receives such a payment[1]. Throughout life a man periodically has obligations to provide feasts and to perform ritual acts for which an important element is the slaughter of one or more animals. In most instances, certainly for any important ceremony, an ox must be provided; but it is axiomatic in Jieland and common in Turkanaland that a man does not slaughter one of his own beasts but always begs from someone else, later providing a cow in exchange. Here again a stock-associate is approached, not any member of society fortuitously. Stock disease is ever present in Jieland, and herds are sometimes gravely depleted by a local epidemic. Though depletion of the herds by disease is far less common in Turkanaland there is equal peril of severe losses due to the failure of pastures, which is only a slight danger for the Jie. The 'owner', in rebuilding his herd, seeks help from his stock-associates. Periodically a man takes advantage of his rights to beg the gift of an animal or two—possibly for no special reason other than the mere desire for animals, possibly to obtain a new bell-ox, bull, goat-buck or ram. In normal social life there is a more or less continuous giving, receiving and exchanging of animals, mainly for essential requirements, but partly also for its own sake in order to make recurrent expressions of vital relationships.

The general category of stock-associates can be divided into two classes—those with whom a man's relations are especially close and lasting and with whom reciprocal rights involve gifts of cattle,[2] and those with whom a man's relations are relatively distant, and which tend to diminish through time if not die away altogether, and with whom reciprocal rights involve only the gifts of a goat or two. Cattle rights exist in reference to close agnates, close maternal kin (chiefly the mother's brothers), close affines (fathers-, brothers- and sons-in-law) and bond-friends; goat (and sheep) rights exist in reference to other maternal and affinal kin, and to minor bond-friends, and, in Jieland, to clansmen. In practice this line of differentiation is not so precise or easy to demarcate, but the principle holds nevertheless. An especially friendly clansman or a wife's half-brother may on some occasion come into the cattle-giving class, for

---

[1] See also below, p. 200.

[2] Following Turkana conceptions, camels are grouped with cattle for all social and ritual purposes. They are 'large stock' in contrast with goats and sheep.

instance; a mother's brother may in a particular case fall into the goat-giving class.[1] The cattle-giving class of stock-associates comprises of course those persons with whom relations are more intense, more important and more reliable, and which persist during a man's lifetime and may even be continued by his sons. It may appear a grossly materialistic concept of either the natives or myself to attempt, as it were, to measure social relations in terms of the nature and value of gifts made and received, but concerning this certain points must be made. In the first place I am adopting the native viewpoint here. If one asks a man which people seem most important to him as an individual, he will enumerate the cattle-giving class of stock-associates; and if one enquires why these people are so important, the ready answer is, 'They are the people who help me and give me cattle at certain times.' The Jie and Turkana are a practical-minded people—as perhaps most Africans are in real life—and for them a relationship is of significant value in so far as it allows the transfer of stock when required, remembering, however, that gifts of stock create reciprocal obligations. It is not only what an individual can obtain, but also what he must give—rights are balanced by obligations. This constant process of giving and receiving stock is for the native dictated by the occurrence of social situations when a man has need of stock for which his own herd is insufficient. For instance, a man cannot produce the whole of a normal bridewealth payment from his herd, or at least not without producing serious economic difficulties by removing the producers of milk, blood and meat supplies. He is, therefore, essentially dependent on his stock-associates for help, on the tacit understanding of the guarantee of his help to them severally in the future.

Stock-association is a form of co-operation and mutual insurance, and through it a man maintains a range of significant inter-personal relations within the wider society in which he lives. Stock-association is the core of social life through which an individual maintains himself as a full social being and not merely an isolated unit or even the member of a small, isolated group.

Whilst, like the people themselves, we may regard stock rights as a reliable index of the strength and importance of social relations, neither we nor they deny in any way the other values inherent in a

---

[1] It would, however, be unusual for a mother's brother to give only one or two goats on important occasions. He might make a gift of fifteen to twenty goats for his nephew's bridewealth, for example, instead of one or two cattle.

person's closest relations. In Jieland, residential ties and the day-to-day co-operation in affairs large and small that results from intimate, face-to-face relations amongst close agnates (extended family) and within the small clan-hamlet are of real and considerable importance. Partly connected with such small-scale community relations, but extended also to the whole range of stock-associates, is the provision of hospitality and general assistance. A man can be sure of getting food and shelter and a welcome at the homestead of any of his stock-associates. He can attend their feasts as a guest. He or his wife can beg grain or seed or other foodstuffs when these are scarce. His wife can call upon their womenfolk to help her in gardening work in return for beer, milk and porridge. Of some importance in pastoral affairs is the right to ask permission to use a water-hole in the dry season.[1] A poor man may put his cattle in the camp of some stock-associate when he has insufficient to warrant a separate camp of his own. Two or more stock-associates sometimes keep all or part of their herds in joint camps. In order to lessen the risks of disease (and formerly of raiding), men like to spread their stock amongst the camps of stock-associates, taking some of their animals in return. In judicial affairs the responsibilities of close relationship are not confined only to assistance in the payment of compensation, but under the indigenous system of self-help, included also the duty of lending verbal and, if necessary, physical support. An accused man might offer forcible resistance to the demands of his accusers and would expect his stock-associates to support him. On the other hand an injured person would back up his demands for compensation by actually going to seize the number of animals believed to be justified in the situation. Indeed, a man who could only put up a weak show of force was likely to be compelled to submit to the opposite party; and in any case force, or the threat of it, was the only method of implementing the efficient resistance of unjust demands or the payment of just compensation. The support of a man's stock-associates in all this was partly a matter of their friendliness with him, the allegiance they owe him; and partly it resided in the fact that if compensation had to be paid they themselves would be liable to contribute animals, and if compensation was to be received they were entitled to shares. Today in Jieland, with the abolition of self-help and the institution of native courts, the aspect of physical support has largely disappeared; nevertheless, the obligation to assist remains,

[1] See pp. 37-8.

both in contributing towards compensation and in giving moral and vocal support.

In Turkanaland, because of ecological conditions, the position is not the same. There are no permanent settlements, nor are there permanent, perambulating groups of families or other units. The ties of common residence, daily co-operation and face-to-face relations in the local neighbourhood always tend to be temporary and exiguous. A man's stock-associates are not linked to him by ties of a residential, economic or pastoral nature; his neighbours at any one time may not necessarily include any of his stock-associates, and seldom more than one or two out of the total category. He will not see many of them for lengthy periods, nor will he be aware of all their movements and activities, for they are likely to be scattered widely and arbitrarily over a large area,[1] and both his and their locations change fairly frequently. The relationship of stock-association therefore consists primarily in mutual assistance on the more important occasions of individual social life. For much of the time relations are dormant, being reactivated as occasion requires. In this connection an aspect of the system peculiar to the Turkana is important. If a man receives a female animal as his rightful share in a stock-associate's in-payment (notably bridewealth) or as a gift, a series of exchange gifts is begun which is ideally inextinguishable. If he receives a cow, he should later return one of its female calves; later again he himself may claim a female calf of that latter animal in maturity. These secondary claims are not necessarily made by a man because of any particular need at the time, although in fact he has a strong right if he is in need. Often, however, it is a matter of keeping the relationship going—'keeping the pot boiling', as we might say colloquially. In this way a fairly constant and persistent series of exchange gifts is maintained additional to the exercise of rights at critical times of need. It is not only, of course, a matter of the gifts as such, important though they are, but more significantly it keeps stock-associates in touch and helps to prevent relations fading out through prolonged inactivity. Not only are rights claimed and obligations accepted, but at the same time a certain amount of personal contact is maintained through visiting and accompanying hospitality. It provides a continuous reason for interest and concern in the state of the herds of a stock-associate.

Occasional pastoral co-operation may occur between stock-

---

[1] Cf. Figure 17.

associates in a similar way to that in Jieland. The obligations of support in judicial affairs also exist; indeed, in Turkanaland, where there is no established court system yet, these obligations are rather more important as most disputes are settled in the traditional manner.[1]

Before examining some of the details of the various types of stock-associates in the two societies, two salient points must be emphasized. Firstly, a man's stock-associates are specific to him alone; they are a category of people related in certain ways to him, and in no manner do they form a corporate group. By the inclusion of affines and bond-friends, not even full-brothers have the same actual category of stock-associates; or, to be more precise, their categories differ in quality. For instance, a man has very close affinal relations with his sister's husband, and he is also the affine of her husband's brother; but the latter relationship is by no means so close, nor so reliable in times of need. A man often, but by no means always, maintains relations with the brother of his bond-friend, yet everyone acknowledges that they are less intense and valuable. Theoretically a man maintains affinal ties with all the close agnates of his daughter's husband, but in practice most of these ties are recognized only in the breach, unless there exist special considerations of friendship. Relations with a stock-associate's brother or half-brother or cousin are indirect; they presuppose the link of one or more people in between. As between other members of a man's category of stock-associates there are slight if any relations at all, certainly no specific recognition of responsibilities, rights and obligations. For example, a man has little or nothing to do with his half-brother's maternal kin, and probably does not know much about his brother-in-law's bond-friends. The cluster of stock-associates only comes into operation in relation to one individual, and then those people do not usually come together as a body at any one time or place. When a man wishes to marry he must himself visit each of his stock-associates in turn to seek their support and material assistance. One may not even know what another has given; they are unlikely all to turn up at the wedding. The exercise of rights periodically to beg an ox for ritual purposes, or an uncastrated male animal, is purely an individual

---

[1] Homicide almost alone must be dealt with by administrative officers in their capacity as magistrate, and a headman must report all cases. Other disputes appear to reach officers only where disputes are long drawn out or where one party feels acutely maltreated by an indigenous settlement.

affair of which other stock-associates know nothing, nor are they in any way concerned. The second point to be made is that social relations involved between stock-associates have no legal content whatsoever. That is, using the term 'legal' as understood in this present account, rights cannot be supported by the use of force, the only indigenous judicial mechanism known, nor in the native courts, the modern instrument of law. This holds even for those close agnates who are members of one's own extended family but stand outside the house (Jie) or the nuclear family (Turkana). Rights with reference to all stock-associates are maintained essentially by the factor of reciprocity. A right is balanced by an obligation such that the social relationship consists in mutual assistance and mutual support. The failure of one partner in the relationship to stand by his obligation can only be met by a similar refusal of the defaulter's rights, and the whole relationship may end. One cannot compel a stock-associate to fulfil his obligations, although one may appeal to his moral sense, and to the social values inherent in the relationship. But if the relationship is not a legal one, neither is it wholly a moral one. It has a vital moral element, yet that is in practice insufficient to maintain it on its own. The basic sanction contained within this type of social relationship is its essential value by virtue of reciprocity. It is this sort of sanction that Malinowski designated 'legal'.[1] It is contended here, however, that it is necessary to distinguish between a social sanction of reciprocity and one of the use, or the threat of the use, of force—ultimately physical coercion. There are well-recognized crimes such as stock-thieving, adultery and homicide (to name only the serious ones), the ultimate sanction against which is force. In this account the sanction of force is called a legal sanction, and the rights and obligations such a sanction upholds are legal ones.

Affinal and Maternal Kin, and Bond-friends

Although essentially similar in principle, the quality of affinal and maternal relations is not the same in the two societies. Affinal kin are of the greatest consequence to Turkana, whilst maternal kin are relatively less important; on the other hand, in Jieland maternal kin are perhaps rather more valued than affines.

Affinal kin are held in greater esteem and affection than perhaps any other body of kin, in Turkanaland, not even excluding close

---

[1] Malinowski, B., *Crime and Custom in Savage Society*, London, 1926, p. 58, and *passim*.

agnates. I have often asked men who in their own circle of relationships they like best and value most, and invariably, whatever the estimate of the rest, close affines are placed first. Turkana speak with great enthusiasm about their affines, which is in marked contrast with their normal phlegmatism. It is suggested here that this importance derives from several related sources. In a society like this, where the nuclear family is so important, the institution of marriage is regarded as of the utmost significance and value, and its stability as quite vital to the maintenance of the unit. This great emphasis on marriage[1] produces a corresponding stress upon affinal relations. In conjunction with this attitude is the large size of bridewealth normally and traditionally given at marriage, which heavy transfer of stock in itself produces stock-relations of great significance. In addition, the cultural norm is for a man to seek to establish his independence of his closest agnates and in this way to set up his own nuclear family and homesteads and to obtain full control of his share of inheritance. In this tendency to move away from agnatic kin, with whom at the time there are relatively automatic relations outside the primary control of the individual, there is a compensatory movement towards affinal kin, in affection and frequently in actual geographical terms—especially towards a wife's father and brothers. In a very practical way, on first becoming independent, a man more often seeks the help of a close affine than of any other kinsman, even to the extent of sharing a joint homestead. At such a time he usually has relatively small herds and finds it economically useful to ally himself with someone else, providing always that his new independence is not thereby threatened. He leaves his brothers in order to assert his status, and this is not endangered by living with affines. At the same time he is strongly drawn towards them, for they are the most important stock-associates specific to himself alone, and at this stage these affinal ties should have become well established. The important position of the wife in the new nuclear family also tends to put a premium on ties and affections between her husband on the one hand and her father and brothers on the other.

Amongst the Jie, where community life is valuable and persistent and where moreover there is little or no possibility of movement away from one's close agnates and one's clansmen, affinal kin do not gain the outstanding importance found in Turkanaland. Neverthe-

---

[1] Divorce is practically unknown in both societies. Adultery is as grave a crime as homicide.

less, they are significant members of the 'cattle-giving class' of stock-associates.

Terminologically, all affinal kin are grouped together in one category—*ekamerun*, pl. *ngikamerak* (masculine forms)—and ideally a man maintains relations with all of them, including the affines of his agnates. In practice, however, his close affines, those upon whom he sets greatest value, are the fathers and brothers of his wives and the husbands of his sisters and daughters.[1] Agnates of these men are regarded as distant affines[2] who come into the 'goat-giving class' of stock-associates. Similarly, from the obverse viewpoint, the closest affines of a man's agnates come into this lesser class.

The process of marriage will be referred to in Chapter 8; apart from the vital fact of the transfer of bridewealth, the significant feature is the series of ritual which is explicitly performed to ensure the success and fertility of the marriage, but which simultaneously involves the joint participation of the new affines with a gradually increasing co-operation and friendliness formally expressed. At this period relations are established which are to persist for a lifetime with an acknowledged and tremendous potentiality for mutual assistance in all manner of social and individual matters. Not the least part of this consists of the claims which either party may make upon the other for gifts of animals. A man can normally rely upon an affine for a cow or female camel at least. Affines take a particular interest in each other's future marriages and are often principal supporters at those events. A wife's father or full-brother is the conventional person to represent a man at his own or his daughter's marriage.

Affinal relations, from the point of view adopted in this account, tend to be asymmetrical. A wife's father or brother, and to a rather smaller extent the father or brother of a son's wife, are 'superior' affines; conversely a sister's or daughter's husband is in an 'inferior' status. A superior affine's claim is greater, or can less easily be refused or reduced by a man, than his own claim against that affine; and similarly his own claim is greater against an inferior than *vice-versa*. In Turkanaland a man can scarcely consider refusal of a superior affine's demand for a cow or camel towards his bridewealth, whereas

---

[1] In Jieland, because of the importance of the house, close relations usually extend to all men of houses into which a man or girl of one's own house has married. Cf. pp. 224-7.

[2] *Ekamerun loice* (Turkana); *ekamerun lodoice* (Jie)—'lesser affine'.

a superior himself might not only be free of such an obligation but, if the groom is fairly wealthy, he might be actually given an animal at the time of the wedding. When Aleri married his fifth wife he sent messages to the husbands of his two sisters and three daughters that they should attend the wedding and bring with them a cow towards his bridewealth. This they did, and, because of their status of inferiority, they were not able to join in any of the ceremonies and celebrations and remained conspicuously outside the crowds.[1] Yet on the same occasion Aleri gave several gifts to his own superior affines who enthusiastically joined in all the events. 'You cannot refuse your "big affine" anything,' said one Turkana, and much the same may be said of the Jie.

With his wife's brother or sister's husband, once the marriage has become well established after a few years, a man often maintains extremely cordial relations of a practical equality, equivalent indeed to fraternity with none of the latent tensions that are involved in real brotherhood. Brothers-in-law may frequently, for larger or shorter periods, share a joint cattle camp (Jie) or a joint chief- or secondary-homestead (Turkana). A brother-in-law is pre-eminently a person whom one can trust and rely upon, even to the extent of allowing him temporary control of one's herd. There is commonly considerable affection between the pair of men, and this relationship is one of the most valued amongst these people. There is not the difficulty of superiority and age difference as with a father-in-law, nor of tension and rivalry as with an agnate. The two men are often of the same generation, about the same stage of personal development and with similar but not competing interests and problems. There is in addition the strong emotional bond via the sister-wife.

It is to be emphasized that not only for an inferior affine but for all affinal kin in general the actual relationship finally established arises out of the genuine efforts that the men put into it. Notwithstanding the significance of the high bridewealth and of marriage,

[1] This case was particularly notable for me since one of Aleri's sons-in-law was well known to me. In age, this man, Imana, differed little from Aleri, and he was at least no less wealthy. Imana was a man of considerable personality and reputation, and was normally afforded a leading position in affairs. On this occasion he took but a minor role in the final bridewealth discussions—a time of much public and private debate and histrionics beloved by Turkana—nor did he take any part in the dancing and feasting. Upon my enquiries, he replied, 'Aleri is my big affine so I just sit [i.e. remain a spectator]. I am afraid to dance or eat meat; it is his marriage and I am small [inferior].' Imana had walked at least twenty miles to attend this event; he gave Aleri a female camel, and stayed several days.

men do not feel that an affinal bond can develop its potential values unless each party wishes for them and strives to obtain them. One must endeavour to put the satisfaction of obligations first and thus to earn the right to make successful claims in turn. Even for a superior affine the element of moral compulsion may be a double-edged weapon which, if unwisely used, can rebound upon him. A father-in-law may have a greater claim upon his daughter's husband, but it is not entirely an automatic right; most certainly it remains related directly to his own attitude to the relationship and his willingness to help. There is a clear and high moral ideal of affinal relations of mutual assistance, affection and sympathy, and Turkana in particular constantly and consciously aim at it. Very many do in fact have notably cordial relations with their affines, and with one or two of the total range in particular, and they find in them one of the most stable elements in their nomadic and rather isolated life.

Therefore, although the notion of superiority and inferiority exists and makes affinal relations asymmetrical, yet there is at the back of it the essential factor of reciprocity; a lesser right is balanced against a greater obligation, but there is specific recognition of this give-and-take. In any case this asymmetry is not to be overemphasized, especially in relations between older men, whatever the nature of the formal bond. Such is the friendliness, sense of ease and strength of long-established ties and interests between affines that a stranger (native as well as alien) finds it difficult if not impossible to ascertain from general behaviour who is in the 'superior' position.

The importance of a man's *maternal kin* stems directly from a recognition of his dual origin, which is not by any means extinguished by the social emphasis laid on agnatic descent. As will be seen presently, a woman is assimilated to her husband's clan and family and therefore neither she nor her children can be said in any way to belong to her natal group. Nevertheless, affectionate ties persist, and they are especially strongly supported by the important affinal relations between the husband-father and his wife's kinsmen.

In Jieland the general pattern of relations with maternal kin is founded in childhood. A first and second child is always born and initially reared at the mother's father's (or brother's) homestead, and all children, with their mother, are frequent and welcome visitors to his homestead. They come to regard it as their second home, and a place where they are almost as free and privileged as at their father's homestead. Maternal kin are conventionally, and most usually in fact also, benevolent, generous and essentially friendly people who make no claims to a position of authority over the child, nor at the early stage do they make material claims. In Turkanaland, owing to the dichotomy of the nuclear family, where brother and sister are often separated for long periods, and the geographical separation after her marriage, relations between the man and woman are not particularly prominent unless there happen to be especial ties between him and her husband as already described.[1] This general situation is reflected in relations between a man and his sister's children. Ideally the Turkana prototype of a mother's brother is the same as in Jieland, but in practice relations commonly fall short of this—not, however, in the sense of any antagonism, but as a faint reflection of the ideal.

Because of the comparative lateness of marriage (about the age of thirty for a man's first marriage) an adult man does not usually have a living mother's father, and the idea of him is always coloured by childish memories. An adult man's maternal relations are largely directed towards his mother's full-brothers. These are the men who were formerly most closely linked with his mother as an unmarried girl and who most benefited by the receipt of her bridewealth. Owing to the fissiparous process in an extended family, a mother's half-brothers and paternal cousins belong to houses specifically distinguished from that of her full-brothers in terms especially of stock-ownership but also in extra-familial interests and relations. Half-brothers consider themselves as distinct from her as they are from her full-brothers who yet remain within the extended family, and they exercise and acknowledge only minor claims in relation to her, her husband and her children. The mother's brother-sister's son relationship (*mamai-locen*) is therefore the essential one, and rights obtain to each party in virtue of the common, direct link of the sister-mother. Nevertheless, this does not presuppose an equivocal status of a married woman, for she is quite definitely a member of her husband's and sons' house and family; within, that is, the orbit of their nexus of stock rights and ritual obligations.[2] The mother's brother-sister's son relationship is therefore, as it was in the latter's

---

[1] A mother's brother is of course a father's brother-in-law. Since polygamy is the norm (see Appendix to Chapter 8), there is a range of wife's brothers, as also of sister's husbands. A man does not maintain equally close relations with them all, and a few come to stand out above the rest. If a son's mother's brother happens to be one of the father's closer brothers-in-law, then the son tends to inherit his father's good relations.

[2] In Jieland, the married woman becomes involved in her husband's residential system also.

childhood, not one of onerous prescription but one of mutual affection, interest and benevolence. Nowhere in the relationship is there any element of compulsion, but throughout there is an emphasis upon mutual consideration and the desire voluntarily to help one another and to maintain the relationship at an ideally high moral level. The mother's brothers exercise claims against their neices' bridewealths and accept an obligation to contribute towards their nephews' bridewealths. At all times each party feels the privilege of seeking the other's assistance, not the least form of which is in gifts of animals.

The general content of the relationship is extended to the mother's brothers' sons, but when the mother's brothers are dead and their sons become differentiated into separate houses, maternal relations frequently fall away or even entirely atrophy in practical effect. Maternal relations are essentially founded on brother-sister affections and interests which disappear with their deaths. They contain only a modicum of reciprocal rights and interests which can be usefully inherited and guarded after their time.

Amongst the Turkana, even more than in the case of affines, the reciprocal rights pertaining to a mother's brother and sister's son are potential and must be established by the genuine efforts of both parties. There is, therefore, a wide variation in these relations. A maternal uncle is chiefly important, if at all, to a younger man who is seeking his independence. It is common also for a widow to take her children to live with or near one of her full-brothers, who becomes temporary guardian to them. Relatively few middle-aged men have a surviving maternal uncle, and in any case, as a man grows older he tends increasingly to lay more emphasis on his closer affinal kin—those with whom he has himself established personal bonds and with whom he feels the links of stock-association to be stronger and more fruitful. In contrast, the Jie wife normally maintains close relations with her brothers, and a man grows up to think of them as very near kinsmen. Also they are usually near in a geographical sense.

Bond-friends[1] are the only type of stock-associates whose ties are not coincident with kinship, but which in virtue of reciprocal stock rights have for both Jie and Turkana a 'pseudo-kinship' quality. A bond-friend is a person with whom one informally contracts such rights for reasons of mutual convenience and trust. In Jieland there

---

[1] 'Bond-friend'—*lopai* (Jie), *lopei* (Turkana).

is usually a strong element of genuine and proved friendship, but not always so in Turkanaland. For both peoples there is something nearly approaching a business agreement. A bond-friend will give one a cow or ox (or camel) for some purpose on the tacit understanding that at another time he can obtain a return gift. There is no strictly formal basis of the relationship; it is not established by any legal or ritual act and consists primarily of this link of reciprocity. In this, of all stock-relations, if a man does not reasonably meet his obligations he will quickly forfeit his own rights and the association fails, for there is nothing at all to support it. Bond-friendship can be contracted with any man, irrespective of age, social position or residence. In Turkanaland especially, but also in Jieland, considerations of wealth enter into it, for a man does not wish to ally himself to someone considerably poorer than he is, and from whom, therefore, he may find difficulty in obtaining his due return and a fruitful relationship in general. A wealthy man never finds it difficult to make new bond-friends, but a poor man is usually acceptable only to similarly poor men.[1]

When a man is in need of stock for some important purpose he tends to approach anyone who he believes is likely to help him. If he has close friends he may attempt to persuade them to help. They have no compulsion to accede to his request, and some refuse on the grounds of insufficiency of the friendship, or current inability to afford help, or unwillingness further to extend the range of stock-association. Here and there, however, over the course of years some men will agree to give an animal. It is recognized by both men that the gift creates a reciprocal obligation and is in fact the beginning of a potentially unceasing chain of exchanges and other assistance. In Turkanaland, in many cases, however, the bond is begun when a comparative stranger seeks hospitality and later begs an animal.[2]

With a firmly established bond-friend one only gives and begs large stock, usually not more than one beast on any occasion. Within reason one can normally depend on such a person. Since the whole relationship rests on its obvious mutual convenience, care is needed not to overtax it by the too frequent exercise of rights nor by a one-

---

[1] For instance, one wealthy and influential Turkana complained to me that men were 'always' [*sic*] trying to begin bond-friendship with him because his wealth and reputation were widely known. As an elderly man he was no longer anxious to assume new bonds except under the most favourable circumstances. Thus he was eager to have me as a bond-friend because, like all Europeans, I was supposed to be inexhaustibly wealthy.

[2] For a case in point see *Survey of the Turkana*, pp. 104-5.

sided exercise. Either party is entirely free to break off the bond, or to allow it to atrophy; on the other hand many bonds persist throughout a man's lifetime and may even be continued by his sons. On the whole, a man is always seeking to establish new bonds, and even young, unmarried men have at least two or three. Through these ties a man is able to extend the effective range of his personal relationships and his stock-associates beyond the relatively restricted and automatic ties of kinship. A man with many bond-friends becomes less dependent upon formal ties where these become irksome or are made difficult by tension and rivalry.

Today, with the disappearance of inter-tribal warfare, bond-friendship extends across tribal boundaries. In Jieland I met no man over the age of thirty-five who had not several alien bond-friends, and most Turkana had one or two in the tribes nearer to their own region.[1] It is probable that even in the old days Jie had bond-friends amongst the Turkana, and vice versa. Some bonds are established for trading purposes primarily, especially by the Jie with the Labwor people to the south-west.[2] Of course, no bond-friendship is entirely a matter of stock rights, for there is always much visiting, hospitality and assistance in general ways.

Amongst the Turkana one of the main elements of bond-friendship is not directly connected with stock rights, but because of its importance in the pastoral system it inevitably affects and strengthens stock-association. Because of the unreliable nature of the rainfall and seasons, no Turkana ever feels quite secure in his dry-season pastures, most particularly his mountain grasslands. In any year he may have to quit his conventional area, exhausted of vegetation, and seek alternative pastures elsewhere. In the later part of the dry season such movements are not easily made, and normally a man must go to an area where someone will stand surety for him in local, informal discussion.[3] Kinsmen will serve this purpose, but their locations are fortuitous and do not necessarily cover all the alter-

[1] The small size of Jieland is doubtless the differentiating factor here.

[2] The Labwor Hills were and are the chief market-centre where pastoral products can be exchanged for agricultural produce, pottery and ironware. The Jie have now extended the system to the eastern Acoli. A man finds it easier to trade in the market area (there being no formal markets) via a bond-friend. During the latter part of the 1950-51 dry season I estimated that at any one time about one-third of the older men of the Kotido district were away staying with Labwor and Acoli bond-friends, often remaining for several weeks. Similarly, Turkana go up to Karamoja or Suk or into the Sudan.

[3] See pp. 34-5.

native pasture areas. Through his bond-friendships a man endeavours to ensure that he has a potential supporter in most or all of the areas to which, in any year, he might wish to shift. This is a quite conscious policy, and each Turkana accepts the corresponding liability to help his bond-friends similarly. I discussed this matter with Lokoyen whose range of bond-friends is given, *inter alia*, in Figure 17. As he pointed out, his thirteen bond-friends covered all the reasonable alternative pasture areas open to him in a bad season, to the north and west of his own conventional area; they included one Dodoth through whom extraterritorial advantages might be obtainable in a disastrous year. To the east was barren country and to the south pastures were chronically inferior to Lokoyen's own, but he had two bond-friends there who depended upon him when they wished to move northwards. (See sketch-map in Figure 17.)

Close agnatic kin comprise the fourth principal type of stock-associates,[1] and, as we have already seen, relations here are no less strongly inter-personal than the rest. Jie and Turkana agree that of the whole category of a man's stock-associates their closest agnates are the most important—reciprocal rights are greatest, i.e. gifts of stock are larger in number and frequency, between these men. Ideally, rights and relations in general are inextinguishable, continuing from generation to generation, although amongst the Turkana they gradually atrophy in fact. Non-agnatic relations die out and are not even all continued by the sons of men involved. For example, there has already been noted the falling away of relations of mother's brother-sister's son to the tenuous bonds between father's sister's sons and mother's brothers' sons. Each new generation establishes its own maternal, affinal and bond-friend relations in accordance with the new social circumstances in its own time.

Further, agnatic relations are combined into loose corporate

---

[1] In each tribe there is a category of putatively agnatic kin, viz. clansmen. A man belongs to the exogamous clan of his father. No formal links are known or claimed between Families of the same clan, nor is any clan founder remembered. A woman, at marriage, abandons her father's clan and is ritually incorporated into that of her husband. Clan membership defines the pattern of ritual to be followed through life, especially in connection with marriage and fertility. A married woman participates only in the ritual prescribed by her husband's clan. In Turkanaland, many clans are large (over a thousand adult males) and most are widespread throughout the country. A man has no relations with his clansmen *qua* clansmen. See *Survey of the Turkana*, chapter 8. In Jieland, clans are small (one to eight Families) and each has a firm, residential basis in a clan-hamlet. Most or all clansmen come within the 'goat-giving class' of stock-associates therefore, and an especially friendly one may sometimes beg or give cattle.

groups such that for all members of a group (extended family) their total fields are co-terminous and specifically related to a common patrilineal ancestor and involve the highly significant factor of inheritance and ownership of the herds. Thus the cluster of the most vital stock-associates make up a group which forms something of a stable core in each individual's total field of inter-personal relations and stock rights. Each member of an extended family shares this core in common. For the Jie this core is given additional importance by its residential character; for both peoples a certain ritual inter-dependence is also involved.

Bearing this in mind, it is instructive to compare the emotional and conventional attitudes and values concerning agnatic kin with those concerning maternal kin, affines and bond-friends. In each of the latter three types of relations, bonds are essentially ones of mutual convenience, and depend in practice on the cordiality that can be consciously maintained between the men. As Jie commonly say of the mother's brother, so we may say of all these men—'it is a matter of the heart'. There are, as already pointed out, quite definite and recognized bases of relationships with the mother's brother and affinal kin, but there are not as such any specific, compulsory obligations on their part to assist a man by giving him stock or in other ways.

Clearly, bond-friendship is entirely a matter of mutual convenience and utility grown out of affection and trust. To get the most out of maternal or affinal relationships, indeed almost to get anything at all, a man must work towards that end. He must make conscious and constant efforts to fulfil his obligations to the utmost, and in general to maintain mutual interests and confidence. He may not take any-thing for granted. If he meets a refusal or only a partial accedence to his demands (whether for stock or other assistance), he can entertain little idea of rights which are now being frustrated and denied. His claims are such that if they are fully met he tends to regard it as an act of generosity, not of proper obligations fulfilled. 'You can not compel a mother's brother to give stock for your marriage,' one informant told me. 'It is good and right that he should, but he only gives because his heart is good [i.e. because he is cordially disposed towards you]. If he refuses you can do nothing.'

Relations and therefore rights in reference to close agnates are almost automatically established and maintained by the facts of birth and descent. A man, as a member of an extended family, shares common inheritance with his fellow agnates and holds therefore fairly specific rights and owes similar obligations. This automatic element tends, as already described, to engender friction, jealousy and even open hostility. Yet at the same time a man scarcely feels constrained to demand less than his 'pound of flesh'. Because of the very closeness of agnatic bonds, a man feels the right to interfere and even dictate in his agnate's affairs in a way which he does not, and dare not, in the affairs of, for instance, his affines; yet a man resents his agnate's interferences and their insistences upon their rights and prerogatives, and relations are often filled with tension and trouble. A mother's brother is invariably contrasted more than favourably with a father's half-brother, or a brother-in-law with a half-brother, a bond-friend with a paternal cousin. The mother's brother-sister's son relationship in particular is conventionally held up as all that is excellent in Jie life—warm friendliness, hospitality, selflessness and readiness to help and comfort—and in like manner relations between brothers-in-law in Turkanaland. Half-brothers and paternal cousins are typified as grasping persons who are out for all they can get, and rudely unsympathetic, and probably attempting to deny one's own justifiable claims. One Jie was praising to me his mother's brother, who had given two cattle to his bridewealth. He went on at some length extolling this generosity. I pointed out that in fact three of his agnates had also given two cattle each and that his half-brother had given three cattle. 'Ee, they are of my [extended] family,' he replied. 'It is only right that they give me cattle. Are we not grand-children [i.e. descendants of a common grandfather]? My mother's brother—his family is separate; he need not give, and he gives me two cattle because his heart is good and because of my mother, his sister. It is wonderful!'

Such contradistinctions are of course highly conventionalized as I have noted them here, for in fact by no means all half-brothers and paternal cousins are rapacious and niggardly in their help or affection, nor yet are all mother's brothers or affines benevolent. A man normally finds some of his closest friends and companions amongst his agnatic kin—men with whom he has maintained loyalty, affection and trust since boyhood and which are most likely to continue until death. Some whole extended families are groups of conspicuous amity; although, equally, others are rent by mistrust and rivalry. Nevertheless, these conventionalized descriptions—conventional-ized by the people themselves, that is—do express what is an important aspect in these social relationships, by contrasting the social and personal tensions which arise out of the very close and almost automatic, initial quality of agnatic bonds on the one hand, with on the other the cordiality which results from the general and constant striving to earn the assistance and confidence of maternal and affinal kin.

The Range of Stock-associates

In Figures 16 and 17 are given examples of the range of stock-associates from each tribe. As a rough average a man has about thirty close associates ('cattle-giving'), but the number varies a good deal, from as few as seven or eight to as many as fifty.[1] The number of a man's stock-associates depends not only upon his age but also upon his stock wealth, past and present. A wealthier man is able to marry more frequently and thus to increase the number of his affines, and he finds it easier to make bond-friends. The prestige afforded to the wealthy man as such helps him to retain the good-will of his associates even where reciprocal assistance slackens. A poor man is conversely in a disadvantageous position.

During this account of stock-associates it has been convenient to write of a wife's brother or mother's brother as if there were but one man standing in that relationship, whereas of course there are commonly several such men. We must take note here of the different types of stock-owning unit existing in Jieland and Turkanaland, i.e. the house and nuclear family respectively. Amongst the Jie the head of a house represents his younger full-brothers in all things concerning the herds. Thus when I refer to the 'mother's brother', like the native I primarily mean the 'eldest surviving full-brother of the mother', and *mutatis mutandis* in respect of 'wife's brother', 'half-brother', 'paternal cousin', etc. A sister's son would not normally beg animals from his mother's younger brothers since they must defer to the eldest in all important matters. On the other hand, some stock-relationships involve chiefly a specific individual, e.g. wife's father, sister's husband. In such a case, although that man is not necessarily the head of his house, the relationship is individualized,

[1] One very wealthy and very old Jie had, on his own estimate, nearly sixty close associates. He had five wives, eight daughters-in-law and five married daughters. In fact, it is doubtful if he had exercised rights against some of these associates for many years. His elder sons and deceased full-brother's sons were near middle age and most of the dealings in stock concerned them and their associates, and not the old man in senescence.

FIGURE 16

THE RANGE OF STOCK-ASSOCIATES IN JIELAND

LOWOT, of Locerimu settlement, Kotido district: *c.* 50 years old, 2 wives, about average wealth, head of his house.

Bond-friends	15
Jie 7	
Turkana . . . 1	
Karamajong . . 3	
Dodoth . . . 2	
Labwor . . . 1	
Acoli 1	
Mother's brother	
Full-brother of wife I	
Half-brother of wife I	
Father of wife II	
Husband of daughter	
Husbands of two sisters	
Sister's son (father dead)	
Father of son's wife	
Total of close stock-associates . .	24
(excluding close agnates)	
Close agnates . . .	8
full-brothers . . 2	
half-brother . . 1	
paternal cousins . 2	
deceased cousin's sons 3	
Total of close stock-associates . .	32

In addition Lowot thought that the brothers of the wife of each of his own full-brothers might come within the 'cattle-giving class'.

The 'goat-giving class' was difficult to delimit abstractly.

Referring to his son's marriage and the assembly of bridewealth about two years previously, Lowot detailed 19 clansmen, 2 half-brothers of his mothers, 12 lesser affines, his mother's sister's husband and 2 neighbours of a contiguous hamlet (lesser bond-friends)—37 men in all, many of whom gave only one goat.

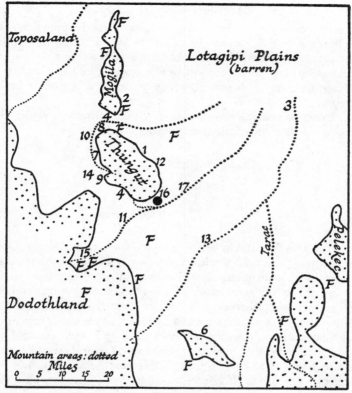

FIGURE 17

THE RANGE OF STOCK-ASSOCIATES IN TURKANALAND

LOKOYEN—aged *c*. 55, wealthy, with 3 wives and full-brother's widow.

North-western Turkanaland: approximate locations in late May 1950. Only the chief-homestead of each associate is shown. At the time this was the cattle homestead in most cases as the wet season had recently set in.

● homestead of Lokoyen   F homestead of a bond-friend

The homesteads of other associates are numbered:—

1. half-brother	10. half-brother of wife II
2. deceased full-brother's son I	11. father of wife III
3. deceased full-brother's son II	12. husband of sister
4. deceased full-brother's son III	13. husband of daughter
5. deceased full-brother's son IV*	14. full-brother of wife III of deceased
6. mother's brother's son	full-brother†
7. full-brother of wife I	15. half-brother of above wife
8. full-brother of wife II	16. husband of daughter I of above wife
9. full-brother II of wife II	17. husband of daughter II of above wife

* This man shared a joint homestead with Lokoyen at the time.
† Lokoyen was pro-husband to this widow.

Together with 13 bond-friends, the total of close stock-associates was 30. For a wealthy man this is rather few, but, as can be seen, there were few close agnates.

referring primarily to him alone. Thus a man approaches his daughter's husband for the gift of an animal, although it is understood that the latter will have to obtain at least the tacit agreement of his eldest brother before the gift can be made. The elder brother in this case reckons his brother's wife's father as a secondary stock-associate.

As an actual example may be taken the circumstances at the time of Locoto's third marriage (see genealogy below):

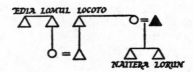

Locoto approached the father of his son's wife, Lomul, for a contribution towards his bridewealth, and was given an ox at the approval of Lomul's elder brother, Edia. Locoto did not formally approach Edia at all. At the same time he sought a contribution from his sister's eldest son, Naitera, and did not directly contact his sister's younger son, Lorun. In fact, when Locoto told me about this bridewealth he made no mention of either Edia or Lorun. He told me, upon my enquiry, that having obtained an ox from Lomul he could not also beg a goat or two from Edia—that is, he could not beg twice from one house. If Lomul had been dead, Locoto would then have begged stock from Edia. In the case of his sister's sons, Locoto said simply that Naitera and Lorun were of one house and therefore he could not also approach Lorun, who in any case could not give animals on such an occasion without Naitera's approval.

In Turkanaland, normally, full-brothers are economically and legally independent of one another, each maintaining his own range of stock-associates separately. In these circumstances, because a man has close relations with, say, one brother of his wife, there is no reason why he should be equally close, in friendliness or reciprocal rights, with the others. Only where a house (in whatever relationship situation) has not broken up and still remains under the leadership of the eldest brother can such terms as 'wife's brother' or 'paternal cousin' have full meaning without further definition.

This raises the question of the determination of practical relations with stock-associates in actual life. This matter has already been discussed briefly in connection with the close agnatic relations of Turkana.[1] In their country, geographical proximity is often important. For example, Lodeki was especially friendly with his chief wife's second brother, Ethin, but had comparatively little contact with her eldest brother. Lodeki and Ethin normally tended to have their goat homesteads in the same area during the dry season and sometimes they lived in the same primary neighbourhood. On at least one occasion they shared a joint homestead for several months. They met frequently, gave one another hospitality and shared leisure pursuits. The elder brother-in-law had his goat homestead conventionally some twenty-five to thirty miles away in the dry season, and he and Lodeki met infrequently. When they did meet, hospitality was no less cordial than between Lodeki and Ethin, because, as Lodeki said, 'We are affines, big ones.' Nevertheless, when Lodeki married again, Ethin contributed a cow and its calf at heel, whereas the elder brother gave only a young ox. Ethin was one of Lodeki's strongest supporters at the wedding, the other brother did not attend.

Whatever their predispositions, Lodeki and Ethin had good opportunity to build up close relations; but the predispositions are also important. With one person a man strikes up a warm friendship; with another, standing in the same formal relationship, he is able to do no more than to maintain the conventions of cordial intercourse applicable to the relationship. There may be mutual incompatibility, and even the formal content of the tie is diminished. A man may tend to live and move near to an associate with whom he is on friendly terms; similarly he tends to maintain a higher level of reciprocal rights with such a person. Because of the nomadic and atomistic nature of Turkana society a man is, as we have seen, often out of touch with many of the men with whom he has formal relations. Inter-personal compatability and friendliness are of course not unimportant amongst the Jie (or indeed in many social situations in all societies) and a man is not usually equally closely linked in practice with all of his brothers-in-law. Amongst the Turkana, however, because of their way of life, these factors are rather more important than for most peoples. Further, a Turkana does not find the important social stability normally afforded by membership of a more or less fixed community (settlement, village, ward, etc.) in sedentary societies. To every formal relationship there is an empirical quality

[1] See p. 190 *et seq.*

which may vary over a considerable range of possible expression, making the bond more or less valuable and persistent. The level of reciprocal stock rights is significantly and consciously related to this.[1]

It will have been noticed that in dealing with the different types of stock-associates I have been chiefly concerned to describe them from the point of view of a single individual. It has therefore been possible to treat, for example, relations with a father-in-law quite distinctly from relations with a son-in-law. For an individual they are of course quite different people; but in relation to his father-in-law, a man is himself a son-in-law, and similarly in relation to his mother's brother a man is a sister's son.

The category of stock-associates is composed of a number of men related in certain ways to an individual, but it also involves a cluster of polar relationships of the type of wife's father-daughter's husband, mother's brother-sister's son, and also paternal cousin-paternal cousin, and so on. For stock-association is primarily a complementary relationship. In terms of rights and obligations, claims and admission of claims, not all of these relationships carry an exact reciprocity. It has already been noted in particular that a wife's father and brother are in a superior status to a man, whilst a sister's or daughter's husband is in an inferior status—the former's claims against a man are stronger than his upon them, whilst the latters' are correspondingly weaker. It was noted further that a wife's brother (or sister's husband) after a few years tends to come on an equal (fraternal-like) footing with a man such that an almost exact reciprocity exists. In the case of bond-friends and of close agnates, relations essentially engender more or less true reciprocity. The mother's brother by virtue of his special link with the mother is conventionally expected to give more than he receives, and contrariwise to be afforded considerable conventional respect. It would be an error to overemphasize this asymmetry, however, for it is often disregarded by people in practice, especially in regard to stock rights. The only type of stock-association where asymmetry tends to persist is that of wife's father-daughter's husband. Elsewhere, if it continues to exist at all, it is demonstrated in terms of respect and deference rather than in the assessment of mutual stock rights.

It must be made clear that in any case exact reciprocity is not

---

[1] There is not space here to discuss this very important topic further. It is unfortunately too often ignored in formal sociological analysis.

consciously calculated arithmetically. The people do not think in such terms. One gives according to one's ability with reference to the particular relationship involved at the time. At the marriage of Logono (a Jie), his mother's brother's eldest son gave a cow towards the bridewealth—a rather generous gift, in fact. Two years later the second of the mother's brother's sons was preparing to marry, but Logono only gave him five goats, for in the meantime the latter's cattle herd had been reduced by over one-half in a rinderpest outbreak. It was not economically possible to give cattle at that time. This was well understood and the goats were accepted in good spirit. There was then no exact quantitative return gift; but in the attitudes expressed and the general feeling of friendliness and cooperation the notion of true reciprocity remained.

One further general point calls for comment. It will be clear that if a man has thirty or more stock-associates there may well be times when he is visited by several of them at the same period, each seeking a gift of stock for some purpose, e.g. for bridewealth during the early part of the wet season. With the best will in the world he cannot normally afford to give, for instance, two head of cattle to an agnate who is getting married, and a cow or ox to several other stock-associates, in addition to the gifts other members of the stock-owning unit may wish to make from the one herd,[1] not to mention gifts of goats and sheep to secondary associates. In any case a man may very probably be building up the herd with a view to his own next marriage, or that of his brothers or one of their sons. Obviously the line must be drawn somewhere in order to prevent undue depletion of the herds. In practice it is not easy to say where that line is to be drawn, and no hard and fast rule can be detected. Each set of circumstances is different, and each 'owner' attempts to meet his proper obligations as best he can without too seriously retarding his own legitimate ambitions and requirements. As far as I could ascertain, a close agnate is seldom if ever entirely refused assistance, even in those extended families where tensions and rivalries are greatest. The bonds of agnatic kinship are too strong, and to deny a half-brother or cousin a cow or ox for his bridewealth would (except in cases of severe poverty) be tantamount to the denial of kinship itself—on this both Jie and Turkana are emphatic. If at all possible a mother's brother and a close affine would not be refused

---

[1] I.e. full-brothers and adult sons in the Jie house; adult and autonomous sons in the Turkana nuclear family.

either. A wife's father or brother (superior affines), like close agnates, can scarcely be refused except in genuine poverty. Other affines and maternal kin may have to accept a few goats in lieu of cattle. A bond-friend might perhaps be temporarily refused altogether. Such modifications of obligations or even outright refusal do not break up the relationships involved—at least not on the first occasion, though repeated refusals will lead to the atrophy of the association. The natives appreciate the inevitable difficulties, as witness the remarks of one Jie, Ekidor, after a fruitless visit to his bond-friend. 'I begged a cow,' he said, 'but Lotiron [his bond-friend] refused—he refused to give me goats also. Ee! he is to marry soon, this season, and will not give me cattle. And his affine, the brother of his chief wife, he also will marry soon, and one cannot refuse a big [i.e. close] affine when he comes to beg. No! And Lotiron's half-brother has to pay an illegitimacy fine and he has begged two goats. Last month a bond-friend [of Lotiron] came from Turkanaland and he drove away a bull-calf. And again, Lotiron's eldest son had to perform ritual and he must give a cow for the ox he took from his mother's brother. Lotiron's headman comes for the tax—there are many men in that house to pay tax; an ox must be sold. Lotiron is to marry soon—he cannot give me a cow now. There are no [hard] words. I shall go another time, and visit him; he will give me a large cow. That will be good.'

As in this case, a man is usually aware of, or can readily discover, the liabilities of his stock-associate, and he can then judge whether the current refusal is justified or not. As Ekidor intimated, a close affine comes before a bond-friend, and no one resents such evaluation. Thus, if there is no set scale of precedence of stock-associates, yet there is a rough notion of those who can scarcely if ever be refused, and of others who can be persuaded to reduce their demands or may be put off for the time being. In many if not all cases considerations of affection and friendliness may override this rough classification at various points. Most certainly, any stock-associate who in the past has fulfilled his obligations especially handsomely will not be forgotten at a time when some scaling down or refusal of claims must be made.

CHAPTER EIGHT

MARRIAGE AND BRIDEWEALTH

THIS chapter contains an account of the most important case of transaction in stock as a concrete example of the operation of relations between stock-associates, both those within the extended family and all others. The payment of bridewealth involves the essence of the principles of stock-ownership and of all the relationships in which reciprocal rights over stock are important, both on the side of the giver of the animals and on the side of the receivers.

Of course, marriage is not the only occasion when the system of stock-association is set into operation. It has already been explained[1] that in both societies there is a more or less continual begging, giving and exchanging of animals for a multitude of social and economic purposes, and even for no purpose at all other than the ubiquitous and permanent desire for stock and the wish to exercise valued relationships. In addition, the important institution of judicial compensation involves the co-operation of the stock-associates of the principals, and not only in the matter of paying and receiving stock but also in the actual social mechanism of the process of settling a dispute. However, the payment of bridewealth is far more common than the payment of compensation, and exceeds the numbers of animals which change hands in other ways. Serious disputes are not common in either Jieland or Turkanaland and the payment of blood-money has largely ceased with the enforcement of European notions of murder. For this reason also it was not possible to collect the vast amount of data concerning compensation payments that was usually so readily forthcoming concerning bridewealth.

The people themselves recognize the focal importance of bride-

---

[1] See p. 197 ff.

wealth and I always found that it was impossible to discuss Family or kinship relations without becoming involved in discussions relating to bridewealth. This condition has been given due recognition in this book by my repeated references to bridewealth assembly and distribution as indices of important social relations. At times of marriage and the concomitant transferences of stock, rights in herds and the social relations involved are reassessed, reiterated and crystallized. Such times are critical points in individual and Family histories.

Logically, also, an account of family and kinship relations should include some mention of marriage, since through that process a new family unit is founded and two previously unrelated groups of people are brought together in close relationship. In both societies the wife who becomes a mother is the point of differentiation in the stock-owning unit and ultimately in the extended family; and in both societies affinal relations are of great significance.

Marriage Regulations

It is not intended to attempt a full analysis of marriage and the marriage-situation in the two societies. Nevertheless, some mention must be made concerning marriage regulations because of the interesting light they throw on the nature of stock-association.

Formal regulations are of two kinds—those pertaining to an individual as the centre of a web of kinship and those pertaining to him as a member of a clan. A Jie or Turkana must not have sexual relations with or marry a girl with whom he can trace a blood (cognatic) link; neither may he have such relations with a girl belonging to his father's or mother's father's clan—and, in Jieland, also his father's mother's or mother's mother's clans.[1] These are set rules sanctioned by supernatural punishment and also public moral opinion; more important is the intense horror and indignation that contravention would arouse amongst a person's kinsfolk. Marriage is out of the question, of course, for even the idea of it would be immediately quashed by the kinsmen of either party, and a man could not go against their opposition, even were he willing to risk the supernatural danger, because he depends upon them for contributions to his bridewealth and for ritual and general support. In fact,

---

[1] These are the clans into which those women were born. It will be remembered that Jie clans are considerably smaller in size than Turkana clans. On the whole, consanguineal bonds are longer remembered in Jieland than in Turkanaland.

I have never heard of even sexual relations within the restricted range, though my information here is perhaps insufficient.

There are in addition certain houses and Families into which a man would not marry although not prevented on legal or supernatural grounds. Primarily he would not marry a girl of the natal house[1] of another wife or his or of his full-brothers. This, as any native will explain, is because it would be extremely foolish to marry into a house with which one's own house already has close affinal relations. 'Your wife's sister is like your [own] sister,' said one informant, and then went on in a very practical manner to explain that he would want to beg contributions towards his bridewealth from such close affines when he wished to marry; but he could not beg stock from the very people to whom he would have to give the bridewealth, for that would be absurd. This practical prohibition is extended to all houses into which a man or girl of one's own house has married, and for precisely the same reasons. Other members of one's own Family (i.e. of different houses) also should not take a spouse from those houses. Whereas, however, a man should not marry into the whole Family from which he, his full-brothers or their sons have taken a wife already, or into which their sisters or daughters have married, this extension does not apply rigidly to other members of his own Family. To give an example: men should not marry into the house of their sister's husband, nor should their half-brothers and cousins; also they themselves should not marry into their brother-in-law's whole Family, whereas their agnates may. Thus a man *may* marry the half-sister of the wife of his half-brother. This permissible union sails very close to the wind, and it is not welcomed that two Families should be linked by more than one marriage. It does occasionally occur, for then 'the cattle do not become mixed', or at least not seriously. Previously existing affinal ties are, relatively speaking, so indirect and distant that they are not a rigid practical bar to marriage.

In the light of the theme of this book I wish to emphasize that the people themselves define and explain these restrictions on marriage in terms of pre-existing reciprocal rights over stock which would conflict with the rights bound up in the new social relations to be established by marriage.

[1] The 'natal house' of a woman is that into which she was born, and is contrasted with the 'marital house' which she joins as a wife. For a man there is of course no distinction. Similarly for a woman there are natal and marital Families and clans.

MARRIAGE AND BRIDEWEALTH

There is a further reason for these prohibitions. Whilst marriage is primarily contracted in order to found a family and a domestic group, there is in native minds always the idea of linking the two Families, specifically the two houses, in a relationship that should be fruitful in social life thereafter. To make this link twice over would be a foolish waste of the opportunity to make a new link elsewhere, and therefore an unnecessary restriction of a man's field of stock-associates. Similarly, one does not wish to marry a bond-friend's close female agnates.

These restrictions are based quite consciously on sociological grounds. The incest taboos are, for most people, purely set rules to be obeyed without question, though the external observer may in fact perceive reasons on an analytical level. For those natives who have thought out the situation the two sets of restriction appear to be similar, and they can be brought together in the remark of many informants, 'You do not marry your own people,' i.e. all your stock-associates, and not only your consanguineal kin. Outside this range social relations are impermanent, often indirect and not based on the recognition of reciprocal obligations. To marry into this range is thought to introduce a new and important system of relations where an already established pattern exists, thereby threatening the stability of the total relationship structure and needlessly limiting its expression. To marry an affine is conceived to be as wrong as to marry a kinswoman; indeed it may be considerably more foolish, since affines are all well known and affinal relations are normally actively maintained and valued, whereas many prohibited kins-women are related in a remote genealogical way and they and their agnates are not connected in active relations. In Turkanaland a man can scarcely even know of more than a small number of these clans-folk, and few Jie know all the girls of their mother's mother's clan, for example, unless its hamlet is geographically close to their own clan-hamlet. In discussing these matters, natives place both sorts of prohibitions in a single category; but whereas they will speak laconically of the incest taboos, they invariably stress the significance of these other regulations at some length.

There are no other restrictions upon sexual relations or marriage by virtue of social position, e.g. membership of age-sets, or settlement and district (Jie), or territorial section (Turkana). Neither are there any types of preferential marriage of a formal nature. The factor of relative wealth may be individually important, especially in Turkanaland. Since a man is always thinking of the consequent affinal ties to be established by his marriage, he does not care to ally himself with a family much poorer than his own from which he can expect relatively less asistance in the future. This is particularly noticeable at the two extremes—the very wealthy and the very poor. Analysis of marriages amongst wealthy stock-owners shows a marked tendency towards affinal links with other wealthy owners.

Marriage[1]

For the Jie and Turkana marriage is not just a single legal act of making a girl the wife of a man, but it is a long ceremonial process which begins with the preparations for the wedding and whose explicit object is the ritual, spiritual and social creation and establishment of the marital union, and to ensure the fertility of the woman and the welfare of her children. In Turkanaland the process is completed between two and three years after the actual wedding (i.e. the formal acceptance of bridewealth) when the first child of the union has been reared to the walking stage. In Jieland the process is completed not less than five years after the wedding, for at least two children have to be similarly reared.[2] In both societies the total process culminates in the ritual incorporation of the woman into her husband's house, Family and clan, at which time she finally abandons her natal affiliations.

The marriage process consists of a number and variety of events which take place in a strict order such that the completion of one allows preparations to go forward for the next. Each event is consciously related to a further stage in the process. Some of them are of vital ritual significance, some are of importance in establishing and cementing affinal relationships, and some appear almost trivial, scarcely to be raised to the level of a stage of this process. An example of the latter is the naming of the first child and the ceremonial provision of the baby-carrying sling of sheepskin—a common enough event in primitive societies. But even such an event is performed with due ceremony at the relevant time and by conventionally determined people from either side of the union. It is regarded as a new stage in the development; that is, the birth of the child is a further step in the woman becoming a 'full-wife' and in uniting her with her husband and his house. It also marks a further step in the linking together of the new affines.

[1] A full account is given in my 'Jie Marriage', *African Affairs*, lii, 1953.
[2] Until just before this time a Jie wife remains at her father's homestead.

MARRIAGE AND BRIDEWEALTH

In fact, there are two interwoven processes; one is the development from unmarried girl, to bride, to 'bride-wife' (*nateran*), to
mother, to 'full-wife' (*aberu*); the other is the gradual binding
together of the husband with his wife's father and full-brothers, and
to a lesser degree the houses and even the Families of each. By the
time the process is completed, the marriage union and the surrounding affinal bonds have been firmly established, emotional adjustments
settled, and the woman has an assured status and role in her new
house and Family.[1] Only when the wife and her children are incorporated into the man's group is marriage completed; then, the
natives say, '*Adowun akotan daang*—the whole marriage is finished.'

Amongst the Jie there are some fifteen successive stages, beginning with the formal request of the girl in marriage and ending with
her ritual incorporation. Most of them require the slaughter of
animals for ceremonial feasts, and many of them necessitate the co-
operation of clan elders on both sides. As usual, Turkana ritual is
neither so rich in detail nor so frequent in occurrence, but the basic
pattern is the same. In both societies the exact pattern of the process
is defined by clan membership. In general the process is essentially
similar, in each tribe, for all clans; but many clans differ in the actual
details of ritual prescription and a few clans call for one or two extra
stages. Some of the stages are determined by the man's clan and some
by the bride's father's clan.

Bridewealth

Strictly legally, it is the transfer of bridewealth (literally, 'stock of
marriage') in the name of the groom to the relatives of the bride
which causes a girl to become a wife, although not, as we have seen,
a full-wife. As one Jie put it—'You know a woman is married if
stock have been given. How do you know a wife if there are no
cattle? Other men go away when they know about the stock.'
Occasionally when recording genealogies I have been unsure
whether some woman is married or not, and invariably my query
was answered in the form: 'Stock have been given. She is a wife.'

The prime, extrinsic features of legal marriage are the man's
sexual monopoly over his wife and authority over her children. On
the reverse side, the wife gains the opportunity to bear legitimate

---

[1] It should be noted that a married woman can be incorporated into her husband's
group when she has successfully reared one or two children; the latter accomplishment
also founds a new yard in her husband's house. The two events are closely correlated.

children and the rights of support and protection from her husband, and she and her children obtain rights in his herds. The norm of domestic union is of course provided within the framework of marriage, which is conveived of as establishing such co-operation.[1] Nevertheless, it must be emphasized that the transfer of bridewealth and its formal, public acceptance is but one stage of the total marriage process, though a critical stage in the eyes of all people. The marriage can only be completely established by the due performance of the ritual and ceremonial acts already mentioned.

The public declaration of the transfer and acceptance of the bridewealth is clearly marked. In Jieland the bride's father permits his share of the stock to be driven into his cattle kraal, followed by the groom and his supporters, who perform ceremonial dancing and drink beer. In Turkanaland the declaration is made as the 'marriage-ox' is driven by the groom's people and slaughtered in the central kraal of the bride's father's chief-homestead. At this time a Turkana bridewealth will amost always have been handed over in full, but in Jieland usually one-sixth to one-quarter remains outstanding.

Bridewealth is payable only in domestic animals. Large stock are quite essential, and I have never heard of a marriage where they were not included. Normally goats and sheep are also considered essential; but in Jieland, herds of small stock have been so depleted by disease in recent decades that sometimes a bridewealth is accepted without them.[2] The average number of stock involved is roughly the same in each tribe—about fifty large stock and about one hundred small stock.[3] The range, however, is considerable. In my Turkana records the range is between five and eighty large stock, and from none to over three hundred small stock. In my Jie records there are eleven cases over seventy cattle and five cases less than thirty. Concerning small stock in Jieland, most cases which occurred more than ten or fifteen years ago contained well over one hundred small stock, mostly

---

[1] In Turkanaland, permanent domestic and economic co-operation between a man and woman also occurs outside marriage—through concubinage. See *Survey of the Turkana*, pp. 218-22. A Jie may have a mistress for many years, with whom he tends to live; but almost always the couple eventually marry. Many Turkana concubines never marry.

[2] Old men told me that during and after the catastrophic rinderpest epidemic of the 1890's, one or two cattle only were given in bridewealth.

[3] For the Jie I have records of forty-eight authentic bridewealth transactions, and the average number of animals in these is fifty cattle and one hundred and twenty-nine small stock. For thirty-five cases in Turkanaland the averages are forty-seven cattle and camels and eighty-eight small stock. Occasionally, at the request of a bride's father, a Turkana groom may include a donkey or two.

about two hundred and a few over three hundred; most of the more recent transactions have involved less than one hundred, many less than fifty and some none at all.

There are no particular conventions concerning the constitution of a bridewealth. About half of the stock should be females, and two or three bell-oxen should be included as a mark of respect to the bride's father. No bull is necessarily required and one is only infrequently included. Poor-quality beasts may be rejected or an extra cow requested as a make-weight when they are accepted.

The first point of significance in connection with this survey of bridewealth is that large numbers of stock are normally involved— very considerably more than are involved in the comparable institutions in many parts of eastern Africa.[1] I suggest that the very size of Jie and Turkana bridewealths tends to make the system more flexible. Where only five or six cattle change hands, the addition or subtraction of an animal, or the type and condition of one of them, would appear to be highly important and liable to foment discord between the parties. For Jie and Turkana the question of a single ox or cow is scarcely likely to raise serious difficulties: where some fifty animals are being transferred the relative value of one of them, or of an additional one, tends to be less. Few men are prepared to risk endangering the marriage and affinal relations over one beast, though perhaps many might over ten beasts. In any case the Turkana in particular, but the Jie also, can always include an extra five or ten goats to placate disgruntled recipients.

The second point of general significance is that any bridewealth is made up of a large number of contributions, and that on transfer it is divided amongst a large number of recipients. Jie will say that a man can afford to marry if his house has about twenty cattle to spare—i.e. leaving enough animals in the kraal, after payment, to provide milk and blood for the people of the house. The rest of the cattle are obtained by the groom from his stock-associates—and similarly in the case of small stock. This method of assembling a

[1] No clear correlation can be found between the general stock wealth of a tribe and the average size of bridewealth given by its members. For instance, the nomadic Fulani, who must be at least no less wealthy than the Jie, give only three or four bulls (F. W. de St. Croix, *The Fulani of Northern Nigeria*, Lagos, 1945, p. 38). Schapera states that the Tswana tribesmen give about ten cattle, yet the Ngwato at least are far wealthier than the Jie (cf. Schapera I., *A Handbook of Tswana Law and Custom*, Oxford, 1938, p. 140). Amongst these tribes, unlike the Jie and Turkana, a whole system of property relations and rights is not brought into play. There is a pressing need for a classification and comparative study of the institutions grouped together under the blanket term 'bridewealth'.

bridewealth involves a system in which a large number of people have an interest in the man's marriage, both at the time of the wedding and afterwards. Further, they have an interest, or have an existing interest renewed, in that man himself. In collecting contributions to bridewealth a prospective groom approaches upwards of forty or fifty people. There have already been distinguished the differences between 'cattle-giving' and 'goat-giving' classes of stock-associates, though of course the distinction is not at all rigid. Most men who are associated with the groom can afford to give a goat or sheep, most particularly in Turkanaland, where small stock are so plentiful. Examples of the composition of bridewealth are given in Figure 18.

FIGURE 18

THE COMPOSITION OF BRIDEWEALTH

(a) An example from Jieland:

Groom	21	
Half-brother	3	
Full-cousin I	4	
Full-cousin II	2	
Father's half-brother I	5	43
Father's half-brother II	3	
Half-cousin I	1	
Half-cousin II	2	
Half-cousin III	2	
2 clansmen (1 head each)	2	
Mother's half-brother	1	
4 bond-friends (1 head each)	4	

Total 50 cattle

Analysis:

Groom's house	21
Rest of his Family (8 houses)	22
All others	7

Notes.—This bridewealth was given in about 1930 at the first marriage of a young man whose father and father's full-brother were dead, and whose full-brothers were only youths. There were therefore no close affines from whom to seek assistance. The mother's full-brother was also dead. In addition there were 100 goats and sheep transferred.

(b) An example from Turkanaland:

Groom	22 cattle	
	4 camels	
Full-brother	3 cattle	
	1 camel	
Half-brother	1 cow	
	1 camel	40
Father's full-brother	4 cattle	
	1 camel	
Father's half-brother	2 cattle	
Half-cousin	1 camel	
Mother's brother	2 cattle	
Wife's full-brother I	2 cattle	
Wife's full-brother II	1 ox	
Sister's husband	1 camel	
6 bond-friends (1 head each)	6 cattle	

Total 52 large stock

Analysis:

Groom's nuclear family	26
Rest of his house	4
Rest of his Family	10
All others	12

Notes.—This bridewealth was given at the second marriage of the groom. His half-brother had had independent homesteads for several years, and the (younger) full-brother had been independent for two or three years. Approximately 100 small stock were also transferred, and, at the special request of the bride's mother, 3 donkeys.

MARRIAGE AND BRIDEWEALTH

The potential groom himself is responsible for the collection of the animals, and he receives little assistance from his father or full-brothers even at his first marriage. He must visit the homestead of each associate from whom he feels he has the right to beg stock.[1] At each homestead he both informs the associate of his intended marriage, seeking approval, and makes his claim for animals. This process may take a considerable time—many months in Turkanaland, where the population is so widely dispersed. Even a Jie will have to visit bond-friends living in other tribal areas. For Turkana, however, hundreds of miles of travelling are involved in addition to the repeated visits of the girl's father for bridewealth discussions. An actual case may illustrate this and at the same time it may show the nature of stock-association relations in that nomadic society. Akorio was living at his chief-homestead near the Koteruk river (central Turkanaland) in wet-season quarters in 1949. He visited his mother's brother, who was living in his goat homestead on the lower Kosibir river at the time about thirty miles away, though in fact Akorio had thought that he was elsewhere and had therefore made a longer, roundabout journey of about fifty miles. The maternal uncle promised to give a cow, and after a stay of a few days Akorio set off with his maternal cousin to the cattle homestead on Muruapolon mountain. From there he finally returned home to Koteruk. This single trip, involving his mother's brother's approval and the gift of a cow, entailed some one hundred and thirty miles of walking and took about fourteen days. He also made at least one other trip to Muruapolon (but to another part) to fetch his own cattle and another cow contributed by a bond-friend. The total time taken to assemble the whole bridewealth extended from early March to about the middle of August; and at that latter date further arrangements had still to be made so that his half-brother's contribution (seven cattle) should reach the place of the wedding at the same time as Akorio himself. In addition, he had made several visits to the girl's father, some twenty-five miles away, for discussions concerning the bride-wealth.

The reverse side of the transaction is the distribution of the bride-wealth. Here no one man ever handles the whole herd of animals

[1] A stock-associate does not automatically give animals, but one must go and beg him: *akilip*—literally 'to beseech'. In the process of begging, the conditions of the stock-relationship and past favours are all discussed, and the reciprocal, kinship and moral elements are reiterated and emphasized.

handed over. The bride's father acts as spokesman for the recipients, although he (or, in Jieland, his house) gets the lion's share of the stock. He informs the suitor how many animals are demanded by each prospective recipient. The suitor, or the head of his house, hands them over directly to each of these people on the day of the wedding. Stock which are not going to the homestead of the bride's father are driven off with little ceremony.

The group of recipients is not so large as the group of contributors. Only close agnates (i.e. the bride's extended family), close maternal kin and close affines may claim shares in the bridewealth. Affines tend to be on the borderline and are sometimes omitted if the number of stock is small; but so strong are affinal bonds that it would be thought discreditable not to allow a claim for a cow or ox in most cases. In this context such affines are the fathers and brothers of the wives of the bride's own father and brothers. In Jieland the husband of the bride's sister has a special claim which must be noted here. A man has a definite claim against the bridewealth of his wife's sister next to marry, to the extent of up to twenty cattle; and in addition, when his wife eventually comes to live with him at his homestead, she (and therefore he) receives gifts of a few cattle and goats from her father or brothers. These are all legal obligations no less than the giving of bridewealth itself, and they further strengthen the contract between a man and his wife's natal house.[1]

Close maternal kin (chiefly the mother's brothers) and members of the bride's Family are considered to have been jointly responsible for the establishment of her yard (or house) and its herd. She is the daughter of 'our sister' and 'our brother' respectively. The mother's herd came chiefly from the herd of the house and thus by extension from the Family herd; but there have been certain contributions to it by her father and brother. Further, a native would say, the father's

---

[1] Thus a groom eventually gets back as many as half the number of cattle that he originally handed over in bridewealth. For example, Logwela gave forty-seven cattle for his wife, and when her sister was married about a year later he received eighteen cattle from the bridewealth. Four years later his wife went to live with him permanently and brought with her from her father, two cows, an ox and a bull-calf. A total of twenty-two cattle were thus given to Logwela, compared with the original transfer of forty-seven cattle plus small stock. In the unlikely event of divorce only the balance, twenty-five cattle, would be returnable. Since that time there have been several occasions when Logwela and his full-brother have received from and given to these affines animals for various purposes. These, however, were in the normal run of affinal relations and had no direct connection with bridewealth given for the wife in question. This particular legal custom does not occur amongst the Turkana.

Family provided the stock which established the marriage union, but the mother's Family provided the mother herself. The daughter, now a bride, is, as it were, a product of the activities of both groups of people as well as the sexual union of the man and woman.

The moral claim which a man has upon his mother's brother is reciprocated by the latters claim against the bridewealth given at the wedding of his sister's daughter. Close agnates habitually co-operate in each other's out-payments and share in all in-payments. That is a principle of Family relations. Both these close maternal kin and close agnates of the bride can jeopardize the success of a marriage of which they do not approve—that is, mainly one which does not produce what is felt to be an adequate share of stock. 'The children [of the union] will become ill and die,' is the conventional formula. Occasionally I have been told that the bride would not be able to bear children at all. In fact, no one was ever able to give me an instance when such a calamity occurred, and it would seem to be only a conventional statement of the moral principles involved in the operation of the kinship system. Kinsmen who were dissatisfied might refuse to join in subsequent ritual in the marriage process and could presumably therefore affect its efficacy. Again this never occurs in practice, although the co-operation of kinsmen in this ritual is taken as a sign that everyone is satisfied and desire only a successful outcome of the marriage. Jie and Turkana emphasize this, both amongst themselves and to the external enquirer. A wedding is sometimes delayed because some kinsman feels that his just claims are being overlooked. This pattern of claims is a direct reflection of the kinship system, and the complex of stock-relations that involves; therefore the just satisfaction of the claims is one of the bases of that system and its component relations.

People more distantly related to the bride and her father have no claim on the incoming bridewealth. A man may legitimately go to beg contributions to his bridewealth from the wide range of stock-associates, as we have seen, but that establishes no reciprocal obligation on the part of the man to give all these people shares of bridewealth coming into his house—e.g. for a sister or daughter. The reciprocal element lies in the obligation the man has to contribute stock to the bridewealth of his erstwhile contributors when they themselves are desiring to marry, or to make a gift for some other purpose.

When the girl's father has given the suitor's representatives his preliminary approval of the match, he must then consult her kinsmen, obtain their approval and listen to their demands for stock. Now, such demands are not purely arbitrary, for there is an approximate number of animals appropriate to each type of relationship. These 'ideal' figures vary only slightly from informant to informant and are roughly similar for each tribe. They form a conventional basis from which bridewealth demands can be developed on each particular occasion. In many cases they will be reduced in the final numbers, and sometimes they are exceeded. Below is given the estimates of a Turkana informant of about average wealth who was thinking in terms of the distribution of a possible bridewealth connected with his own Family. It is roughly typical of normal expectations. Figures here are for large stock only.[1]

> Father—about 15 (in addition a special allotment is probably made to the bride's mother (3 or 4 cows or female camels) and to her mother's co-wives (1 or 2 cows)).
> Father's elder brother—at least 5.
> Father's younger brother—4 or 5.
> Father's half-brother—1-3.
> Father's paternal cousin—1 or 2.
> Mother's brother—1-4.
> Close affines—possibly an ox or cow.

Two examples of the distribution of bridewealth are given in Figure 19.

Various factors are involved in the translation of this optimistic ideal into practice. In the first place the actual claim a man may make is directly affected by the current conditions of his relationship with the bride's father and brothers. A mother's brother (say) who has been generous and kind to the bride's brother in the recent past will feel able and will be allowed to put forward a strong claim and to reject a reduction of it for any reason. A half-brother who has been niggardly of assistance formerly will scarcely be encouraged in the same size of claim as another half-brother who has been reasonably generous and with whom relations are cordial. Enough has been said in earlier chapters of this book concerning the way in which rights between kinsmen, or between stock-associates, are established and maintained, and here it is sufficient to note yet another example of this system of reciprocity.

[1] All relationships mentioned in this account of bridewealth are given with reference to the bride and groom respectively.

FIGURE 19

THE DISTRIBUTION OF BRIDEWEALTH

(a) An example from Jieland:

Full-brother	20	
Mother	15	42
Sister II (unmarried mother)	4	
Sister III	3	
Half-brother	3	4
Half-sister	1	
Half-brother	3	
Full-cousin	1	
Father's half-brother	2	
Mother's brother	3	
Father's elder sister's husband	2	
Father's younger sister's husband	1	
Sister I's husband	20	

(The figures 42 and 4 are bracketed together as 52.)

Total 78 *cattle*

Analysis:

Brother's house	42
Rest of Family (4 houses)	10
All others	26

Notes.—This bridewealth was taken in my presence in 1951. The bride's full-brother was head of her house. On the day of the wedding 67 cattle were handed over, but some of the remainder were received within 10 days of that event. The brother of the wife of the bride's full-brother received no cattle on this occasion but he took 11 small stock. The remaining 17 small stock were taken by the bride's brother.

(b) An example from Turkanaland:

Father	14 camels
	5 cattle
Father's brother I	5 camels
	5 cattle
Father's brother II	3 camels
	4 cattle
Father's half-brother I	2 camels
	3 cattle
Father's half-brother II	1 camel
	2 cattle
Father's full-cousin II	2 camels
	2 cattle
Son of father's full-cousin I	1 camel
	1 cow
Mother's brother	4 camels
	2 cattle
Father's sister's son	1 cow
Father of brother's wife	1 camel
	1 ox

(The items bracketed together total 50.)

Total 59 *large stock*

Analysis:

Father's nuclear family	19
Rest of father's house	17
Rest of father's Family	14
All others	9

Notes.—This bridewealth was handed over in my presence in 1950. The groom and his close associates were all wealthy camel owners, hence the unusually large proportion of these animals. No small stock were transferred—a most uncommon occurrence in Turkanaland. This was due partly to the large number of cattle and camels given, and also because flocks of goats and sheep were small.

Secondly, a bridewealth demand, as presented initially to the suitor and his supporters by the girl's father at the formal joint assembly of the two groups of kindred, is based quite consciously and directly on what the girl's people estimate that the others can give. This is an explicit tenet of Jie and Turkana law.[1] That is, a

[1] The same principle applies to the assessment of judicial compensation, e.g. in cases of homicide or adultery.

wealthy man, or the son of a wealthy house, will be expected to give relatively more than a poor man, irrespective of the wealth of the bride's people. The size of bridewealth is not a fixed quantity. A groom gives, and desires to give, as many animals as he can muster. It can seldom, if ever, happen that the girl's people have not an excellent idea of the size and state of the suitor's herds and those of at least his extended family. Such things are more or less common knowledge, especially in Jieland, and they can in any case be easily ascertained. Consequently, in reckoning up the total bridewealth demands a man who insists on his full number of animals (by ideal standards) may be quickly reminded that the suitor is not wealthy enough, and that therefore the claim must be reduced. In other words, demands must be made to fit supply.

There may also be special claims on any particular bridewealth, the fulfilment of which necessarily reduce the number of animals available for other people. Mention has already been made of the legal claim of the husband of the bride's next oldest sister in Jieland. For reasons of great friendliness someone outside the normal range of recipients may be allowed a claim by the girl's father. In Turkana-land the 'namesake'[1] of the bride may rightfully claim a cow if he is living near enough at the time to learn what is afoot.

Finally, ideal claims must of course be adjusted in the light of the number of claimants in any particular case. There may, for instance, be several independent maternal uncles in a Turkana bridewealth case, and their individual shares may well be reduced below that which a single uncle could reasonably expect. On the other hand, there may be no full-brothers of the bride's mother alive, and a half-brother could not usually expect to claim their full share. Thus more animals are available for others. The fewer close agnates, then on the whole the larger is the share of each. Thus the distribution of a bridewealth depends upon the number of animals to be received and a balance of claims of all the people with recognized rights.

One fact emerges quite clearly from analysis of bridewealth transactions. The herd of the groom provides the largest single contribution to an out-payment, and the house (or nuclear family) of the bride takes the largest single share of an in-payment. This agnatic

[1] The 'namesake' is the man who gave his name to the girl. It is a recognized custom amongst Turkana by which two men are linked together, i.e. the 'namesake' and the child's father, and may be regarded as a form of bond-friendship. See *Survey of the Turkana*, p. 106.

emphasis is strengthened if the total contributions and shares of the respective Families are compared with those of all other stock-associates. Another feature is (though this cannot be easily shown here) that in almost all cases every house (or nuclear family) of each Family involved contributes to or receives shares in bridewealths. Indeed, we may go further and state that as a very general rule all of a man's stock-associates contribute something to his bridewealth. Some bond-friends may, on a specific occasion, decline to give the customary ox or cow.[1] In the case of other stock-associates, relations need to be excessively strained before a man does not give something, or before his conventional claim is entirely repudiated. On the other hand there is of course a good deal of room for the manipulation of the numbers given or allowed in expressing the cordiality (or conversely the antagonism) operative in the relationship. For instance, in the case of the first half-cousin in example (a), Figure 18, the man in question did not refuse to give an ox (the least valuable type of large stock), but he refrained from contributing the same number as the other two paternal cousins (his own half-brothers) or from giving a bell-ox or a cow. In fact, he and the groom were personally on bad terms at the time, and he did not really agree to the marriage.

The final number of animals actually transferred results from a lengthy series of discussions—between suitor and girl's kin on the one hand, and amongst the girl's kin themselves on the other. In Turkanaland particularly the process of discussion is frequently long drawn out because of the difficulties of communication over long distances and where people are likely to shift their locations. In all this the girl's father (if the father is dead, the head of her house in Jieland, and her eldest full-brother in Turkanaland) plays a central part, acting as a focus of discussion for both parties. Once he has approved of the match and the suitor shows proper conduct and energy in assembling bridewealth, the father is largely instrumental in forging the compromise between the suitor's offer and his own kinsmen's demands. He is, by this time, definitely thinking of the new affinal ties that are being created and wishes to do all that he can to establish them successfully. Almost invariably the demands of the girl's kin are higher than the suitor's offer and the father sets

---

[1] It is unusual for a bond-friend to give small stock if the relationship is well established, and it has been seen that a man is sometimes compelled to refuse his bond-friend's request. See pp. 221-2.

about reducing the former and increasing the latter, frequently tending to favour the suitor. This common benevolence on the part of the girl's father does not preclude him from demanding as high a bridewealth as possible, and most suitors go away from the first discussions with instructions to obtain more animals. In any case, say Turkana, it would not do for a father to accede too quickly to the suitor's offer. It would appear as if he were anxious to be rid of his daughter and were not giving sufficient attention to the claims of his stock-associates; and in the superior status of potential father-in-law he can enjoy the luxury of compelling the suitor to make renewed offers and entreaties. No Jie or Turkana in this position wishes to forgo the pleasure of lengthy discussion, proposal and counter-proposal connected with the large-scale transfer of stock.

To give bridewealth according to one's ability means that the groom must be prepared to surrender a very large proportion of his herds—or his father or eldest brother must do so for him. Turkana say that so long as a man has a bull and a cow he has a herd, and that much he must retain after giving bridewealth. This is of course a very considerable exaggeration, for few if any men would be prepared to impoverish themselves so greatly, nor is it expected of them. The Turkana are almost entirely dependent on their herds for food and many other normal necessities, and to alienate all the stock would be to subject the groom's nuclear family to grave privation, indeed to starvation, without even the opportunity to beg or borrow milch animals from stock-associates who have just made contributions to the bridewealth itself. Although the Jie situation is easier (there is an alternative food supply), nevertheless, as in Turkanaland, a groom should retain sufficient animals to ensure a moderate milk supply, although a degree of stringency must be expected. Part of the significance of the institution of bridewealth lies in its heavy burden, by the depletion of the family and house herds, which in itself gives a value to the marriage union thus contracted. The natives are aware of this, and they always show great pride concerning the size of their bridewealth payments, for they are a measure of their efforts and of the importance they attach to marriage. The sacrifice of highly valued stock is for them explicitly correlated with the great significance of marriage—a significance which comes primarily, I suggest, from its integral part in the Jie house, and far more so in the Turkana nuclear family, the basic and somewhat isolated family and stock-owning unit.

MARRIAGE AND BRIDEWEALTH

The general disposition of a man to trust and assist his daughter's suitor at this time is a direct consequence of native attitudes towards the whole transaction. A suitor is not only expected to give according to his ability and wealth but he on his side consciously wishes to do so. He attempts to assemble as large a bridewealth as possible, consistent with basic economic requirements, and he spends many weeks begging and cajoling his stock-associates. It is a matter of genuine pride to give as large a number of animals as possible and it will bring him favourable opinion and esteem, not only in society at large but more importantly with his father-in-law and brothers-in-law. Needless to say a father wishes to receive as large a bridewealth as possible, for that allows him generously to meet his obligations to his stock-associates, and also enables him to proceed with plans for the future marriage of himself or his sons. However, Jie and Turkana are so deeply aware of the value of affinal relations that a son-in-law who has assembled as many stock as he genuinely can, even though the total be relatively low, is welcomed as a person who can be trusted for the future. Many men have told me that conscientiousness is to be valued above sheer wealth in a son-in-law. The ethical and practical considerations are happily in accord. This underlies all bridewealth discussions. Although superficially they may be lengthy and keen, underneath there is a quite specific idea of compromise. The outward disagreements are only partly real. In a conventionalized way they express the obvious difficulties and structural opposition between two formerly unrelated parties who are feeling their way to a new balance out of which profitable affinal relations may emerge. Men say that outward disagreement is chiefly the result of the father-in-law exercising and emphasizing his superior status and demonstrating his power to be magnanimous towards his son-in-law. There are, of course, cases of rapacious fathers-in-law and of deceitful, niggardly suitors; but they appear to be a small minority who are unreservedly condemned by public opinion. A man who practises duplicity or refuses compromise in bridewealth discussions can scarcely hide the fact for long, nor can he expect to lay the foundations of normal affinal ties. Bridewealth discussions are not therefore carried on in an atmosphere of near hostility, hard bargaining and bitter feelings such as are reported amongst some African peoples. Jie and Turkana norms of affinal relations and hard bargaining are parts of an antithetical value system.

Others of the girl's kinsfolk, however, may well feel less altruistic towards the suitor. They are less concerned with whom their kinswoman is to marry and with the success of her marriage. Their affinal relations with the suitor will not be especially close, so that they do not feel the great need to establish them firmly at this time. The girl's maternal kin, in particular, will have almost negligible relations with her husband and his agnates. These kinsmen are therefore chiefly concerned with obtaining what is felt to be their legitimate shares. The girl's father has to plead with them to secure a reduction. I have recorded several cases where the father has actually reduced his own demands in the face of the obduracy of a kinsman in order to accommodate the suitor and prevent the marriage foundering.

One final point calls for comment concerning bridewealth in the present context. It has been consistently argued in this book that the senior full-brother (in close conjunction with his juniors) of a Jie house, or the head of a Turkana nuclear family, alone has the authority to alienate stock, and that he, representing the group, receives all in-payments. Sometimes, as we have seen,[1] a junior member of the group is approached by a man with whom he is directly associated and with whom his seniors have relatively less connection. Thus a younger brother in a Jie house will be approached by his own wife's brother for a contribution to the latter's bridewealth; and in such a case he makes the appropriate gift, but always at the ultimate approval of his eldest brother, the head of the group. In some cases, however, more than one member of a house, or nuclear family, gives to or receives a share in a bridewealth. For example, the head of a house will make the proper gift to a half-brother who is preparing to marry, but a junior brother or even an adult son may give an additional animal. This occurs where especially friendly and intimate relations exist between the prospective groom and this junior member, such that the latter desires to express his feelings through the extra gift. Usually he will give one of his own bell-oxen, over which it is generally recognized that he has something like individual control; although if the house were relatively poor he would be unlikely to make the gift without the agreement of the head. Alternatively, the head might seek to suppress the quantitative affect of the gift by a corresponding reduction of the house's normal contribution. Conversely, the junior man may receive an animal over and above the ordinary share taken for the house as a unit by the senior full-brother.

[1] Cf. pp. 215-8.

Even women may be detailed as receiving shares of bridewealth, in addition to those animals received by the male head of the group; although, as both Jie and Turkana so often remark, 'Women do not own stock.' The chief category of such women are the mother of the bride and the mother's co-wives, but a sister and even a half-sister may sometimes be included (cf. Figure 19, example (a)). This again is a way of expressing a special relationship between the bride and these womenfolk inside her own group or between her group and another closely related one. It is chiefly a matter of conventional respect.

All such shares belong to the common herd of the group, but become attached to the yard of the person concerned—e.g. to the yard of the younger full-brother's mother or wife, or to the yard of the woman recipient. That is, these additional animals are put into the allocation of the appropriate yard; but they are no more owned by that yard, or the particular member of it, than are any of the other animals attached to it. Besides the expression of friendliness or respect, this custom is also a method indirectly to increase the share of bridewealth going to a particular group. Thus the cow allowed to the friendly half-sister is in reality an extra animal for the house of the bride's half-brothers. The essential unity of house or nuclear family remains unaffected by this custom.

APPENDIX

THE INCIDENCE OF POLYGYNY

(a) Jieland

Approximate Age of Men	Number of Wives							Total Men
	0	1	2	3	4	5	6	
30-45 . .	9	69	9	2	2	0	0	91
Over 45 .	0	19	23	9	7	3	1	62
Total Men .	9	88	32	11	9	3	1	153

Total men in sample—153
Average number of wives per man in total sample—1·6
aged over 45—2·3
aged 30-45—1·1

For a Jie man, marriage below the age of 30 is rare. For instance, in the Kotido district, out of approximately 140 men between the ages of 18 and 30, only 6 had married.

(b) *Turkanaland*

Approximate Age of Men	Number of Wives							Total Men
	0	1	2	3	4	5	6	
20–30 . .	13	9	1	—	—	—	—	23
30–40 . .	3	20	14	7	1	—	—	45
40–50 . .	—	5	8	1	7	1	—	22
Over 50 .	—	—	7	5	2	3	1	18
Total men .	16	34	30	13	10	4	1	108

Total men in sample—108
Average number of wives per man in total sample—1·8
aged over 30—2·2
aged over 40—2·9

These samples are compiled from genealogies and some census data recorded during the course of normal field-work enquiries. They refer only to men who were alive when I personally knew them, and in all cases include all wives, living and dead. To the best of my knowledge no widows, unmarried mothers or concubines are included, though a few may have escaped proper identification.

It is not possible to make more than a tentative hypothesis concerning these high rates of polygyny. 'Widow-inheritance' is not a factor, for strictly speaking it does not occur in either society. The East African Native Census, 1948, gave 8671 males and 9540 females for the Jie—i.e. about 1·13 females per male. These figures scarcely suggest a complete answer. No demographic statistics are available for the Turkana. It may be suggested that a possible explanation lies in the fact that in all generations previous to that now growing up the death rate of male children and young men was rather higher than that for equivalent females. With the end of warfare and of the periodic famine years (both likely to have affected males relatively more than females) the male death rate may now have fallen. If this argument is tenable, the present generation should show a decline in the polygyny rate; but it is as yet too early to tell, since modern conditions have scarcely existed for more than a single generation.

According to informants, elderly Jie men today have about the same number of wives as elderly men in the old days, but this is not easy to check due to the particular nature of the genealogical memory of the Jie. Reliable Turkana informants said that in pre-British days there were scattered cases of men who had over ten wives. In those days it was possible for an exceptional Turkana to amass large herds as the results of raiding—herds which only to a limited extent had to be shared with close kin. Inevitably, then as now, herds were 'invested' in wives.

CHAPTER NINE

CONCLUSION

I

FROM the foregoing accounts it is clear that there are many fundamental similarities and certain decisive differences between the property-kinship complexes of the Jie and Turkana. In this concluding chapter an attempt is made to bring the two accounts together in order to establish the chief points of similarity and to seek some explanation of the important divergences.

I begin from the premise that in each society under review there is an institutional complex of 'stock-association' which in many details as well as in basic principles follows a common pattern. In either tribe, a man is the centre of a specific field of inter-personal relations based on ties of kinship and bond-friendship, and these relations are chiefly, though not wholly, expressed and maintained through a system of reciprocal rights in respect of domestic animals. As the native sees it, any kinship relation can, and indeed should, be made the vehicle of property rights, and such rights come to have a significance of their own which transcends the initial kinship bond, and they become the principal factor in the determination and persistence of relations. Thus a man can say, 'He is my cousin [mother's brother, etc.] therefore he should give me a cow when I am in need'; but this changes, and he says, 'Because I gave him a cow formerly, he should now give me a cow.' The original *raison d'être* of the rights and the initial standard is provided by the kinship tie, and ideally there is a norm of rights corresponding to each such tie. However, through time and by a process of mutual adjustment between the pair of individuals, ideal rights are modified by the explicit principle of reciprocity so that two identical kinship ties are not the same in practical content and expression. The kinship tie alone does not afford a right to obtain animals, for that right is directly and continuously dependent upon the nature of the fulfilment of obligations in the past and upon the acceptance of liabilities for the future. 'If he does not give you stock, you do not give to him. He is not like your mother's brother now,' said a Turkana informant in illustration of this point. A genealogical bond in itself is a relatively arid thing and it requires to be activated by the exercise of rights and satisfaction of obligations. Of course, kinship means more than propery rights. It means also affections and interests, assistance and support (morally and physically), and co-operation in work and leisure; but, as a Jie informant put it, 'He is a good person who gives you stock. You like him very much; you help him.' In other words, like the kinship bond itself, concomitant ties of affection and co-operation tend to become sterile if the property relations fall through, and they are explicitly stimulated by the exercise of mutually satisfactory rights. It is significant that the one type of stock-associate who is not a kinsman—the bond-friend—is often classed as if he were. We saw that the *sine qua non* of bond-friendship lies in reciprocal gifts of stock, and although a certain affection and other assistance goes with it, the bond is rather like an informal business contract which cannot long withstand the non-fulfilment of obligations. The relationship is fundamentally one of mutual convenience and satisfaction. Yet the common attitude, as expressed by one informant is, 'Your bond-friend gives you a beast; and he comes to beg and you give him a cow. He is like [one of] your own people [i.e. kinsmen], he is like a cousin.' He gains a pseudo-kinship quality because of the property relationship, so nearly are the two equated by the native.

On the other hand, of course, if kinship gains social meaning from its property content, the latter is initially determined by the nature and proximity of the kinship bond. A native does not expect to claim so many animals nor to make so frequent demands upon a cousin as upon a brother, nor upon a mother's brother's son as upon a sister's husband. One kinship bond contains the seeds of greater rights (but also therefore greater obligations) than another. Further, the degree of generosity depends not only upon the fulfilment of obligations in a given kinship situation but also in part it depends upon (and is re-flected in) affections and friendliness, or tension and antagonism, and, in Turkanaland, upon the frequency of communication and contact.[1]

[1] The frequency of contact itself partly, but not wholly, is a result of the friendliness or hostility of personal relations. As we saw in Chapter 6, contact may be a result of fortuitous movements in nomadic life.

CONCLUSION

Thus, analytically speaking, there are three interrelated elements of any relationship of this nature: the initial bond of kinship, which presupposes a certain ideal standard of both rights and sentiments—the reciprocal rights as established in practice through time—and inter-personal sentiments. Kinship provides the starting-point, and the other two elements react upon one another to create the actual total relationship. In this book chief interest has been centred upon the nature of reciprocal rights, for kinship relations have been principally regarded as property relations. This approach was originally suggested by the attitudes of the natives themselves. Rights and obligations are for them the central expression of any important bond between two people, and the giving and receiving of stock is not a mere symbolization of relations. There is not only an actual transfer of animals, but they are transferred for a practical, social purpose and use, and not merely as objects of ritual or ideological value. When a man begs animals he most usually wishes to undertake some social transaction—to make up a bridewealth, or to pay compensation, or to perform some essential ritual act, or to provide a feast; or he wishes to obtain a good animal to rear and use as a bull (or bull-camel, buck-goat or ram) or as a bell-ox (or dance-ox). The value of reciprocal rights lies therefore in the practical necessities and ambitions of social life. Theoretically it might be possible for a man to play his role in society, using only stock from his own herds; but as the Jie and Turkana system exists, this is out of the question. Those animals which are received as shares of in-payments or which, less frequently, are begged for no especial and immediate purpose are in fact ear-marked for future transactions and in themselves establish corresponding obligations and, in general, keep the system going. Their essential value comes from the actual or potential value in use. By the gift of an animal to a stock-associate for some purpose of his, moreover, a man makes a practical contribution to the social life and development of that associate. He is not merely given moral and ritual support, valuable though these are, but is in part provided with the actual means with which to accomplish the given end, and without which that end is unattainable. That is, men are linked together in order that each may fulfil his own social role through the use and disposal of property.

To sum up: whatever else is presupposed by kinship, such a bond, for both the Jie and the Turkana, establishes the right to claim animals and the obligation to give them, the right being a direct

CONCLUSION

consequence of the obligation. Reciprocity comes to be a second basic support of the relationship, so that in practice each type of kinship bond operates within a wide range of expression. Further, the total field of a man's stock-associates is specific to him alone, for not only is his range of kinship different from that of all other men (and in this range I include bond-friends), but the nature of reciprocity established is primarily a matter between himself and each of his associates individually. The total field of a man's kinship and the co-terminous field of property relations in no way attain the quality of a corporate group, either in thought or action.

In either tribe, however, people related through close agnatic kinship form a distinct, persistent group—the extended family. For all members of an extended family the cores of their fields of stock-associates are identical. In addition to the general principles of connection between kinship and stock rights, another significant factor emerged from analysis—that is, inheritance. Rights are thought of not as based initially on agnatic kinship alone but also as stemming from a particular notion of inheritance which provides a kind of joint ownership of the single herd of a common ancestor in the last or last but one generation. This is, of course, a special expression of kinship ties. Because one's herd formed part of what was a single herd at some time in the past, genealogically posited, one exercises rights against and acknowledges obligations to the owners of other parts of that same herd. Moreover, the nearer the time of common inheritance—the closer, that is, the agnatic link—the greater the rights and obligations. Thus the extended family is a group of interrelated stock-owners who in one way or another recognize common sources of their herds. This factor of inheritance is one of the chief qualities which mark off agnatic ties from ties of wider kinship. Again, however, the initial basis of rights is modified in practice by the conditions of reciprocity. The effective relations which result from two identical agnatic links are not necessarily the same.

In this connection, ownership of stock must be clearly distinguished from the exercise of certain rights against them. There is a basic 'stock-owning unit' in each tribe—the 'house' in Jieland and the 'nuclear family' in Turkanaland—within which, subject to the privileges of seniority, rights are largely communal and egalitarian, and administered by the head of that unit. Legally the group of Jie full-brothers, or the independent Turkana man, owns the stock by

247

right of inheritance, but the privileges of ownership are conferred upon the wives and children. Beyond the narrow confines of this unit there is no greater stock-owning unit or individual. Rights between these 'stock-owning units' are not commanded by ultimate force—that is, they have no legal content for the native. Rights are ultimately dependent upon the fulfilment of obligations. Inter-unit relations are largely carried on by their heads, and emphasis is laid on the mutual adjustment of inter-personal relations between pairs of agnates. This means, at least in so far as property relations go, that there are no corporate groups beyond the stock-owning units, which possess stock, exercise rights and meet obligations, or through which rights, are put forward. The structural articulation of agnatic kinship within the extended family does not primarily produce inter-acting corporate groups but principally categories of mutual rights between individual owners. We have seen the slight importance of the house-line in Jieland and of the various agnatic sections in Turkanaland in group action, and it has been shown how rights and effective relations frequently cut across formal structural lines.

It was pointed out that in certain respects both the Family as a whole and its various sections do sometimes emerge as active corporate groups, chiefly in a ritual connection, though the Jie Family is also a residential group with a degree of economic and pastoral co-operation. It was shown further that in Jieland the Family and its sections are not the basic ritual groups and that residential, economic and pastoral co-operation also extend beyond them to clansmen and others. In Turkanaland there is, of course, no question of the insignificance of residential ties and of economic and pastoral co-operation, and though the Family there is the widest active ritual unit, yet ritual is relatively unimportant, being meagre in content, infrequent in practice and always subservient to the state of agnatic relations and the exigencies of pastoral movement.

Within the structure of the extended family in each tribe the principle of descent and inheritance via the mother—the 'house-principle'—is of fundamental importance. Each stock-owning unit is internally differentiated according to maternal affiliation; and rights, interests and affections follows those lines. With the meta-morphosis of the unit itself, stock are inherited on the same basis and in accordance with pre-existing allocations. A reflection of the house-principle is to be seen in the tenuous relations within the house-line —that is amongst the descendants of a grandmother. Another

CONCLUSION

important common principle of family organization has been strongly emphasized: not only men, nor yet only agnates or even all relevant agnates, are included in an extended family or any of its sections. Sisters and daughters marry and become incorporated into other groups elsewhere, renouncing all stock rights and ritual obligations and privileges in connection with the herds of their natal group. Conversely, wives are incorporated into the extended family of their husbands, and there they found new sections which in due course become stock-owning units in their own right. Although relations and rights are chiefly exercised by men, yet not only have women certain general rights, particularly within the stock-owning unit, but they have social roles of fundamental importance in the total structure and development of the extended family.

A general but significant feature of similarity between the extended families in the two countries lies in their limited genealogical range and in their structural isolation from like groups. Ideally the extended family is based on the grandfather of the current adult males, and beyond this founder little or no genealogical knowledge is remembered—though for different practical reasons in either tribe. There is a conscious if somewhat vague notion that mutual rights based on agnatic kinship and common inheritance die out between people whose agnatic linkage is more indirect than through a common grandfather. This principle is expressed in rather different ways in each tribe. The Jie demonstrate it quite clearly to the observer by the implicit values inherent in the process of re-amalgamation and the fictionalization of specific agnatic ties. It appears to be essential to them to rationalize the system of effective relations and rights to the ideology of descent from a common grandfather, for it is at least not inconceivable that these relations could be equally well maintained within a wider span of kinship or even with an admission of the absence of known genealogical ties.[1] This does not happen, for the grandfather has a traditional role in the moral system of kinship and inheritance which justifies actual reciprocal rights. Amongst the Turkana, if an even narrower genealogical span does not exist, known agnates other than the descendant's of a grandfather are most usually beyond the confines of the effective Family.

---

[1] Such a group, within which precise genealogical links are not always known, is the 'matrilineal group' of the Thonga of Northern Rhodesia. Cf. Colson, E., 'The Role of Cattle among the Plateau Thonga of Mazabuka District', *Rhodes-Livingstone Journal*, xi, 1951, pp. 13 *et seq.*

CONCLUSION

This structural importance of the grandfather is given general recognition in other features in both societies.[1] It may be of significance that the grandfather is on the fringe of, or just beyond, an individual's personal memory, such that this ancestor comes to symbolize the relatively distant past as against the recent past of the fathers' generation. As study of such features would, however, go beyond the limits of this present account and does not appear to be essential to its understanding. It is sufficient here to note the structural similarity.

I have made here only a brief review of the basic similarities of the property-kinship complex of the Jie and Turkana, and it is not necessary to consider all the details which have been given in previous chapters. It is hoped that the approximately parallel accounts will have been sufficient in themselves to demonstrate the many points of agreement. One other point may be noted in conclusion. The field of stock-associates, with its important core of the extended family, provides for each man in each society the range of his peculiarly individual, social action; for these kinship-property relations cover the whole category of persons with whom a man is connected in a distinctive way, on an inter-personal basis, beyond mere acquaintanceship, or casual companionship or through the requirements of general (rather than individual) ritual interdependence.[2] They comprise his body of friends and supporters, and establish his individual social status.

II

It is clear that these significant similarities arise out of the specific historical connection between the two tribes which has been outlined elsewhere.[3] The common legend of former unity and subsequent cleavage is in itself well supported by the sociological affinity. The two sets of factors are mutually consistent. The claim

---

[1] For example, children are named after a 'grandfather' and obtain their ox-colour from him in Jieland. See my article, 'Bell-oxen and Ox-names amongst the Jie', *Uganda Journal*, 1952. In the age-set organization of both tribes, grandfathers and grandsons are brought into structural opposition with the intervening generations, so that the sets of one generation are logically succeeded by those of the generation next but one. Cf. my article, 'The Age-set Organization of the Jie tribe', *The Journal of the Royal Anthropological Society*, lxxxiii, Part 2., and *Survey of the Turkana*, chapter 12.

[2] Such general ritual interdependence involves participation in tribal rain-making, for instance.

[3] See my paper, 'The Karamajong Cluster', *Africa*, xxii, Jan. 1952.

of common origin is also most strongly borne out in a multitude of major and minor cultural and sociological features which cannot be described here, and which are largely shared with other members of the Karamajong Cluster.[1]

The question then arises—What has caused the important differences in the property-kinship complexes of the two peoples? It is tempting to regard Jie society as a kind of base-line from which Turkana society has developed its individual pattern, for the Jie are the descendants of that part of the old, unified group who have remained more or less within the same geographical region to this day and whose society shows many signs of considerable conservatism. There is, of course, no real justification for this, for it is impossible to discover whether modern Jie society is approximately the same as it was at the time of the secession of the proto-Turkana; nor can it be discovered in what ways or for what reasons it may have changed. It is fairly certain that at some time after the cession of the proto-Turkana, the remainder of the old Jie tribe migrated some thirty miles westwards; and later there was a further cleavage as another section seceded—the forebears of the contemporary Toposa and Donyiro tribes. The Jie have also for a long time been hard pressed by more powerful enemies on almost four sides of their territory, which condition is likely to have had some effects. Quite apart from such features, however, there can be no real justification for the denial of internal development, either as a continuous factor or in particular occurrences.

These rather obvious remarks are included here because in contrast with the obvious and important changes of conditions which the Turkana have encountered after their secession—ecological and demographic, and through culture contact to the alien east—the Jie appear almost to have remained static. For lack of good reason to the contrary, however, it is suggested that both societies of today are particular developments of a former initial society whose outlines cannot be known. On the other hand, it is possible to establish and

[1] Such features of similarity range from a common language to similar styles of male head-dress, from common clan and personal names to common initiation ceremonies. They involve also notable negative qualities, such as the absence of specific land and water rights, the unimportance of magic as a social instrument, or the almost complete absence of folk-stories, myths, riddles and similar oral heritage. There is no doubt, either for the Jie and Turkana or for the present writer, that the two peoples are very closely related; and the legend of common origin affords an eminently satisfactory explanation of this situation.

describe the different conditions in which each society now operates, and to attempt to draw some conclusions upon that basis. We cannot be sure that we have thus discovered all the factors that have existed to bring about contemporary differences—indeed, we can be reasonably certain that we have not. Nevertheless, in the light of the great importance of some of these factors (chiefly ecological ones) we may be able to obtain some satisfactory results.

The most striking external difference between the Jie and Turkana is in respect to their ecological systems. These have been briefly discussed in Chapter 2 and it is only necessary to make some general remarks before going on to a consideration of the effects of ecological diversity. The Turkana inhabit what is mainly an extensive, semi-desert country wherein vegetation is so poor that herds must be shifted fairly frequently in order to obtain adequate pasturage. Even with this degree of mobility it is not possible for large numbers of stock, and therefore large numbers of people, to live together. Population density is low,[1] and because of the particular type of nomadic system few inter-personal contacts are continuous. Each stock-owning unit (nuclear family) is a self-determinant pastoral unit, moving more or less independently of like units, and there is no fixed community life anywhere.

The Jie, in marked contrast, inhabit a small territory rather richer in natural resources than Turkanaland, and the bulk of the population are permanently clustered in an intensively settled area. The extended family normally lives in a single homestead. Thus residential ties, face-to-face relations and everyday co-operation in work, leisure and ritual are important in social life generally and in kinship affairs in particular, and the whole social system has a certain stability not found in Turkanaland.

In Turkanaland, the stock-owning unit is relatively isolated, and not only from a purely structural viewpoint but geographically and pastorally, and for long periods of time. There are only exiguous, temporary connections with relatively fortuitous neighbours. A man's category of stock-associates is spread over a wide, irregular area, and spatial relations frequently change. It is not usual for a man to live near more than one or two of his associates, perhaps none at all sometimes, and certainly none permanently. This gives a peculiar quality to kinship relations amongst the Turkana, for such relations receive little or no support and expression in fairly constant and

[1] See pp. 42-3.

CONCLUSION

repeated co-operation and face-to-face contacts. Kinship relations come to mean intermittent, irregular contact at the critical points in social life and individual development. Because these critical occasions usually involve matters affecting the use and disposal of stock, the aspect of property relations comes to the forefront. For the rest of the time—and quantitatively for a far larger portion of the time—kinship tends to be of little consequence outside the stock-owning unit. In Jieland, kinship is not so nearly subsumed by property relations. The extended family is a compact, residential unit, and because of the restricted area of settlement it is possible for men to maintain fairly constant contact with the rest of their stock-associates. Property rights and other aspects of social relations give each other important mutual support.

Perhaps the most notable difference between the effective Family in the two tribes is in respect of their development through time as the generations succeed one another. Groups of so small a genealogical and numerical range are particularly sensitive to this inevitable succession, which sensitivity is increased by the particularly inter-personal nature of relations. Rights and relations between agnates are not organized at any group-level above the stock-owning units, but between man and man as heads of such units. As men die and are succeeded by their sons, such relations must be begun afresh in a sense. A new system of interrelations containing an articulation of new stock-owning units and new alignment of rights must be established.

It has been shown that as a stock-owning unit breaks up, an existing system of relations has to be re-adjusted in the light of the results of inheritance. Men or groups of men, with their wives and children, who had formerly been constrained to maintain a unity of stock-ownership, close co-operation and a degree of equality, now become legally independent, holding their own herds. Rights and relations are no longer determined by inescapable, superior authority, but come to rest upon reciprocity and mutual toleration. A *modus vivendi* must be established wherein each kinsman can be of assistance to another without thereby claiming to control the other's external activities. There is not an easy or rapid re-adjustment, and considerable tension may result. This process has been examined in some detail in earlier chapters and it is essentially similar in both tribes. The end-result is, however, different. Amongst the Jie the stage is normally reached, sooner or later, where re-adjustment is made and tensions are largely resolved, and interrelations become stabilized at a new level wherein the unity of the total group is maintained. Co-operation and common interests are retained by residential and face-to-face association in everyday life. Reciprocal rights persist and there is little or no tendency for cleavage to occur; indeed, a premium is put upon continued unity. As genealogical links become extended, they are re-defined in conformity with the ideal of descent from a common grandfather. This rationalization follows and does not precede the re-adjustment of relations and the continued, effective unity of the group. An important factor in this process has probably been the relatively static population of the Jie before the present generation. Effective, co-operating, agnatically based groups tended not to increase in size, and the numbers of people involved were not too large either to make continued relations and rights unwieldy or to encourage the severance of any of them without considerable loss.

In Turkanaland, the dispersion of the extended family leads to the atrophy of more distant and weaker relations following the same sort of re-adjustment. Through difficulties arising from geographical separation and communication, such relations tend to die out, not necessarily or wholly as a result of continued tensions and problems of re-adjustment but through increasing disuse. The group obtains no permanent, underlying unity of constant co-operation and close contacts. Each succeeding generation of sons tends to establish its own field of relations in which the sons of the father's closer agnates are near the periphery and the sons of his more distant agnates are omitted. In this sort of nomadic life, conscious and considerable efforts have to be made by a man if he wishes to maintain relations with his kinsmen; the lower the standard of reciprocal rights and of intermittent co-operation, then the less worthwhile it becomes to continue those efforts. We have seen earlier the connection between inheritance and subsequent rights (p. 181). What was a potentially fruitful relationship between two half-brothers is of much decreased value to their sons, who are half-cousins. In the next generation relations atrophy altogether, for there is little to maintain them and all the social difficulties of nomadic life are against them, unlike the context of similar relations amongst the Jie.

This basic distinction between the Jie and Turkana—re-amalgamation and rationalization of agnatic links on the one hand, and cleavage and atrophy of relations on the other—comes from the difference between the compact, settled population and the mobile, dispersed population. How are these differences to be explained? Clearly this raises the problem of environmental influences and ecological systems.

Let us return for a moment to the principles of pastoralism, which are the same in both tribes. First, there are no individual or group rights in land or water[1] and therefore no restrictions as to where any animals are herded and moved. Secondly, because of the legal independence of the stock-owning unit there is no superior authority over the head of that unit to determine the dispositions of its stock in the pastures. However closely related, a member of one unit has no more right or power to control the movements of the herds of another unit than he has to control the use of that stock in social transactions. Control goes only with legal ownership. Now, this does not have any great effect upon the Jie Family, for there are always the permanent homesteads, the bases of the senior man, of domestic life and of all the important social activities and relationships. These bases are not disrupted by the movements of the stock camps, for the latter are, sociologically, relatively minor appendages of the former. The Family remains essentially a compact, residential group, with its roots in the ancestral homestead and settlement. In Turkanaland, however, the homesteads are the very units of pastoral movement, and that movement follows the same lines as amongst the Jie. Each stock-owning unit is independent; it can and does move according to the decisions of its head as he seeks to provide for the herds as seems best to him. There is no permanent base of any kind, and although to a certain degree annual movements tend to become conventionalized into a cyclical routine, yet the vagaries of climate and vegetational resources allow of no precise, pre-determinate location at any time of the year. Following their independent courses, homesteads and their inhabitants become dispersed in an ever-changing pattern which now brings some relatives near together and now scatters them far apart. That is to say, dispersion of units of the Family in Turkanaland is not wholly an ecological phenomenon, for it has roots in the structure of the group itself and in the principles of stock-ownership and control. Other semi-desert areas contain pastoral societies whose nomadic systems are not the same as that of the Turkana. The pattern may be, for example, one of corporate kin groups controlling sections of pasturelands to the relative exclusion

---

[1] Temporary rights in developed water resources lapse with disuse. In any case, holes dug in water-courses are destroyed each time there is a flow of water. See pp. 37-8.

of others. Such kin groups may be organized in an interlocking segmentary system. Then it is likely that the solidarity of such groups is high and the possibility of dispersion of near kin correspondingly low. This appears to be the case amongst some of the North African Bedouin tribes. The point to be made is, that whereas a semi-desert environment has certain limiting effects upon a primitive, pastoral society—quite decisive effects in some ways—yet it is not possible to posit any fixed sociological structure because of this. There can be no real question of an environmental determination of society. The Turkana system exists as it does because it has the same sociological origin as that of the Jie; it differs from that of the Jie because of the different conditions in which it operates. This is where environment has its effect. To a considerable extent it determines the sociological development of the given structural and legal pattern. That pattern is to be taken as given, its origins and early development lost in time.

There are therefore two sets of factors determining the contemporary kinship system of the Turkana. One is environmental: owing to poverty of vegetation and vagaries of rainfall it is not possible either for there to be large concentrations of population nor for groups of people to remain settled or even to maintain an established pastoral routine which follows a fixed course and allows of the stabilizing of contacts and communcations. This is a general influence on social life, and does not in itself bring about the dispersion of any specific groups of people such as extended families. In other arid regions, where population is no less thinly distributed, kin groups do keep together and operate within fixed territories. Here we come to the second set of factors, of a sociological nature. Due to the absence of rights in pasturelands and of organized control of pastoral movements, and the legal independence of nuclear families within the extended family, the leaders of these families are able to move as and where they like. Unlike the similar Jie situation, however, such movement affects not merely the economic administration of the herds, it involves also the concomitant movements of the owners of the herds and their dependants. This leads not only to the dispersion of the herds, as in Jieland, but also the dispersion of the people attached to them and who are kinsfolk. We come back, therefore, to the fundamental difference between these two peoples. The Jie maintain established, permanent bases of Family life unaffected by contemporary principles of land-use and stock-ownership; whereas the Turkana can nowhere retain permanent bases, whilst the same principles of land-use and stock-ownership bring about a dispersion of population. In this the independence of the stock-owning unit, bound by no superior power, connected to like units principally by reciprocal rights, is the key to both the similarities and differences between the two tribes.

In Turkanaland, as we have seen, legal and social independence comes, by extension, to be defined in terms of geographical separation and the establishment of homesteads and pastoral routines. The kinship-property structure, through environmental necessity, causes the dispersion of the Family and the separation of homesteads. In turn, this separation comes to be taken as an index of independence and to obtain therefore a value of its own beyond mere necessity. Further, separation expresses not only property-owning independence but also the tensions and maladjustments which accompany the assumption of it. A stock-owner not only has the ability to operate independently, but because of tensions between himself and other (agnatically related) owners he is encouraged to exercise his independence by spatial separation.

To put it another way, it may be said that in the Turkana Family there is not only necessity but opportunity for separation, and by that separation a man's independence is assured and emphasized. Amongst the Jie there is the firm basis of settled life, and in any case there is little opportunity to effect geographical separation in so small a territory, whilst there is a good deal of incentive to retain the values of the established home. Very occasionally a man may renounce his rights in the ancestral homestead and the continued daily support of his close agnates; but in the vast majority of cases too much is at stake and a man hesitates to 'outlaw' himself in this way. There is so much to lose; and the whole situation is supported by ties of essential ritual co-operation in conjunction with a fixed ritual grove in the settlement. In contrast with the Turkana, very great emphasis is laid upon the value, even the necessity, of the continuity of relations in the permanent homesteads, hamlets and settlements. This emphasis may lie behind the continued unity of the Jie house compared with the Turkana house, which later becomes no less dispersed than the Family itself. Like the Jie, the Turkana recognize the moral unity of full-brothers and of their herds, and to a limited extent there is structural opposition to corresponding groups of half-brothers, especially at first. But neither the house, nor its precursor, the yard, ever obtains the great unity that is so obvious and so important amongst the Jie. Because of the dual-homestead organization of the stock-owning unit, a yard is normally separated from some of its allocated stock, and its members are frequently if not usually divided between the homesteads so that full-brothers may not live and work together. One brother herds cattle in the mountains whilst another herds goats in the plains. When the yard becomes a house it still fails to achieve a unity at all comparable to that of a Jie house. Brothers tend to remain separated, divided amongst different homesteads, working under different conditions with different social contacts. Again, there is no specific base for a house. Eventually even the unity that does exist is mainly destroyed as each brother establishes his own homestead and pastoral routine. Even should he wish, there is little opportunity for a Jie younger brother to move away and become independent of his senior. He could only, one supposes, do it by 'outlawing' himself not only from his house but from his whole extended family and settlement; he would need to forfeit his most important social rights and his status gained by birth and maintained through residence and co-operation. By remaining in the ancestral home a younger man must acknowledge his subordination to his eldest brother. Even in Turkanaland if two full-brothers live in a single homestead the elder assumes, and is allowed to assume, authority. In Jieland such authority is never lost because of the essential factor of the common focus of the permanent base. In Turkanaland there is every opportunity for separation and a certain degree of necessity, and in their different homesteads the elder's authority and the total unity quickly diminish.

There remains some doubt in the writer's mind whether the above analysis is entirely satisfactory. Amongst the Jie the unity of full-brothers, together with their wives and children, is the keystone of social structure. It is given the highest moral evaluation by the people themselves, and only extremely rarely indeed does any serious threat to it occur. I was not able to discover any case where house solidarity had been permanently destroyed, although there were a few cases where extended families had partly broken up.[1]

---

[1] The Jie know little about the details of Turkana social organization, and generally assume it to be the same as their own. It was interesting, therefore, to note the great surprise with which they listened to my stories of Turkana full-brothers who live permanently separated, with younger men independent of their senior.

CONCLUSION

Despite the ecological conditions and social opportunities in Turkanaland, it still appears somewhat difficult to appreciate why full-brothers attain such a complete legal independence of one another. In the ritual and ceremonial spheres the unity of the Turkana house is marked, for a man can do little in that connection without the support of his brothers; and, for instance, if he or a member of his nuclear family is in ritual danger, the threat is believed to extend throughout the whole house. Yet the essential fact remains that, in property ownership and administration, brothers become quite independent of each other. Even in such cases where a pair of brothers frequently live near together and occasionally maintain a joint homestead there is a decisive division of the herds, and the younger man feels himself able to go against the wishes of his senior and to move away should disagreement become unpleasant. Only very few older men continue to live near to their full-brothers, and it is not considered particularly laudable to do so. It would appear that some other factor of social change has operated at some time which cannot now be discovered. If Turkana society is considered by itself, there seems to be no inconsistency between the dispersion of the extended family and its larger sections and the dispersion of the house. There is a common pattern which in itself would call for little comment. It is only in comparison with Jie society that the discrepancy arises. Of course, it is arguable that the type of Turkana house follows the original pattern and that the especial unity of the Jie house is a development after the time of cleavage. On this point there is no evidence, neither is it known what the comparable situation is amongst the Karamajong or Dodoth.[1] A *prima facie* case could be made out for this proposition based on the notable unity and compactness of settlement life in contemporary Jieland. Speculation is fruitless, however; we must merely accept the present situation as it is, whilst taking note of the decisively different ecological conditions in the two societies.

III

Emphasis has been given to ecological differences between the two tribes, and their influence has been traced in the notable differences

---

[1] These two tribes appear in many ways to present situations in between the extremes of the Jie and Turkana. Cf. my 'The Karamajong Cluster'.

CONCLUSION

in the structure and development of the extended family in each case. There are, however, other external differences which must be noted. One such factor is the fairly recent territorial expansion of the Turkana in contrast to the probably prolonged static settlement of the Jie. During at least the last two generations 'colonization' in Turkanaland has involved perhaps half of the population, and of course those who remained behind have not been unaffected. In accordance with the independence of nuclear families, migration occurred largely through the individual movements of these groups due to the desires and inclinations of their heads. Colonization has therefore been an important contributory factor to the dispersion of extended families and the speedy atrophy of agnatic ties.[1] This general process is probably now ended, for colonization is complete and further expansion prevented by the *pax Britannica*. Today its effects remain important, particularly in the west and north-west, but also in the north and south; and remnants of grand families can still be discovered in those regions from which migration occurred. It is likely that, for a time at least, these large-scale movements have emphasized the inherent differences between the Turkana and Jie. The general atmosphere of dispersion and disintegration in Turkanaland may diminish in succeeding generations, and differences from the Jie may become less pronounced.

Another factor which may have had its effect upon the Turkana is their contact with alien tribes to the east—Marile, Rendile, Samburu and Suk. It is fairly certain that by intermarriage large numbers of these aliens were absorbed into the Turkana tribe. Turkana admit this, and their contemporary physical characteristics give some support.[2] It is not possible, however, to estimate the effects of this from a sociological point of view, and in particular in respect of the kinship-property complex. There is no adequate account of any of these alien tribes in these matters. It is known, for instance, that the camel was introduced from the east some time after the secession from the Jie, and the latter have never obtained these animals. The Turkana have adopted the camel as a species of cow which can live in grassless semi-desert, and they use it exactly the same as a cow.[3] No particular cultural elements appear to have been taken over with

[1] Cf. Chapter 6, p. 184 ff.
[2] See footnote 4, p. 5.
[3] That is, camels are a supply of milk, blood and meat, and also leather. Animals were obtained as a result of raiding, not by trade, and this may explain why associated cultural features were not obtained concurrently.

CONCLUSION

the camel, though to the east, for example, camels are used for pack-purposes. At least until considerably more data are available for these alien peoples there must remain a gap in our complete under-standing of present Turkana society. There may in fact have been relatively little culture diffusion.

The coming of the European and the *pax Britannica* have had their effects in contemporary tribal society, though as yet on the whole these have been relatively unimportant. Apart from the end of war-fare, neither tribe had been appreciably affected by the new Colonial régime. In a more general treatment of the two societies the cessa-tion of warfare itself would call for some investigation, but in the spheres of kinship and property relations its effect has been of minor significance. The Turkana remain loosely administered and there have been exceedingly few of the usual 'modern developments'. In view of the extent and poverty of the country and the thin distribu-tion of its people, the handful of Government officers have been able to do little more than maintain a *status quo*. In any case a great deal of their time has been and continues to be taken up by inter-national affairs on the Ethiopian border.

It was mentioned in Chapter 2 how the early military adminis-tration in Jieland immobilized the bulk of the population which had hitherto taken part in the transhumantic pastoral system. As far as can be seen, thirty to forty years later, this has probably intensified Family unity now that it is no longer partially disrupted for several months each year by relative dispersion in the western pastures in the second half of the dry season. Apart from this, Government policy before 1939 was merely a conservative attempt to maintain a peaceful *status quo*. After the Second World War, in Jieland (as part of the Karamoja District of Uganda) 'modern development' got under way, but it has not yet had time to produce particular effect upon the existing social system. One important feature of post-conquest times has been the new, rapid increase in population, which has nearly doubled since 1919.[1] This is due mainly to the end of warfare, increased material prosperity and, by the introduction of new sources and supplies of foodstuffs, the end of periodic famine years. Again, it is too early to see the effects of these changes, for they have only occurred during about one generation. To have a general effect they will require the passage of two or three genera-tions when they have permeated right through the whole extended

[1] See p. 123.

CONCLUSION

family. It is tentatively suggested that, with increasing numbers, cleavage within the Family may become more frequent. It is possible, too, that an increasing individualism may result from the developing cash economy, which may support the effects of increasing population. This takes us into the realm of speculation, however, away from the reasons for contemporary differences between Jie and Turkana. At the time when my research was carried out, at least the more significant similarities and differences had no relation to recent changes in either tribe, and I would emphasize again that the indigenous systems which I have described were in full operation.

IV

For both the Jie and the Turkana there are two distinct aspects of livestock as property—one, legal, and the other, social. From the legal point of view a herd of cattle or a flock of goats must be owned by one person or a small group of persons—in the terminology used in this account, the 'owner' may be a group of full-brothers under the authority of the eldest, or (following the dispersion of the Turkana house) the head of a nuclear family. If a native is asked who owns a given herd of stock, a Jie will give the name of a house, or of the eldest brother of a house, or both; according to the degree of differentiation in the house, a Turkana will give either the name of a house and/or the eldest brother, or the name of the head of a nuclear family. The point is that there is no doubt in a native's mind who is the 'owner' or what ownership means.

In more developed societies legal power resides in some system of courts to which appeal may be made and from which support may be obtained in respect of property ownership and legal rights. The courts and the political system which upholds them have the power to enforce rights both by their official announcement of judgment and if necessary by commanding the use of force to compel their observation. That is legal which, if necessary, is upheld in the courts. In societies such as Jie and Turkana, where no courts and rulers existed indigenously, legality is less readily definable. It has been assumed throughout this present account that any act or right is legal which is or can be supported by the use or the threat of the use of physical force according to accepted public moral agreement in the society. It is left entirely to the individual concerned to take the appropriate action and to summon the support of his particular

262

associates to that end, for society itself is not organized to take corporate or state action. Nevertheless, such actions of force are not arbitrary but obtain a fundamental legitimacy from general tribal morality. Thus he who seizes or attempts to seize the goods of another man, or to compel a certain act, for no good reason, is not acting legally; if he does that in accordance with accepted moral standards he is acting quite legally and receives the tacit support of society at large. Legality stems essentially from morality and is in practice that part of rightful behaviour sanctioned by physical force. Not all moral standards have a legal coefficient nor even necessarily those which are given the highest regard in society. Moral standards which have legal effect are such as to give a certain minimum of security and stability in the society. Thus they chiefly concern life and property and are largely of the category 'thou shalt not' rather than 'thou shalt'. This has no reference to the efficiency of the use of force, which is another matter altogether.

Legal ownership of livestock means that the 'owner' has absolute control over those animals; he can use or dispose of them as he desires; he can herd and water them and move them about as he sees fit. No one can compel him to give animals away or to herd them in another locality or in any way to administer them differently. Powerful persuasion there may be at times; frequently there is the acknowledgment of an obligation to people in respect of some right or privilege obtained from them, but this reciprocity has no legal content. This situation is modified only in one particular. An 'owner' has certain inescapable obligations to society at large to provide an animal occasionally for ritual purposes which are intended and believed to benefit the whole tribe or at least large portions of it. In Jieland, if the seniormost elders of a district or of the whole tribe demand from a house an ox for slaughter at, say, a rain-making ceremony, there is no chance of refusal. In Turkanaland, if a diviner announces that the High God demands the slaughter of a certain animal if rain is not to be delayed, the 'owner' of such an animal cannot ultimately refuse it. In both cases the sanction is partly a supernatural one, but it is supported by what is considered a legitimate use of force by society in seizing the required beast,[1] and

---

[1] In Jieland the elders may order men of junior age-sets to go and take the required animal; in Turkanaland the diviner might give a similar order, or in righteous indignation men may take it upon themselves to seize the animal. I write deliberately in the present tense here, for this is current procedure.

CONCLUSION

sometimes an extra one is taken at the same time by way of punishment.

It is of interest to note that in Jieland, with the establishment of permanent courts under the authority of the Colonial Government, the definition of legal ownership has remained unaltered, although native confidence in these courts is, so far, too small for many cases to come forward under indigenous law and custom.

By this form of stock-ownership there are no legal rights in a herd beyond those of the 'owner' and his (or their) wives and children. It is this form of legal ownership which establishes the independence of the stock-owning units in each tribe.

From the non-legal point of view, however, there is a wide range of what may be called 'social' rights and obligations which are not sanctioned by force (and which are not enforceable by the modern Jie courts). These are the rights existing between stock-associates. From a sociological point of view property is not an indivisible entity residing with one person or a small group. It is a cluster of rights appertaining to some object. Only by cutting himself off from his society and his fellows can a legal 'owner' avoid obligations to other people. A person normally seeks certain things from society—co-operation, assistance, affections, company, security, pleasure, opportunity for development, for altruism, for power, etc.—and for these things he must and does offer part of his own assets, i.e. his legal property. He wishes to exercise rights against others, therefore he must accept certain obligations towards them. Amongst both the Jie and Turkana such rights usually spring from some kinship bond[1] which provides an initial standard of assistance and co-operation; but, as we have seen, this standard comes to be modified in each individual case on a basis of reciprocity. An obligation is consciously balanced against a right that has been realized in the past or that may be exercised in the future. This is, of course, not a sociological necessity, for rights could continue to be ordered on the basis of a fixed kinship or other social bond. It is not intended to suggest that kinship is unimportant to these two peoples; for the initial establishment of rights and obligations is a direct consequence of a kinship situation; and that relationship system remains important not only in reference to stock rights but also concerning attitudes, affections, general co-operation, ritual interdependence and the like. Kinship is, however, not an independent social factor. In this enquiry into the

[1] Bond-friendship is an exception to this.

264

CONCLUSION

nature and development of property rights it has been shown that rights between kinsmen (other than co-members of a stock-owning unit) are not legal rights, and that they are not an automatic consequence of kinship alone. Rights are not identical between a man and each of two others related by kinship in the same way. The balance of reciprocity establishes a separate level in each case on an inter-personal basis.

INDEX

INDEX

C50587